100

W9-BOZ-220

GRANTA

SCIENCE

16

Editor: Bill Buford
Assistant Editor: Graham Coster
Advertising and Promotion: Jennie O'Connor
Associate Editor: Todd McEwen
Executive Editor: Pete de Bolla
Design: Chris Hyde
Editorial and Office Assistant: Carolyn Harlock
Editorial Assistants: Michael Comeau, Margaret Costa, Melanie Franklin, Piers Spence, Vicky Ross
Photo Research: Tracy Shaw
Photo Editor: Harry Mattison
Editorial Board: Malcolm Bradbury, Elaine Feinstein, Ian Hamilton, Leonard Michaels
US Editor: Jonathan Levi, Granta, 13 White Street, New York, New York, 10013

Editorial and Subscription Correspondence: Granta 44a Hobson Street, Cambridge CB1 1NL. (0223) 315290.
All manuscripts are welcome but must be accompanied by a stamped, self-addressed envelope or they cannot be returned.

Granta is photoset by Lindonprint Typesetters and Hobson Street Studio Ltd, Cambridge, and is printed by Hazell Watson and Viney Ltd, Aylesbury, Bucks.

Granta is published by Granta Publications Ltd and distributed by Penguin Books Ltd, Harmondsworth, Middlesex, England; Viking Penguin Inc., 40 West 23rd St, New York, New York, USA; Penguin Books Australia Ltd, Ringwood, Victoria, Australia; Penguin Books Canada Ltd, 2801 John Street, Markham, Ontario, Canada L3R 1B4; Penguin Books (NZ) Ltd, 182-90 Wairau Road, Auckland 10, New Zealand. This selection copyright © 1985 by Granta Publications Ltd. Page 256 constitutes a continuation of copyright page.

Cover by Chris Hyde

Granta/ISSN 0 14 0017 3231 is published quarterly for $22 by *Granta,* 13 White Street.
2nd Class postage pending at New York, NY. POSTMASTER: send address changes to GRANTA, 13 White Street, New York, NY 10013.

ISSN 0017-3231
ISBN 014-00-8593.9

Published with the assistance of the Eastern Arts Association

Contents

ATOMIC DIPLOMACY
Gar Alperovitz

A penetrating account of American diplomacy and military planning in the final years of World War II

In this newly revised and detailed analysis, Gar Alperovitz discusses the motives, doubts, hesitations, and ultimate decisions that led to the American use of the atomic bomb against Japan. Complete with a new introduction and additional chapters on the role the atomic bomb played in the beginning of the Cold War, **Atomic Diplomacy** is a landmark work of revisionist history and essential reading for those interested in the history of modern war and peace.

"In the best traditions of historical scholarship . . . an extremely thorough and imaginative exercise in historical research." ——*The Nation*

Elisabeth Sifton Books • Penguin
$7.95

THE ACCIDENT
Dexter Masters

It took Louis Saxl only eight days to die at Los Alamos in 1946

Doctors watched over him, wondering what had been on Saxl's mind when his hands slipped. Was the accident really unavoidable? In this fascinating story of the beginning of the great atomic project, Dexter Masters writes not only of the making of the bomb, but also of the horrifying reality of radiation and its effects on the human body. Even more frightening now than when first published in 1955, **The Accident** is an extraordinarily prescient novel about science and scientists, top-secret experimentation, the government, and, above all, "progress."

"Honestly and lyrically written, ineffable moving . . . a triumph" ——*Harper's*

PENGUIN BOOKS $6.95

Perspectives On Our Time and Our World

On Writing and Politics 1967–1983
GÜNTER GRASS

In these essays, the renowned German author speaks out on the irresponsibilities of the New Left, against repression in both East and West, on the sudden death of the Prague Spring, on utopian novels and his own *Tin Drum*, on the legacy of Auschwitz. Translated by Ralph Manheim. **A Helen and Kurt Wolff Book.** *$13.95*

A Perfect Peace
AMOS OZ

Set on a kibbutz in the mid-1960s, this powerful novel tells the story of a young man in rebellion against the only world he knows. In exploring the nature of Jewishness and the condition of modern Israel, Oz brings alive the sights and sounds of his native land. Translated by Hillel Halkin. **A Helen and Kurt Wolff Book.** *$16.95*

One Earth, Four or Five Worlds
Reflections on Contemporary History
OCTAVIO PAZ

In these wide-ranging political essays, Paz examines the West's crisis of confidence: terrorism, student unrest, faltering prosperity, consumerism and hedonism, the failings of Western and Soviet leaders. It is a book of rare sensitivity by a writer known for his intellectual independence and integrity. Translated by Helen Lane. *$14.95*

HBJ *Harcourt Brace Jovanovich, Publishers*
1250 Sixth Avenue · San Diego, California · 92101

CHICAGO

WORKERS AT RISK
Voices from the Workplace
Dorothy Nelkin *and*
Michael S. Brown

This is a powerful and moving documentary of workers routinely exposed to toxic chemicals. More than seventy of them speak here of their jobs, their health, and the difficult choices they face in coming to grips with the risks of their work.
    "Innovative *and* perceptive."
— *Nature*
Cloth $20.00   248 pages

Now available in paperback:

PRINCES AND PEASANTS
Smallpox in History
Donald R. Hopkins

The ravages of smallpox — once mankind's most feared scourge — have changed the course of history. Hopkins tells the astonishing story of this dread infection, recounting its devastating effect on the prosperous and the poor in every inhabited continent on earth, from its suspected prehistoric origins to its eradication by the World Health Organization in 1977.
    "A book that will astonish, delight, flabbergast, shock, and impress." — Harry Henderson, *Medical Tribune*
Paper $12.95   400 pages   b&w illus.

THE DISCOVERY OF INSULIN
Michael Bliss

"Bliss's excellent account of the insulin story is a rare dissection of the anatomy of scientific discovery, and serves as a model of how rigorous historical method can correct the myths and legends sometimes perpetrated in the scientific literature." — Nicholas Wade, *The New Republic*
    "The story of insulin's discovery ought to be a novel. . . . Bliss's splendid account is just as absorbing as any fiction." — *Isis*
Paper $9.95   304 pages   36 b&w illus.

The University of **CHICAGO** Press

5801 South Ellis Avenue, Chicago, IL 60637

OLIVER SACKS
EXCESSES

'**D**eficit' is neurology's favourite word—its only word, indeed, for any disturbance of function. Either the function (like a capacitor or fuse) is normal—or it is defective, or faulty: what other possibility *is* there for a mechanistic neurology, which is essentially a system of capacities and connections?

What then of the opposite—an excess or superabundance of function? Neurology has no word for this, because it has no concept. A function, or functional system, works—or it does not: these are the only possibilities it allows. Thus a disease which is 'ebullient' or 'productive' in character challenges the basic mechanistic concepts of neurology, and this is doubtless one reason why such disorders —common, important and intriguing as they are—have never received the attention they deserve. They receive it in psychiatry, where one speaks of excited and productive disorders— extravagances of fancy, of impulse . . . of mania. And they receive it in anatomy and pathology, where one speaks of hypertrophies, monstrosities, of teratoma. But physiology has no equivalent for this: no equivalent of monstrosities or manias. And this alone suggests that our basic concept or vision of the nervous system—as a sort of machine or computer—is radically inadequate, and needs to be supplemented by concepts more dynamic, more alive.

This radical inadequacy may not be apparent when we consider only deficits or loss, but it becomes immediately obvious when we consider, as we do here, their *excesses*, for these are characterized almost violently by dynamism, bursting and burgeoning. Then we see at once how traditional neurology, in its mechanicalness and its emphasis on deficits conceals from us the vivid 'go' of cerebral functions—at least such higher functions as those of imagination, memory and perception. It conceals from us the very life of the mind.

The themes of the two pieces that follow are closely linked in my mind. Indeed, I wrote them at a single sitting in an all-night restaurant near my home, and originally entitled them 'Frenzy I' and 'Frenzy II'. Here they are, then—twins, a brace of frenzies.

A Matter of Identity

'What'll it be today?' he said, rubbing his hands. 'Half a pound of Virginia, a nice piece of Nova?'

Evidently he saw me as a customer. He would often pick up the phone on the ward, and say 'Thompson's Delicatessen'. 'O, Mr Thompson!' I exclaimed, 'and who do you think I am?'

'Good heavens! The light's bad—I took you for a customer. As if it isn't my old friend Tom Pitkins . . . . Me and Tom,' he whispered in an aside to the nurse, 'was always going to the races together.'

'Mr Thompson, you are mistaken again.'

'So I am,' he rejoined, not put out for a moment. 'Why would you be wearing a white coat if you were Tom? You're Hymie, the Kosher butcher next door. No bloodstains on your coat though. Business bad today? You'll look like a slaughterhouse by the end of the week!'

Feeling a bit swept away myself in this whirlpool of identities, I fingered the stethoscope dangling from my neck.

'A stethoscope!' he exploded. 'And you pretending to be Hymie. You mechanics are all starting to fancy yourselves as doctors, what with your white coats and stethoscopes—as if you need a stethoscope to listen to a car! So, you're my old friend Manners from the Mobil station up the block, come in to get your boloney-and-rye . . . .' Mr Thompson rubbed his hands again, in

---

This story is a companion piece to 'The Lost Mariner' (*New York Review of Books*, 16 February 1984), which is also an exploration of memory and amnesia and their relation to a man's life and identity. Jimmy, the 'lost mariner', in consequence of a profound memory-loss due to Korsakov's syndrome, not only forgot things as soon as they happened but had a *retrograde* amnesia going back to 1945. Thus, although he was nearly fifty when I met him, he felt himself to be a youth of nineteen, and was marooned in a remote but to him *now*-seeming past.

his salesman-grocer's gesture, and looked for the counter. Not finding it, he looked at me strangely again. 'Where am I?' he said, with a sudden scared look. 'I thought I was in my shop, doctor, my mind must have wandered . . . . You'll be wanting my shirt off, to sound me as usual?'

'No, not the usual. I'm *not* your usual doctor.'

'Indeed you're not. I could see that straightaway! You're not my usual chest-thumping doctor. And, by God, you've a beard! You look like Sigmund Freud—have I gone bonkers, round the bend?'

'No, Mr Thompson. Not round the bend. Just a little trouble with your memory—difficulties remembering and recognizing people.'

'My memory has been playing me some tricks,' he admitted. 'Sometimes I make mistakes—I take somebody for somebody else . . . . What'll it be now—Nova or Virginia?'

So it would happen, with variations, every time—with improvisations, always prompt, often funny, sometimes brilliant and ultimately tragic. Mr Thompson would identify me—misidentify, pseudo-identify me—as a dozen different people in the course of five minutes. He would whirl fluently from one guess, one hypothesis, one belief to the next, without any appearance of uncertainty at any point: he never knew who I was, or what and where *he* was—an ex-grocer, with severe Korsakov's, in a neurological institution. (Korsakov's syndrome is due to degeneration of minute relays in the memory circuits of the brain. Described by Korsakov in 1887, it is often the result of chronic alcoholism.)

He remembered nothing for more than a few seconds. He was continually disoriented. Abysses of amnesia continually opened beneath him, but he would bridge them, nimbly, by fluent confabulations and fictions of all kinds. For him they were not fictions, but how he suddenly saw, or interpreted, the world. Its radical flux and incoherence could be tolerated, acknowledged, for an instant, but there was also this strange, delirious, quasi-coherence, as Mr Thompson continually improvised a world around him with his ceaseless, unconscious, quick-fire inventions: an Arabian Nights world, a phantasmagoria of ever-changing people,

11

figures, situations and of continual kaleidoscopic mutations and transformations. For Mr Thompson, however, it was not a tissue of ever-changing, evanescent fancies and illusion, but a wholly normal, stable and factual world. So far as *he* was concerned, there was nothing the matter.

On one occasion, Mr Thompson went for a trip, identifying himself at the front desk as 'the Reverend William Thompson', ordering a taxi, and taking off for the day. The taxi-driver, whom we later spoke to, said he had never had so fascinating a passenger, for Mr Thompson told him one story after another, amazing personal stories full of fantastic adventures. 'He seemed to have been everywhere, done everything, met everyone. I could hardly believe so much was possible in a single life,' he said. 'It is not exactly a single life,' we answered. 'It is all very curious—a matter of identity.'

M r Thompson's Korsakov's syndrome had exploded just three weeks before, when he developed a high fever, raved, and ceased to recognize all his family, and he was still on the boil, was still in an almost frenzied confabulatory delirium, continually creating a world and self, to replace what was continually being forgotten and lost. Such a frenzy may call forth quite brilliant powers of invention and fancy—a veritable confabulatory genius—for such a patient *must literally make himself up (and his world) every moment.* We have, each of us, a life-story, an inner narrative, whose continuity, whose sense, *is* our lives. It might be said that each of us constructs and lives a 'narrative', and that this narrative *is* us, our identities.

If we wish to know about a man, we ask 'what is his story, his real, inmost story?', for each of us *is* a biography, a story. Each of us *is* a singular narrative, which is constructed continually and unconsciously by, through, and in us—through our perceptions, our feelings, our thoughts, our actions; and, not least, through our discourse, our spoken narrations. Biologically, physiologically, we are not so different from each other; historically, as narratives, we are each of us unique.

To be ourselves we must *have* ourselves: possess, if need be re-possess, our life-stories. We must 'recollect' ourselves, recollect the inner drama, the narrative, of ourselves. A man *needs* such a narrative, a continuous inner narrative, to maintain his identity, his self.

This narrative-need, perhaps, is the clue to Mr Thompson's desperate tale-telling, his verbosity. Deprived of continuity, of a quiet, continuous, inner narrative, he is driven to a sort of narrational frenzy: hence his ceaseless tales, his confabulations, his mythomania. Unable to maintain a genuine narrative or continuity, unable to maintain a genuine inner world, he is driven to the proliferation of pseudo-narratives, in a pseudo-continuity, pseudo-worlds peopled by pseudo-people.

What is it *like* for Mr Thompson? Superficially, he comes over as an ebullient comic. People say, 'He's a riot.' And there is much that *is* comic, but not just comic: it is terrible as well. For here is a man who, in some sense, is desperate, in a frenzy. The world keeps disappearing, losing meaning, vanishing, and he must seek meaning, *make* meaning, in a desperate way, continually inventing, throwing bridges of meaning over the chaos that yawns continually beneath him.

But does Mr Thompson himself know this, feel this? After finding him 'a riot', 'a laugh', 'loads of fun', people are disquieted, even terrified, by something in him. 'He never stops,' they say. 'He's like a man in a race, a man trying to catch something which always eludes him.' And, indeed, he can never stop running, for the breach in memory, in existence, in meaning, is never healed, but has to be bridged, to be 'patched', every second. And the bridges, the patches, for all their brilliance, fail to work: because they *are* fictions which cannot serve for reality, while also failing to correspond with it. Does Mr Thompson feel *this*? Or, again, what *is* his 'feeling of reality'? Is he in a torment all the while, the torment of a man lost in unreality, struggling to rescue himself, but sinking himself, by ceaseless inventions that are themselves quite unreal? It is certain that he is not at ease; there is a tense, taut look on his face all the while, as of a man under ceaseless inner pressure; and occasionally, not too often, or masked if present, a look of open, naked, pathetic bewilderment. What saves Mr Thompson in a sense, and in another sense damns him, *is* the forced or defensive superficiality of his life: the way in which it is, in effect, reduced to a surface—brilliant, shimmering, irridescent, ever-changing—but for all that a surface, a mass of illusions, a delirium, without depth.

And with this, no feeling *that* he has lost feeling (for the feeling he has lost), no feeling *that* he has lost the depths, that unfathomable, mysterious, myriad-levelled depth which somehow defines identity or reality. This strikes everyone who has been in contact with him for any time: under his fluency, even his frenzy, is a strange loss of feeling, the same feeling or judgment which distinguishes between 'real' and 'unreal', 'true' and 'untrue' (one cannot speak of 'lies' here, only of 'non-truth'), important and trivial, relevant or irrelevant. What comes out torrentially in his ceaseless confabulation has finally a peculiar quality of indifference . . . as if it didn't really matter what he said, or what anyone else did or said; as if nothing really mattered any more.

A striking example of this peculiar quality of indifference was presented one afternoon, when Mr Thompson, jabbering in his fluent way about all sorts of people who had been improvised on the spot, said 'And there goes my younger brother Bob past the window,' in the same excited, but even and indifferent tone, as the rest of his monologue. I was dumbfounded when a minute later a man peeked round the door, and said, 'I'm Bob, I'm his younger brother. I think he saw me passing by the window.' Nothing in Mr Thompson's tone or manner—nothing in his exuberant, but unvarying and indifferent, style of monologue—had prepared me for the possibility of . . . reality. William spoke of his brother, who *was* real, in precisely the same tone, or lack of tone, in which he spoke of the unreal—and now, suddenly, out of the phantoms, a real figure appeared! Further, he did not treat his younger brother as 'real'. He displayed no real emotion, was not in the least oriented or delivered from his delirium. On the contrary, he instantly treated his brother as unreal, effacing him, losing him, in a further whirl of delirium. This was intensely disconcerting to poor Bob who said, 'I'm Bob, not Rob, not Dob,' to no avail whatever. In the midst of confabulations—perhaps some strand of remembered kinship or identity was still holding (or came back for an instant)—Mr Thompson spoke of his *elder* brother, George, using his unvarying present indicative tense.

'But George died nineteen years ago!' said Bob, aghast.

'Aye, George is always the joker!' Mr Thompson quipped, apparently ignoring or indifferent to Bob's comment, and went on blathering of George in his excited, dead way, insensitive to truth, reality, propriety, everything—insensitive too to the manifest distress of the living brother before him.

It was this which convinced me, above everything, that there was in Mr Thompson some ultimate and total loss of inner reality, of feeling and meaning, of soul, and led me to ask the Sisters, 'Do you think William *has* a soul? Or has he been pithed, scooped-out, de-souled by disease?'

They looked worried by my question, as if something of the sort were already in their minds: they could not say, 'Judge for yourself. See him in chapel,' because his wise-cracking confabulations continued even there. Doubtless, as the sisters said, he had an immortal soul in the theological sense, and could be seen and loved as an individual by the Almighty; but, they agreed, something very disquieting had happened to him, to his spirit and character in the ordinary, human sense.

For William with his brilliant, brassy surface and the unending joke which he substitutes for the world (which if it covers over a desperation, is a desperation he does not feel), and with his manifest indifference to relation and reality, there may be nothing 'redeeming' at all: his confabulations, his apparitions, his frantic search for meanings being the ultimate barrier *to* any meaning. Paradoxically, then, William's great gift is also his damnation. If only he could be *quiet*, one feels, for an instant; if only he could stop the ceaseless chatter and jabber, if only he could relinquish the deceiving surface of illusions—then reality might seep in; something genuine, something deep, something true, something felt, could enter his soul. It is not memory only which has been so altered in him, but some ultimate capacity for feeling which is gone. And this is the sense in which he is 'de-souled'.

Luria speaks of such indifference as 'equalization', and sometimes seems to see it as the ultimate pathology, the final destroyer of any world, any self. It exerted, I think, a horrified fascination on him, as well as constituting an ultimate therapeutic challenge. He was drawn back to this theme again and again—sometimes in relation to Korsakov's and memory (as in *The Neuropsychology of Memory*), more often in relation to frontal-lobe syndromes (especially in *Human Brain and Psychological Processes*) which contains several full-length case-histories of such patients, fully comparable in their terrible coherence and impact to 'the man with a shattered world'—comparable, and in a way more terrible still, because they depict patients who do not realize that anything has befallen them, who have lost their own reality without knowing it, who may not suffer but be the most God-forsaken of all. Zazetsky (in *The Man with a Shattered World*) is constantly described as a *fighter*, always (even passionately) conscious of his state, and always fighting 'with the tenacity of the damned' to recover the use of his damaged brain. But Mr Thompson is so damned he does not know he is damned, for it is not just a faculty or some faculties which are damaged, but the very citadel, the self, the soul itself. One never feels, or rarely feels, that there is a *person* remaining.

With Mr Thompson, the therapeutic challenge can be summed up as 'only connect'. But our efforts to 're-connect' Mr Thompson all fail—even increase his confabulatory pressure. But when we abdicate our efforts, and let him be, he sometimes wanders out into the quiet and undemanding garden which surrounds the home, and there, in his quietness, he recovers his own quiet. The presence of other people excites and rattles him, forces him into an endless, frenzied social chatter, a veritable delirium of identity-making and -seeking; the presence of plants, a quiet garden, the non-human order making no social or human demands upon him, allows this identity-delirium to relax, to subside. Their quiet, non-human self-sufficiency and completeness allows him a rare quietness and self-sufficiency of his own, by offering a deep wordless communion with Nature itself, and with this the restored sense of being in the world, being real.

The Possessed

Precisely a century ago, Gilles de la Tourette, a pupil of Charcot, described the astonishing syndrome which now bears his name. 'Tourette's syndrome' is characterized by an excess of nervous energy, and a great production and extravagance of strange motions and notions: tics, jerks, mannerisms, grimaces, noises, curses, involuntary imitations and compulsions of all sorts, with an odd elfin humour and a tendency to antic and outlandish kinds of play. In its 'highest' forms, Tourette's syndrome involves every aspect of the affective, the instinctual and the imaginative life; in its 'lower', and perhaps commoner, forms, there may be little more than abnormal movements and impulsivity, though even here there is an element of strangeness. It was well recognized and extensively reported in the closing years of the last century—years of a spacious neurology that did not hesitate to conjoin the organic and the psychic. It was clear to Tourette, and his peers, that this syndrome was a sort of possession by primitive impulses and urges: but also that it was a possession with an organic base—a very definite (if undiscovered) neurological disorder. I have already written about the commoner form of Tourette's and the singular role it may play in a man's life, but there is another more sinister form of the disorder.*

---

* The commoner form is described in 'Witty Ticcy Ray' (*London Review of Books*, 19 March 1981). Ray was a young man of unusual gifts who had had convulsive tics since the age of three and referred to himself as 'witty ticcy Ray'. At first he felt that he was untreatable because he 'consisted of tics.' Happily this proved not to be the case, though the treatment (the drug haloperidol) which suppressed his tics also suppressed a good deal of his animation and creativity too. Finally he opted for a double-existence, taking haloperidol during the week but taking himself off it on weekends. Thus, as I wrote at the time: 'There are now two Rays—on and off haloperidol . . . the sober citizen, the calm deliberator from Monday to Friday . . . and "witty ticcy Ray", frivolous, frenetic, inspired, at weekends.'

17

Tourette himself, and many of the older clinicians, used to recognize a malignant form of Tourette's, which might disintegrate the personality, and lead to a bizarre, phantasmagoric, pantomimic and often impersonatory form of 'psychosis' or frenzy. This form of Tourette's—'super Tourette's'—is quite rare, perhaps fifty times rarer than ordinary Tourette's syndrome, and it may be qualitatively different, as well as far more intense than any of the ordinary forms of the disorder. This 'Tourette psychosis', this singular identity-frenzy, is quite different from ordinary psychosis, because of its underlying and unique physiology and phenomenology. Nonetheless it has affinities on the one hand with the frenzied excesses sometimes induced by L-Dopa, and on the other with the confabulatory frenzies of Korsakov's syndrome. And like these, it can overwhelm the individual.

And yet if super Tourette's, though so blatant in character, is less well recognized than it should be, this is partly a reflection of clinical practice—confining one's practice to the clinic—and shows the need to venture at times into the great world outside it. A clinic is not always the best place for observing disease—at least, not for observing a disorder which, if organic in origin, is expressed in impulse, imitation, impersonation, reaction, interaction, raised to an extreme and almost incredible degree. The clinic, the laboratory, the ward are all designed to restrain and focus behaviour, if not indeed to exclude it altogether. They are for a systematic and scientific neurology, reduced to fixed tests and tasks, not for an open, naturalistic neurology. For this one must see the patient unselfconscious, unobserved, in the real world, wholly given over to the spur and play of every impulse, and one must oneself, the observer, be unobserved. What could be better, for this purpose, than a street in New York—an anonymous public street in a vast city—where the subject of extravagant, impulsive disorders can enjoy and exhibit to the full the monstrous liberty, or slavery, of their condition.

'Street-neurology', indeed, has respectable antecedents. James Parkinson, as inveterate a walker of the streets of London as Charles Dickens was to be forty years later, delineated the disease that bears his name not in his office but in the teeming streets of London. Parkinsonism cannot be fully seen, comprehended, in the clinic; it requires an open, complexly interactional space for the full revelation of its peculiar character, its primitive impulsions, contortions, transfixions and perversions. Parkinsonism *has* to be seen in the world to be fully comprehended, and if this is true of Parkinsonism, how much truer must it be of Tourette's, especially in its most extravagant form in which the individual is virtually possessed by convulsive imitations and impersonations. But I had first to see Witty Ticcy Ray to open my eyes before I suddenly started seeing Touretters in the streets. A very similar situation happened with muscular dystrophy, which was never seen until Duchenne described it in the 1850s. By 1860, after his original description, many hundreds of cases had been recognized and described, so much so that Charcot said, 'How come that a disease so common, so widespread, and so recognizable at a glance—a disease which had doubtless always existed—how come that it is only recognized now? Why did we need M. Duchenne to open our eyes?' By the same token, the Tourette's Syndrome Association, founded in the early seventies with a few Touretters from New York, is now worldwide and has in excess of 50,000 members. *

While walking through New York in 1971, my eye was caught by a grey-haired woman in her sixties, who was apparently the centre of a most amazing disturbance, though what was happening, what was so disturbing, was not at first

---

* Sometimes physicians are the last to recognize clinical phenomena. Thus Hobbes's shaking palsy was described by Aubrey a century and a half before Parkinson. And some of the best descriptions of Tourette's Syndrome may be found outside the medical literature. There is, for instance, an extraordinary autobiographical description of an imitative and antic *ticqueur* in the streets of Paris in 'Les confidences d'un ticqueur' in Meige and Feindel's great book *Tics* (1902), and there is Rilke's description of a strange *ticqueur* ticcing through the streets of Paris in *The Notebook of Malte Lauride Brigge*.

clear to me. Was she having a fit? What on earth was convulsing her and—by a sort of sympathy or contagion—also convulsing everyone whom she gnashingly, ticcily passed?

As I drew closer I saw what was happening. *She was imitating the passers-by*, if 'imitation' is not too pallid, too passive, a word. Should we say, rather, that she was caricaturing everyone she passed? Within a second, a split-second, she 'had' them all.

I have seen countless mimes and mimics, clowns and antics, but nothing touched the horrible wonder I now beheld: this virtually instantaneous, automatic and convulsive mirroring of every face and figure. But it was not just an imitation, extraordinary as this would have been in itself. The woman not only took on, and took in, the features of countless people, she took them *off*. Every mirroring was also a parody, a mocking, an exaggeration of salient gestures and expressions, but an exaggeration in itself no less convulsive than intentional—a consequence of the violent acceleration and distortion of all her motions. Thus a slow smile, monstrously accelerated, would become a violent, millisecond–long grimace; an ample gesture, accelerated, would become a farcical convulsive movement.

In the course of a short city-block this frantic old woman frenetically caricatured the features of forty or fifty passers-by, in a quick-fire sequence of kaleidoscopic imitations, each lasting a second or two, sometimes less, and the whole dizzying sequence scarcely more than two minutes.

And there were ludicrous imitations of the second and third order; for the people in the street, startled, outraged, bewildered by her imitations, took on these expressions in reaction to her; and those expressions in turn were re-reflected, re-directed, re-distorted, by the Touretter, causing a still greater degree of outrage and shock. This grotesque, involuntary resonance, or mutuality, by which *everyone* was drawn into an absurdly amplifying interaction, was the source of the disturbance I had seen from a distance. This woman who, by becoming everybody, lost her own self, became nobody. This woman with a thousand faces, masks, *personae*—how must it be for *her* in this whirlwind of identities? The answer came soon, and not a second too late; for the build-up of pressures, both hers and others', was fast approaching the point of explosion.

Suddenly, desperately, the old woman turned aside into an alley-way which led off the main street. And there, with all the appearances of a woman violently sick, she expelled, tremendously accelerated and abbreviated, all the gestures, the postures, the expressions, the demeanours, the entire behavioural repertoires of the past forty or fifty people she had passed. She delivered one vast, pantomimic regurgitation, in which the engorged identities of the last fifty people who had possessed her were spewed out. And if the taking-in had lasted two minutes, the throwing-out was a single exhalation—fifty people in ten seconds, a fifth of a second or less for the time-foreshortened repertoire of each person.

I was later to spend hundreds of hours talking to, observing, taping, learning from Tourette patients. Yet nothing, I think, taught me as much, as swiftly, as penetratingly, as overwhelmingly as that phantasmagoric two minutes in a New York street.

It came to me in this moment that such 'super-Touretters' must be placed, by an organic quirk, through no fault of their own, in a most extraordinary, indeed unique, existential position, which has some analogies to that of raging 'super-Korsakov's', but, of course, has a quite different genesis—and aim. Both can be driven to incoherence, to identity-delirium. The Korsakovian, perhaps mercifully, never knows it, but the Touretter perceives his plight with excruciating, and perhaps finally ironic, acuity, though he may be unable, or unwilling, to do much about it.

For where the Korsakovian is driven by amnesia, absence, the Touretter is driven by extravagant impulse—impulse of which he is both the creator and the victim, impulse he may repudiate, but cannot disown. Thus he is impelled, as the Korsakovian is not, into an ambiguous relation with his disorder: vanquishing it, being vanquished by it, playing with it; there is every variety of conflict and collusion.

Lacking the normal, protective barriers of inhibition, the normal, organically determined boundaries of self, the Touretter's ego is subject to a lifelong bombardment. He is beguiled, assailed by impulses from within and without, impulses which are organic and convulsive, but also personal (or rather pseudo-personal) and seductive. How will, how *can*, the ego stand this bombardment? Will identity survive? Can it *develop*, in the face of such a shattering, such pressures? Or will it be overwhelmed to produce a 'Tourettized soul' (in the poignant words of a patient I was later to see)? There is a physiological, an existential, almost a theological pressure upon the soul of the Touretter—whether it can be held whole and sovereign, or whether it will be taken over, possessed and dispossessed, by every immediacy and impulse.

Hume, in his *Treatise of Human Nature*, wrote: 'I venture to affirm . . . that [we] are nothing but a bundle or collection of different perceptions, succeeding one another with inconceivable rapidity, and in a perpetual flux and movement'. Thus, for Hume, personal identity is a fiction—we do not exist, we are but a consecution of perceptions.

This is clearly not the case with a normal human being, because he *owns* his own perceptions. They are not a mere flux, but *his* own, united by an abiding individuality or self. But what Hume describes may be precisely the case for a being as unstable as a super-Touretter, whose life is, to some extent, a consecution of random or convulsive perceptions and motions, a phantasmagoric fluttering with no centre or sense. To this extent he *is* a 'Humean', rather than a human, being. This is the philosophical, almost theological, fate which lies in wait, if the ratio of impulse to self is too overwhelming. It has affinities to a 'Freudian' fate, which is also to be overwhelmed by impulse. But the Freudian fate has sense (albeit tragic), whereas a 'Humean' fate is meaningless and absurd.

The super-Touretter, then, is compelled to fight, as no one else is, simply to survive—to become an individual, and survive as one, in the face of constant impulse. He may be faced, from earliest childhood, with extraordinary barriers to individuation, to becoming a real person. The miracle is that, in most cases, he succeeds. For the powers of survival, of the will to survive, and to survive as a unique inalienable individual are, absolutely, the strongest in our being: stronger than any impulses, stronger than disease. Health, health militant, is usually the victor.

DOROTHEA LYNCH
AND
EUGENE RICHARDS
AMAZON

1

I am stunned.

Right under my fingers, as big as a wad of bubble gum, only harder, like the cap on the toothpaste tube. I feel it again, and my stomach jumps up into my chest.

No. Through the apartment, touching the leaves of plants. *No.* Feed the cats. Open the refrigerator. Close the refrigerator. I can't eat. I can't read, can't watch any more of a television movie about a meteor falling straight into downtown Phoenix, people screaming and glass flying, a foolish movie that leaves me gasping. I am thinking of that thing, buried in my breast, breathing and nesting and eating like a fleshy mouth. I call Dr Dragonas. 'But maybe I'm just being silly,' I say. 'I'm only thirty-four. I don't even smoke any more.'

I am supposed to cover a school committee for tomorrow's paper, but I just can't do it. I walk through the streets. It has begun to snow, sifting and hissing against the ground. I smell wood-smoke, someone's cosy fire. My father loved a fire, in all kinds of weather, but particularly in this kind of cold. Silver-haired, with his arm drawn back, snowball in hand, laughing—I have a photograph of him like that. His teeth were exactly like mine, very white and perfectly shaped. To share even the same mouth and nose and drooped left eyelid. Martha, my cousin, died of cancer last year at thirty-three. Twelve years ago, I danced with her brother Bill in a little café just before he landed in Vietnam and was killed. I remember dancing close, because neither of us felt like cousins, and laughing, and the lights turning blue with cigarette smoke.

I sit on the edge of the examining table while Dr Dragonas probes and tests. I would like to rest my head against his shoulder. Pressure against my left breast stirs the ache again, so like a toothache. In his waiting-room, I had felt diseased, a carrier among the pregnant women with their different-sized stomachs. I am young enough to be having my first child. Dr Dragonas discovers a second lump up high in my armpit that has been aching for the last few days like a strained muscle.

What is it? What is it? But he will give nothing away except a shot of Metaxa brandy that he keeps for emergencies. He and the nurse with curly blonde hair take turns calling hospitals, looking for a bed and an operating room.

'Breast resection,' they say into the beige telephones.

Resection. It sounds like refashion, as if they are going to remake my breast. No one says the word 'malignant', or 'tumour', or 'cancer'.

'We'll just put you into the hospital for a few days and take a sampling of those tissues to find out what's going on,' Dr Dragonas says. 'Don't worry, Dorothea, it's just a biopsy.'

Perhaps I am already crying when I get on the elevator in the parking garage, for the man standing next to me looks at my face and then down at his shoes. Rain has begun, and it is bitterly cold. Gene is in New York, photographing. I call my newspaper to tell them I cannot go to work. I need to talk to someone, so I drive to my mother's house. Until I was fourteen, I always thought of it as my father's house. It was my father who defined the boundaries of my life: *his* pear tree, *his* two peach trees, *his* narrow white house with black shutters on a dead-end street in Dorchester, Massachusetts. There was my mother and my older sister Moira and my little brother Billy, of course, but my father was the one. He died in his sleep when I was fourteen.

I stand in the middle of her living-room, still wearing my coat, and my mother stares at me without speaking. Ill with liver disease, her body is swollen and yellow. She is frightened by my tears. The TV blares in the corner because my mother is deaf—*The Odd Couple*—I am interrupting her favourite programme. When it ends, Oscar and Felix are still friends, and I am drunk from a highball my brother has given me.

Back at my own apartment I walk from room to room trying to get myself under control. My cats and plants and books are no protection against the circling black cloud: one aunt, three cousins, four uncles—all of them dead or dying from cancer. But writing the names of the people I love makes me feel better. I sit at my typewriter and make a will, leaving my silver ring and car to Gene; crystal beads to my mother; shell necklace to Tessie, Gene's mother; and an Indian silver bird charm to my friend Eileen who doesn't own many things.

So there is something worse, after all, than your man turning away from you. Your own body turning away, running away with a crazy new life of its own.

The afternoon light is piercing white. Snow colour. The wind is like a blow to our faces. Shivering from nervousness and the cold, I kiss Gene's parents goodbye and slide into the car. Goodbye, goodbye.

Gene smiles at me. 'Don't cry,' he says. 'One would think you're going on a long, long trip.'

'Well, I am,' I answer in surprise, not being clever at all. 'Aren't I?'

Blood sample, lung capacity test for the anaesthesiologist, electrocardiogram, X-rays. A man in a lab coat pulls the chest X-rays out of an apparatus in the corridor that looks like a Coke machine, checking the names written on them. He turns and looks at me in my voluminous hospital wrapper, then down at the X-rays again. Is that mine, I want to ask. Can you tell me if the lumps show?

Pale-faced and worried women in bathrobes walk up and down, up and down in the ward. Shuffling and bent, up, then back again. 'What are you here for?' several of them call over to me, friendly and nosey at once. 'What are you here for?' They are like a Greek chorus. Harpies. 'What are you here for? Have you had yours yet?'

Dorothy across the ward is having her hernia examined by her doctor. 'Don't you ever wear mittens?' she asks him. 'Your hands are so cold.'

The nurse shaves the hairs around my breast. 'The doctor wouldn't be able to see a thing otherwise,' Irene says smiling at me. 'They wear those magnifiers doing a biopsy, you know, and it would look like a forest.' She nicks me a few times, shaving off small moles.

'Would you mind if I felt the area?'

She presses firmly, running her fingers into my armpit where the larger lump aches, all by itself. 'I've felt a lot of breast lumps in my life,' she says, 'and I don't think you have anything to worry about. Aren't you only thirty-four? Well, then.'

The lump is so small I wouldn't have noticed it if Gene hadn't touched me, stroking and kissing in our warm Sunday afternoon bed. A bruise, I thought. A pulled muscle. My period. The next morning my hand found the same soreness and, beneath the soreness, the lump.

Irene turns out all the lights. The snow sprays against the hospital walls, and around me the women breathe like tired animals. The hospital rocks a little in the wind, groans, a large ship getting underway.

At 7.30 a.m. a nursing attendant rolls white elastic stockings up my legs, squeezing my cold feet gently with her warm hands, then wheels me down the hospital corridor to the operating-room. The walls slide by. Gonzo. I am really gonzo on their Demerol, head rocking around. Faces in masks, flowered caps. 'Are you Dorothea? . . . Hello, are you Dorothea? . . . Are you Dorothea Lynch?' And then nothing at all. Blackness. I try to lift my eyelids, one eyelid. Nothing moves. I must be dead.

What is this? What is this pain? Ferocious, tearing open my armpit. I can hear their voices. How can I be dead? I try to wiggle my foot, my finger. Then. It's the doctor making the pain. Dragonas saying, 'Oh, oh. This doesn't look so good.'

When I open my eyes it is night-time, and Gene is alone beside my bed. No results? No results. I try to tell him what I think I heard during the biopsy, but I am too tired.

When I open my eyes, Gene is with my mother and some of my friends. My mother is reading aloud from a children's book, and everyone is laughing. I cannot understand any of it. What has happened? But my mother reads on and on.

When I open my eyes again, Dr Dragonas comes in wearing his overcoat, bringing in the cold night air as he unwraps a red plaid scarf from his neck.

'Well, Dorothea,' he says, standing by the side of my bed, 'you do have the disease.'

Malignant. I awaken in the morning in a fog of medication with the word 'malignant' on my tongue. I say it aloud, though the nurse who gives me a shot for pain will not talk about the biopsy. Dr Dragonas arrives to change the dressings on my breast, and tells me the cut on the left breast was to sample the tumour. The cut on the right breast, a mirror-image biopsy, is done because half of all patients have another tumour in the same place in the other breast.

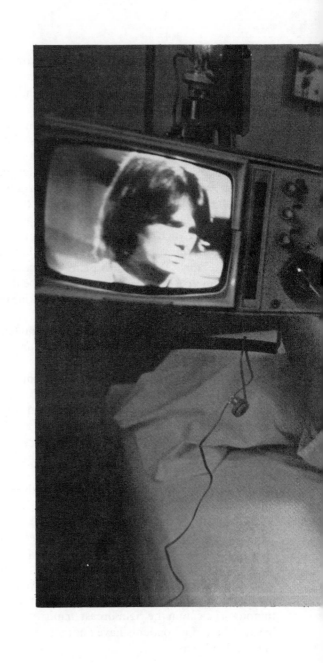

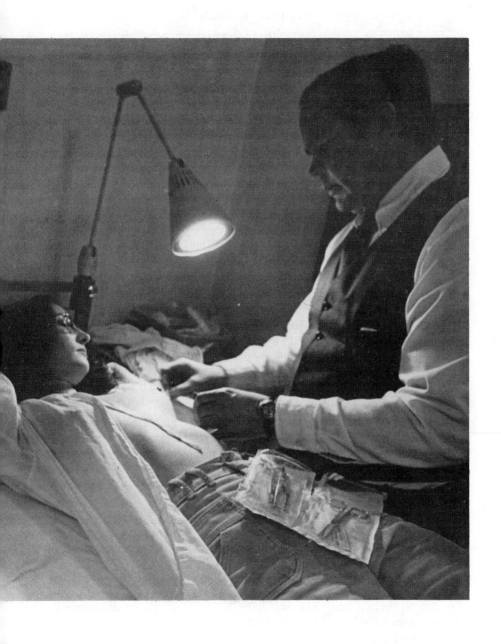

But I don't really understand much of what he is saying: 'Three out of four lymph nodes involved . . . a bone scan to survey metastatic sites . . . then we will plan your protocol.' I put my hands over my face until the nurses come in to move me downstairs. The day passes in a blur of sleep.

Before dawn a large man in a navy blue three-piece-suit wakes me. In a voice so casual and so precise he could be talking about school budgets, Dr Robert Shirley explains that a modified radical mastectomy will remove my left breast and the lymph glands under my arm. Or, I might choose to have primary radiation therapy instead—long needles with radium implants stuck into my breast. 'Maybe not the best thing,' says Dr Shirley, 'what with the possible radiation spray effects that could generate tumour activity in the other breast.'

A radiologist, Dr Kinsella, visits my room next to tell me about this very same primary radiation therapy. Dr Kinsella doesn't know what Dr Shirley, a surgical oncologist, means by a 'spraying effect'. Not in his experience, he says, has it ever happened. 'We would give you twenty-five external radiation treatments, but we would use radiation shields to protect the rest of the body. The implant is a fairly low dosage and only remains in place for a few days.'

I look at the doctors, and I think of undertakers, straight and dark and inescapable. 'Interstitial implant, morbidity, adjunctive chemotherapy.' Listening to them is like trying to decipher the code in my Graham Greene spy stories where finding the answers means saving the hero's life. 'Of course, it's your decision after all,' each doctor tells me. 'Radiation or surgery. You decide.'

Rain, rain. Gene and I spend a cold, wet afternoon searching through bookstores in Harvard Square. Muzak jingles ring over and over; people are shopping for Christmas gifts. We find a book about cancer treatment from which I learn something about chemotherapy, but there are no pictures to show me what a woman with one breast looks like. On the shelves, however, are books of a senile old man dying of starvation, young children with distended bellies crying with hunger, men and women blown apart by bombs.

At home I pore over photographs Gene has made of me: happy family snapshots, fifteen-year-old prom pictures from the days we first began dating, blue nudes, sunset nudes. 'Make a picture of me now,' I tell him. If he takes a photograph today, it will show the bloody scars from the biopsy. Until a few days ago, I didn't know what one looked like. And there must be thousands of women who undergo the slice-and-snip-and-examine without knowing the first thing about it.

We women, how in the dark we are about our bodies and what can happen to them. We ask in whispers in the corner at a party or on the telephone, what does a breast lump feel like? What does cancer look like? Will I be all right?

Gene sits me on one of the mattresses on the bedroom floor. The room is cold. The sun, setting behind the house next door, leaves one bar of light high on the wall. He makes the photograph.

All I want to do is climb into bed with the cats, layers of blankets, and sleep. I wish someone else would visit doctors, look for books, make the right decision. But Gene is like a mosquito, needling, pushing, telling me to get up, get dressed.

He brings me to Dr Peter Deckers, a surgical oncologist at University Hospital, to get a second opinion. Dr Deckers is a huge man with ruffled hair and rumpled clothes. He lightly touches my biopsy wound, and then he sits, stooped a little, reading the pathology reports I have brought along. He agrees with the findings sent over from Boston Hospital for Women.

'If you were my wife, I would tell you to have surgery. And yes, I would follow it up with chemotherapy as added insurance.'

I decide to go ahead with surgery. Treatments with radiation would mean sitting beneath an X-ray machine day after day, waiting for the tumour to shrink, dry up, die. It seems the way to get rid of this cancer is to cut it out from my body. I want to get rid of it quick, quick.

Tonight I cannot sleep. I am obsessed with when that one different voracious cell in my breast first exploded into life. The books say tumours can grow for years before they are detectible to the touch, so I can't help wondering if it was already in place that night we skinny-dipped at Sunset Lake, or when I covered my first news story, or that summer I spent trying to run more than a mile.

Gene lies beside me, restless, wanting sex. How could anyone be attracted to me right now, with my oozing, discoloured breasts and my frozen thoughts? I wish I could explain to him that it isn't just the loss of a breast that's troubling me. It is what the loss symbolizes, a premonition of the day when all the cells in my body are extinguished like cold stars.

'Maybe you should be making photographs of the whole thing,' I tell Gene. 'If there aren't any pictures of mastectomies, maybe you should take pictures of mine.'

'No,' Gene says looking upset. 'No. We have no permission to photograph inside the hospital. And a camera would be in the way when I'm with you.'

'Come on,' I bully him. 'You're always criticizing me and our friends for not recording the important events in our lives.'

'Don't you want to get up and use the toilet?' a nurse whispers. 'You can brush your teeth, but don't swallow any water. This shot will dry out your mouth but make you more relaxed.'

I was warm and calm when I woke, but now the fear returns, coating my tongue with a hot, metallic taste. My heart is chattering away inside my chest. Perhaps I will die of a heart attack before they have a chance to cut me open.

Can you climb onto the cart yourself, Dorothea? How can I climb? I am so dizzy. I feel sick. What? Are you going to be sick? She can't be sick, there's nothing in her stomach. Do you feel sick, Dorothea? Are you Dorothea? Are you Dorothea Lynch? Everyone is in masks. There is Dr Shirley and the Dragon. This is just going to make you go to sleep.

Sunlight and pain, sunlight and voices. The sting of needles, hands forcing me to roll from one side to another, cough, cough again. Bandages tight across the chest, great engulfing fog, pain sharp in my arm, but someone arranges the pillow perfectly, precisely, so the pain can flow away. 'Cough, can you cough, Dorothea?'

A nurse, minutes, maybe hours later, props a tray over my belly, then lifts me up onto the pillow and puts a spoon in my hand. I watch her peel a soft-boiled egg and mash it.

'Eat, eat,' she says.

I would like to tell her I don't like soft-boiled eggs, but I am too tired, and the spoon feels good in my hand. So solid. Real. Yolk sticks to it and to my teeth.

Dragonas and Dr Shirley arrive together, faces shiny from shaving. They tell me they have been in conference. Dragonas is shy, apologetic and smiling too much, as if he has committed some unforgiveable act. He sips from a container of coffee while Shirley unwraps my bandages.

'Look at it, Dorothea,' they tell me, raising me up.

'No. No.' I tell them I can't see without my glasses.

Deep breath. I look down at the purple black line, an eight-inch long puckered, black-stitched cut. There is a drainage tube stuck in a hole in my side that is kept from falling inside my body by a safety pin. The breast remaining is a surprise, its nipple as pink as a girl's pout. Where I had expected a gaping hole and raw flesh, there is a little skin remaining, their attempt to leave as much as possible. Clean, necessary.

In the ward on the top floor of the old hospital, I am the only patient, except for a girl who talks all morning long through my curtains when the nurses draw them around the bed, through my closed eyelids. All afternoon I drift in and out of sleep. I am dreaming some silly dream. A woman carrying a clipboard says she is doing a research project on cancer patients and asks if I smoke cigarettes, drink, have ever taken the pill, eat meat, had X-rays. Gene argues with the head nurse who blocks the camera when he tries to make a picture of me in bed having my hair combed. 'You can't take pictures in here. I don't care what Dr Shirley says, the hospital is the one to give permission.'

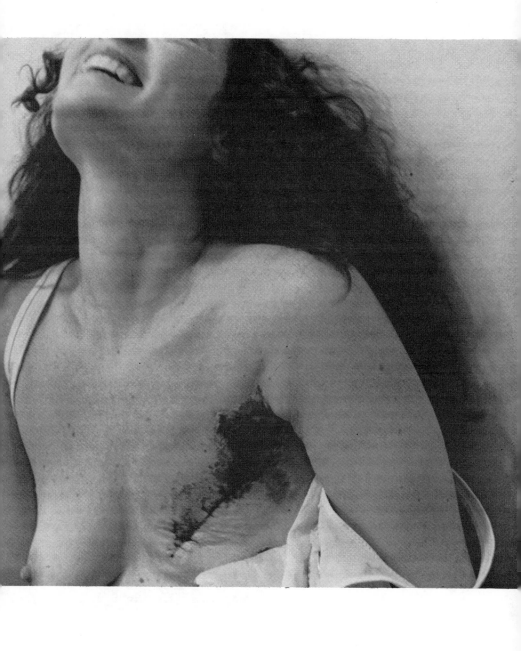

A lady with blonde hair pokes her head into my room, calling cheerfully, 'Hello there, Dorothea. Are you keeping busy? Want me to send the crafts cart along for something to do? What are you writing?' I have no idea who she is. Someone is always walking into my hospital room, acting as if we have already met, old friends and all that. It is the medical professional's way of attempting to put a patient at ease. But it is disconcerting to me not to know to whom I am talking.

The woman eventually introduces herself as Helen; she's a psychologist. I show her my notebooks, explaining that I am writing about what it is like to have cancer. Why? Because writing is what I do. It helps me sort out ideas and emotions and find out what I really feel.

Slowly, deliberately, Helen nods her head, not saying a word. I want her approval, so I keep talking. Surely having cancer is as important as having a baby, or getting married, or sleeping with a man. Women write about those experiences all the time. I speak excitedly of the people who will help me—Dr Dragonas, Dr Shirley, the nurses here. I will ask hospitals to let me talk to other cancer patients.

The hospital psychiatrist, Dr Gates, makes me nervous when he visits later in the day, constantly jotting notes on a pad. He is conducting an independent study on the psychological reactions of breast cancer patients. Answering his questions I am aware of sounding like a Pollyanna. What I mean to say twists away from me.

'Nothing is what I thought it would be,' I tell him, 'not cancer, not dying, not being alive. I feel I've been given a reprieve, like lucky Lazarus, and have returned from the grave. The sound of my own heart is a miracle. The feel of clean sheets against my skin is—'

Dr Gates interrupts to say I am experiencing a medical phenomenon called 'euphoria', quite common after a major operation. What I should expect, he says, is to have sexual difficulties, be shorter-tempered and more impatient with people.

After Dr Gates leaves, I close the door and do twenty-five sit-ups and leg-raises, careful not to crush my swollen arm, working against being a textbook cancer patient, I suppose. I keep wishing he would come back and catch me at it. Ah, one-two-three.

D r Shirley and I go over the chemotherapy procedure for the last time. I will lose all my hair and my menstrual periods may stop. Most people become nauseous, so he prescribes Compazine, and he tells me I might get some marijuana and smoke that as well.

I have been doing some reading on my own, too. My cancer textbook tells me how important it is for the patient to receive the maximum dose of chemotherapy drugs each time. Mathematically, it is all beyond me: tumour-killing cells to the tenth power, to the eighth power, to the sixth power. Each time they dose me, they kill the same percentage of cancer cells that are left circling around in my body, until theoretically my own immune system should kick in, like a faulty furnace, to polish off the last of the little killers.

So many questions I have forgotten to ask Dr Shirley. Just how delicate are my cells, and how can I be sure they will return to normal? What are the long-term effects of these poisons? If I ever have a child, could the egg from which it was produced be genetically damaged? Could I produce monsters now?

'Oh. Oh, wait,' I say, as Dr Shirley begins emptying the syringe containing the chemicals into the vein in my arm. 'Oh, what if my heart should fail? Oh, stop. Stop, stop.'

I hate it. Not even surgery with all its risks and complications seems as deadly as pouring these poisons into my veins. My stomach and bowels tighten with dread. When the doctor touches my hand to encourage me to make a fist, my fingers are ice needles. I cannot stop filling my lungs with air, and still there is not enough oxygen to stave off my fear.

He ties the rubber noose tightly across my upper arm, trapping the veins. Boom-bam, boom-bam, slams my heart, pouring more blood into my veins, swelling them for the needle's sting.

'Are you going to be sick?' he asks me.

'No. It's the taste . . . I can taste the chemical.'

They all look at me, Dr Shirley, Ann the nurse, Margie the aide, and Gene with his camera in his hand, and they wonder what I am talking about. How could I taste the red chemical just beginning to run into my arm? Is my blood already sending a warning to the nerve cells lining the back of my throat, my tongue, all the way to my brain?

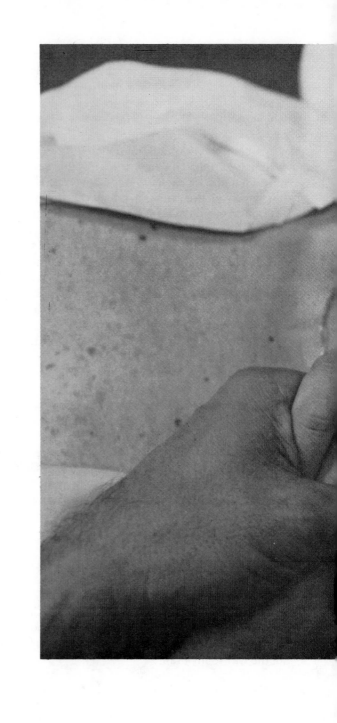

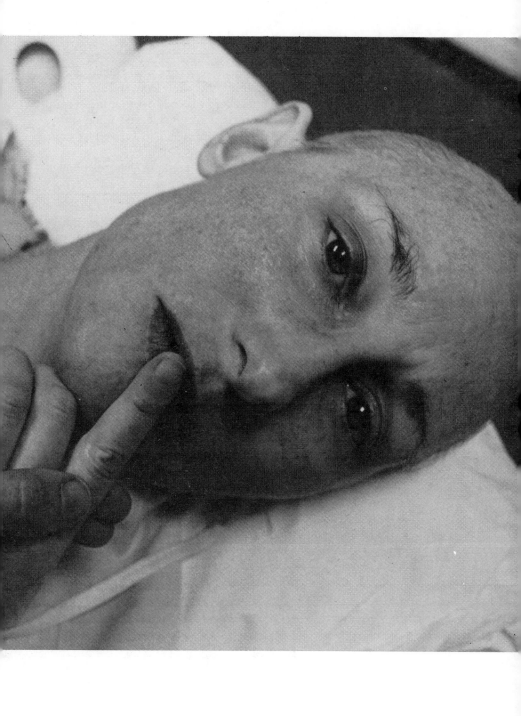

A t the photography school in New York where Gene teaches part-time, a few people ask shyly how I am, and others look sideways at me. A teacher, who had written me several times when I was in the hospital, looks at me and walks away. Maybe she doesn't recognize me in the wig, and I have lost some weight.

But this woman is not unlike the photographer who telephoned a few weeks ago, warning Gene of the dangers of living with a cancer patient. 'Are you going to keep living together?' she asked. 'I mean . . . well, it's transferred from saliva.'

'What is?'

'Cancer. That's how people get leukaemia—they get it from saliva.'

'Where the hell did you get that idea?' Gene screamed at her. 'You're talking about cat leukaemia, cat's saliva. A disease of cats, not people. Cats.'

One of Gene's students at the school asks to see the pictures Gene has made of my hospital stay. 'Do you have a different attitude now?' the student asks me, the photographs spread on the table between us. 'Aren't you going to change your life-style?'

'I couldn't have a much healthier life-style,' I tell him. 'I ran, I'm a vegetarian, and I stopped smoking four years ago. What else am I to do?'

'Yes, but it's your attitude that's important,' he says earnestly. 'There are all kinds of studies that show cancer patients repress feelings and emotions.'

I know what he is talking about. He's saying people cause their own cancers by having the wrong emotions or reactions, sort of the old philosophy of blaming the victim.

I would like to give his pseudo-radical pony-tail a good yank. Ever since I've been in the hospital, well-meaning friends and people I barely know have flooded me with bibles, tracts on holistic therapy, macrobiotic diets, each person wanting to be the one with the answer, the cure. They made me hopeful at first, then tired, tired.

This is it: the fifth and last treatment. I am surprised that I feel so little relief, perhaps because I know I still have one last sickness to get through.

'Hey,' Gene says, holding up his camera, 'we should get a picture of this. This is a celebration.'

I sit on the edge of Dr Shirley's examining table, already nauseated, and smile back at Gene. I don't know what to do or how to look. Finally, I hold up the Amazon T-shirt Gene has given me, remembering what my friend Hollysue said to me in the hospital, 'Now, you're like one of those legendary women warriors—an Amazon. They cut off one breast so they can shoot better with a bow and arrow.'

In July, Gene and I take a vacation at a tiny lakeside cottage in Maine. Adams Lake is full of fat goldfish and water-walkers. I go for my first mile run in eight months, my sneakers slapping against the bare Maine dirt. When I stop to catch my breath, Gene makes a picture of my blood-filled cheeks.

Sunshine, long walks, swimming: this is the kind of Maine vacation I used to share twenty-five years ago with my family. I remember us as we were then and realize my mother must have been nearly the same age I am now. I am standing where my parents once stood, in the middle of my life.

Gene and I sleep on the screen porch, which as a child, I was never allowed to do. All night, moths, big as flowers, hang on the screens.

2

For months now, we have been battering against the doors of officialdom, writing letters, meeting with hospital administrators, board members, lawyers, public relations people and more than two dozen doctors. What could be more natural, I had thought, than a cancer patient wanting to write about other cancer patients?

Dr Lawrence, oncologist and board member at Boston Hospital for Women, is horrified at the idea of our making 'intimate' photographs of his patients, even though one is an old friend. In a letter he circulates to fellow physicians, he calls Gene a pornographer. When we ask Dr Dragonas for help he sees 'no need to rock the boat.' Other doctors beg previous commitments or offer to act as their patients' mouthpieces, rather than let us meet with them in person. We are told that even if patients agree to work with us, our writing and photography will still compromise their 'right to privacy'. 'Patient's right to privacy' is cited again and again as the reason for keeping us out, until I cry in frustration, My God, it's not a secret illness—one out of three Americans will get it. I cannot understand the mistrust, this opposition.

'Patient's right to privacy.' When I hear these words, I think of the heavy drapes that screen hospital beds. The drapes that shield patients from bright lights and the wantonly curious can also be pulled tight to muffle protest and shut patients away from the world.

In desperation, we contact Dr Peter Deckers at University Hospital. Dr Deckers, who had advised me last November on my own cancer, listens to us, really listens, then taking a deep breath exclaims, 'Why not?' His thunderous voice booms even louder, 'Why the hell not? Maybe we will all learn something.'

I turn in the humid night, winding the bed-clothes around myself. Awakened in the darkness, my mother rousing me in the winter morning, 'Dress quickly, hurry, let's hurry.'

'Where are we going, mummy?'

'Don't you remember? You're going to the hospital so the doctor can make your tonsils better.'

I lie still, swallow hard, trying to clear my head of sleep and dreams. Gene has to pull me to my feet. 'The alarm's gone off. It's 4.30.'

Dawn is just a golden streak in the sky when we park our car outside University Hospital. The guard at the front desk checks the identity cards pinned to our coats. The photos show us smiling, aware of our new, officially recognized status. We have been approved to work with patients after all these long, long months. 'Made it,' we say to each other as we head for the elevators to C-5. C building, fifth floor. C for Cancer.

A rustle of sheets, a moan running down into a snore, one wet cough that goes on and on. At 5.30 in the morning the cancer ward is a no-man's-land. The corridor is dim, lined with dark rectangles that are the doors to patients' rooms. Out of the rooms waft the odours of antiseptic, urine, alcohol, the perspiration and breath of a dozen sick people.

We tiptoe along the hall. Gene carries his camera over his shoulder, and I clutch a new notebook as if it were a permission slip. Dr Deckers, bless him, has arranged for us to go on rounds. Waiting is his amiable chief resident, Dr Bill Kelley, and a handful of interns and students who look us over warily. At 5.45 a.m. we begin.

There are two purposes for making rounds, I've been told. One is to check on the condition of patients, the other is for medical students to see and discuss real-life cases. The group files into Mr Nichols's room. Fearful of saying or doing something inappropriate, Gene and I hang back in the doorway. I look at Mr Nichols, a middle-aged man who has a virulent form of blood cancer, and I think of Gene's photo of me after surgery with a terrified face and watery eyes. I feel helpless.

Dr Kelley checks the chart, and asks Mr Nichols if he is in any pain. Then he waves Gene and me forward near the side of the bed.

Mr Nichols holds out his hand for me to clasp. The exhausted, grey face breaks into a smile. 'A story about us would be a wonderful thing,' he says. 'But we must hurry if I'm to be involved. I'm leaving in a few days to get married.'

At this news the medical students and interns crowd closer, whooping out loud and shaking hands with Mr Nichols and with each other. Everyone is laughing, telling marriage jokes. The good spirit is contagious. Two interns introduce themselves, and promise to assist us in understanding other patients' cancer. A medical student puts his arm around my shoulder and welcomes me aboard.

Wednesday morning, and we're back on rounds. I scratch a few notes down as we move along the hallway. B 528, Leon Doucette, 'Still sounding better than he looks.' Grace Kelly, 527, 'Breast cancer metastasized to lung.' Mrs Ziff, F 328, late twenties, 'Acute leukaemia'. In our week's absence from C-5, Mr Andrews has lost another ten pounds; he's lost eighty in the last few months. Mrs St Croix is being readied for a 'middle-sized' operation. Lillian Canning's going home. Mr Farley will receive double doses of radiation, then go home next week. Radiation is being used to shrink Sally Powers's brain tumour and to restore her eyesight. Mrs Powers's room-mate Mary Storelli has died.

'I looked up into the blue sky,' says Sally Powers settling back against her pillow. 'I was going to make some coffee to celebrate the blue sky. But as I went by the curtain of her bed, I sensed that something was wrong. I went to get the doctors, and they said she had been in great pain and was gone. There was nothing to say, so I went back to the room and sent a little prayer out the window to that beautiful blue sky. If you take a picture, please include that bed as a sign of respect for her being gone.'

Gene kisses her forehead, then without talking trails his fingers from her eyelids to her cheeks, beneath her thinning hair to the radiation mark, the purple target there against her skull.

I sneak back to Room 520 to continue my chat with Evelyn Doherty, who made me laugh out loud this morning with her snappy retorts to the medical students' endless questions. She is a peppery, ginger-haired woman, full of funny, bawdy stories about her long career as an obstetrical nurse.

I've been visiting her as often as I can, grateful for the fun we share, though I know that in doing so I am breaking the head social worker's rules that we involve ourselves only with Dr Deckers's and Dr Kelley's patients. Mrs Doherty has a brain tumour metastasized from an earlier breast cancer and now has trouble walking. Her doctor is a neurologist whom we haven't met.

Mrs Doherty is talking about her cigarette addiction, three packs a day right up to the night of her operation, when the head social worker calls me out of the room.

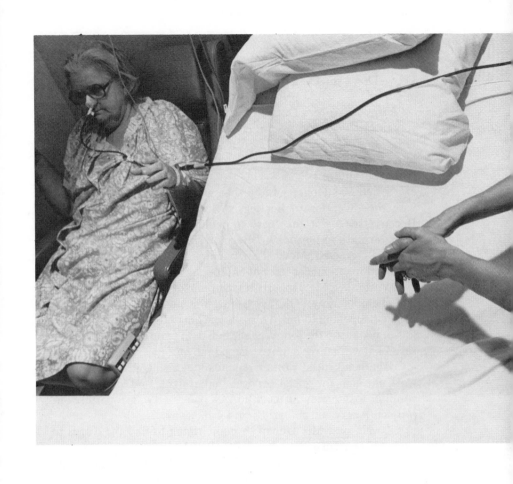

'I wish you wouldn't choose Mrs Doherty,' she whispers, 'She isn't one of Deckers's patients, and she has a brain tumour, you know. Don't you think you are being unfair? She isn't really herself anymore.'

'But I like Mrs Doherty,' I protest. 'I like her. We met on rounds last week and just hit it off.' A second social worker and a nurse approach Gene who's been waiting in the corridor, circling him with their complaints, '—not in her right mind . . . tumour . . . taking advantage . . . .'

I find Mrs Doherty to be sharp-witted and functioning well, with the exception of her legs. Why shut her away from me? Because she's not the 'perfect patient'? Because she's dying? Because she's so outspoken? Because she's critical of some of the care she's received? Medical personnel should dispel half-truths and suppositions about cancer, not mouth new ones.

Yesterday, Mrs Doherty told her nurse about the first time she had chemotherapy. 'Oh, my God, I was petrified. Oh, my God, what's happening to me. This is a teaching hospital, with lots and lots of people on the job. Why the hell didn't you or someone make sure I knew what was going to happen to me?'

The head social worker reminds me, again, that I agreed to work through the social services department, and says that if I continue to interview an unauthorized patient, it will jeopardize our project. Angry and embarrassed, I walk away.

I walk past Mrs Doherty's door, trying to find the words to explain why I can no longer visit her. But there is no sensible way to interpret the hospital's rules, and I cannot tell her the nurses think she is mentally impaired. I pass back and forth in front of the room four times, five times, six, knowing she must be waiting for me. Mrs Doherty is scheduled to be released soon, in two or three days. I tell myself it will be a lot smarter if I get her telephone number and call her at home. Under my breath, I wish her good fortune and goodbye.

3

I sit here crying and crying, unable to pull myself together. My eyes are swollen and my mouth stings with salt. The second shoe has finally dropped. I found a swelling, a lump on the same side where I had my mastectomy. An aspiration into two lymph glands shows malignant cells.

My handwriting isn't mine. I look at the black characters as they move slowly across the page, and I can see the writing is not mine. It's terrifying. I am a character in one of Le Carre's spy novels, or a drug addict, or a schizophrenic who lives in a dozen worlds. But, of course, I am none of these things. What is happening is that the doctors are stealing my brain, bit by bit, and I am co-operating with them.

My handwriting isn't mine. I am thirty-eight, again a cancer patient. Four months ago, in December 1981, the cancer returned in my lymph nodes. They irradiated me, but in April it was back again followed by headaches and weakness on one side of my body. Diagnosis: brain tumours which had to be treated before attacking the lymph nodes with chemotherapy.

So they slapped me down, got a CT scan to find the metastases, and zap—sixty seconds on one side with the linear accelerator, sixty seconds on the other. And, of course, I am taking something called Dexamethasone, which is steroids. But no one tells me the steroids will make me a space-cadet, wheeling around like a pin-wheel, unable to pull a word from my head, to think a coherent thought. When I talk to my friends, I sound like a twelve-year-old, not able to say anything of consequence, yet they look at me as they always have.

I begin chemotherapy again, but this time around I have tried to ask the right questions. It isn't fair for a patient to have to watch such terrible things happen to his body without understanding they are going to happen. One of the three chemotherapy drugs to be used, Methotrexate, can damage the brain. But what a time to tell me—minutes before I am to receive it.

Buzz, buzz, buzz. I am the fly. The noise can't be stopped unless it is I who am stopped. Buzz, buzz. Between the little tumours in my head, the rest of my body, and the outside world there is a barrier of chemicals. I am a fly in a bubble.

Steroids flow in little green pills to my brain, making my food taste awful, water sour. I move as if through molasses. Are there words for what I'm trying to communicate? I ask myself, tearing thoughts apart, puzzling, losing sense. I sound like an idiot. How can you sound so stupid?

Last night I woke up many times and thought of the garden out back. I pictured it growing, filaments reaching, tendrils, hairy protruberances cracking through the soil. I lay awake in bed pulling up weeds, pulling them out like I pull out my own hair—rake and stir; lift it free. All night the windows glowed as if dawn were on the way, but it was ten o'clock, then two o'clock, then three.

I thought of the garden getting stronger, but it was not a benevolent image. The garden outside our house was breathing on its own now.

'Amazon' is from *Exploding into Life*. See Notes on Contributors, page 256, for further details about this book and how it might be possible to contribute to the publication of it.

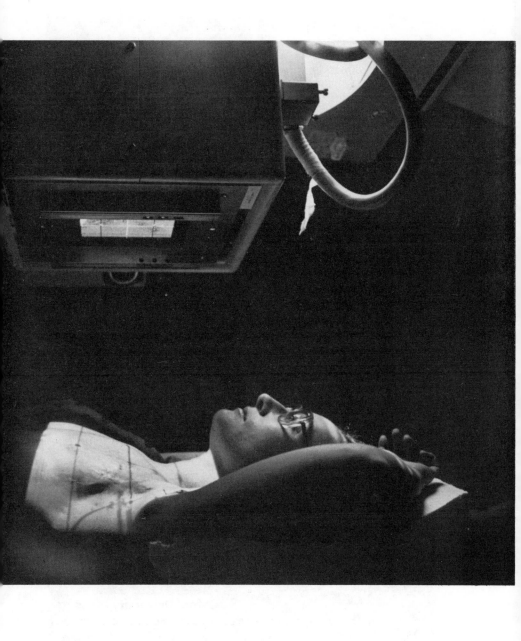

The Limits of Science

Peter Medawar

Explores the largest questions mankind can pose, in a witty and accessible way.   £7.50

Aristotle to Zoos

Peter and Jean Medawar

A personal A-Z of the life sciences compiled in the spirit of Voltaire (and occasionally of P.G. Wodehouse).
£4.95   *Oxford Paperbacks*

The Youngest Science

Notes of a Medicine-Watcher

Lewis Thomas

'one of that precious, tiny minority of scientists who write well enough to convey the beauty and significance of their subject.' **Standard**   £3.95
Oxford Paperbacks

Coming soon . . .

Late Night Thoughts

Lewis Thomas

'thoughtful and elegant collection of essays.' **New Statesman**
Approx. £2.95
Oxford Paperbacks

On Being the Right Size

and Other Essays

J.B.S. Haldane

'comprises some of the very best things Haldane ever wrote . . . masterpieces.' Peter Medawar,
The Guardian   £4.95
Oxford Paperbacks

Order and Surprise

Martin Gardner

'Another collection from the most trenchantly witty of science commentators.' Sean French,
The Sunday Times   £6.95
Oxford Paperbacks

Coming soon . . .

The Sacred Beetle

and Other Great Essays in Science

Chosen and introduced by Martin Gardner

Asimov, Darwin, Freud, Russell, Sagan and Thomas feature in this lively collection of Gardner's thirty-two favourite essays.
Approx. £4.95   *Oxford Paperbacks*

Oxford University Press

Walton Street, Oxford OX2 6DP

THOMAS McMAHON
BELL AND LANGLEY

In later life, Alexander Graham Bell lived in a large house facing the great Bras d'Or Lakes. This house was heated by ten fireplaces in addition to the large one in the main hall. It was built to resemble a French château. There were several round towers, each topped by a cone roof. The main roof was cut through in many places by stone chimneys and dormers, and a wide porch faced the water. Inside were great long runs of ash and cherry panelling. It stood on a sloping point, surrounded by wild grass. Peculiar varieties of sheep could be seen in pastures above the house.

Bell had become interested in sheep breeding. He was attempting to create a strain of sheep in which the ewes had extra nipples. He was interested in the observation that ewes with more than the usual two nipples often gave birth to more than the usual one lamb. He reasoned also that the extra nipples could be used to nourish extra lambs. An elaborate system was being used to keep track of the genealogy of his flocks. The sheep's ears were punched according to a code. Samples of their wool were taken and tested in a machine of Bell's design. A young man standing in the pens wrote down the number of times a ram penetrated a ewe. Every time it happened, his trousers tightened. The ram gripped the ewe, using his front legs like arms. From the way they jittered about in the pen, they might as well have been treading water. The ram appeared to be trying to save himself by climbing on her back. Eventually the ewe stood still and opened her mouth. They both panted like fire dogs.

One summer evening, Bell and his guests Samuel P. Langley and Simon Newcomb had a terrible argument about the righting ability of cats. It had started in the living-room of Bell's house after dinner. Bell and Langley were talking about animal reflexes, as part of their continuing speculations about the future of manned flight. Sitting in a heavily stuffed chair facing an open porch, Bell had said that he thought a nation might defend itself against hostile aircraft by blowing them out of the sky with giant fans. An engine and a propeller could be mounted on a tower, and the draught thus created could be aimed at the approaching enemy. He noted that flying machines had to be made so light that they could be driven out of control by a stiff breeze. He went on to speculate that the limitation on control might well be in the reflexes of the pilot, so that no improvement in the machines themselves could ever allow them to be operated safely in turbulent air.

Langley and Newcomb countered that a cat, dropped on its back, is able to right itself before it strikes the ground. Bell replied that he had heard this said, but he did not believe it since the cat would have nothing to push on as it was falling. With nothing to push on, it could not possibly rotate itself in space. Langley presented an argument in which the tail was used as an inertial paddle. He made use of physical reasoning which Bell could not follow.

Finally the argument was put to an experimental test. One of Bell's children was sent to the barn to round up cats. Oil lamps were brought to the porch, and mattresses were placed on the ground ten feet beneath the porch railings. Dogs ran in circles, barking, as the cats flew through the air. After the cats struck the mattresses, they ran in random directions and couldn't be recaptured. The children enjoyed the game more than the adults. They screamed with excitement as the cats dropped through the dark air into the illuminated space above the mattresses, where observers checked to see how they landed. Some of the children were scratched launching cats, but it was such a pleasure to be throwing cats around without being reprimanded for it that they forgot their wounds. In the end, Bell had to admit that a cat can right itself in mid-air.

Years earlier, when Charles J. Guiteau had shot President Garfield, Bell had offered his services to the President's physicians, who had not been able to find the bullet. As Garfield lay near death, Bell experimented with techniques for finding metal in the body. He placed an electric light, along with a bullet, in the mouth of an assistant, and observed that the bullet cast a shadow on the man's cheek. He proposed that President Garfield should swallow an even more powerful electric light bulb connected to a source of electricity through wires leading from the mouth. The physicians protested that the President was too feeble to swallow weak tea, let alone a light bulb. Bell went back to his laboratory and returned two days later with a modified version of the Hughes Induction Balance. By this time, President Garfield had fallen into a state of septic delirium. None of his physicians had taken the trouble to wash their hands before probing his wounds, with the consequence that extensive infections now inflamed his body.

Bell set up the induction balance by the President's bed. He put an earphone to his ear and asked for silence. Slowly he moved the coil over the surface of the body. A newspaper man standing among the onlookers misinterpreted what he was seeing—later he wrote that Bell had been listening for the bullet with a telephone. In the course of seven hours' work, Bell located not one bullet but twelve. The bullets were arranged in a rectangular pattern over the President's thorax and abdomen. Bell drew a little circle on the skin around the location of each bullet, using a grease pencil. The physicians were dumbfounded, since they knew only one shot had been fired.

Much later, after the President's death, it became clear that the rectangular pattern sensed by the induction balance had been due to the steel springs in the President's bed.

James Garfield died from the infections introduced by his physicians' fingers, not from the bullet wound, but this fact was unknown at the time and Bell blamed himself heavily. He fell into a depression which lasted several years. His inventions of that period took on a manic quality. He coiled a length of wire around his head. A similar wire was coiled around the head of an assistant. He suspected that Thomas Edison might be using this principle to steal his ideas, but he was never able to prove this. He was fascinated by the photoelectric properties of the metal selenium, and thought it might be possible to implant selenium in the eyes of the blind to make them see. He recklessly applied the current from a spinning magneto directly to his own eardrums. He published a paper in a technical journal in which he maintained that a man could save himself from slipping into madness by bouncing on a trampoline. In this paper, he advocated the placement of trampolines in madhouses on an experimental basis to see if the basic causes of mental disease could be reversed. He worked on devices to be used on lifeboats utilizing microscopic quantities of selenium for condensing drinking water from fog.

He wondered if odours might be vibrations between sound and heat.

Through this difficult period, Mabel supported him and encouraged him to come out of his thoughts. She tracked him by the smell of his cigar, often into the attic. Others could depend on their ears to know where he was, but Mabel couldn't hear him because scarlet fever had left her deaf from the age of five. She loved everything about her husband—his originality, his kindness, even his size.

She accompanied him on exploring trips by foot and by boat along the east coast of the United States. They sailed into Bar Harbor aboard the yawl *Flora G. Benthic* and walked along the carriage roads. At Jorden Pond, they sat on salmon-coloured granite rocks and looked up at Mount Sargent. They ate simple food from a basket and watched lens-shaped clouds shadowing the top of the mountain. They talked about their children—their dead infant sons and their live, grown girls. Mabel read her husband's lips. She held his hand and walked beside him in the woods. The carriage roads were paved with gravel and graded to climb in smooth curves around the mountains. Where the roads passed over streams, they were carried by elegant pink stone bridges. Italian labourers had built these bridges to resemble similar ones on the high paths above Udine. Bell enjoyed walking, and let his wife far into his confidence when he held her hand in the woods.

'Don't you think it's peculiar,' he said, 'that I'm becoming more and more famous for the telephone, and more and more ignored for everything else I do? Even my so-called friends think I happened on it by accident, and since then I've contributed little else of value.'

'How do you know what they think?'

'I know.'

'I don't believe you do,' Mabel said. Her speech still had some of the distortions of the deaf voice. 'You don't know what they think because you've fallen out of the habit of being with people.'

This was true. Bell worked alone through the night. His best hours for concentration, he told everyone, were between midnight and four in the morning. He said that new ideas only came to him between these hours, and when they did, they were like recollections of things forgotten. Sometimes he put on his hat and coat at two a.m. and walked ten miles, the way a mourner will do when he is trying to recall the sight of a beloved face. After a brief sleep, he would bathe, breakfast, read a newspaper, and then return to bed until late afternoon.

In the maple groves, Mabel made him see that this was shutting people out. Too much solitude, she said, is risky. It is an opiate. It can promise to refresh a person, and end by destroying him.

Bell looked into his wife's face and was filled with astonishment. If anyone else had said this to him, he would not have taken it seriously. Coming from Mabel, it struck him sharply. He stared at his wife as if he were regarding her for the first time. In speaking of solitude, Mabel would know what she was talking about. Perfect solitude was the private territory of the deaf. Mabel had lifted herself out of it only by making the effort a climber makes when ascending a rope. Every day, she rescued herself afresh. She had become a master speech-reader, and once wrote a celebrated and useful journal article on that subject. Here was a lady full of generosity and good will, but even so, she could not stand to be in the company of other deaf people. Instead, she preferred the naive faces of the hearing. When a deaf person came into the room, she averted her eyes. How selfish this was! How mean-spirited! And yet, she had to do this because such a shock, such a flash of electricity would result if she let that person catch her eye! The deaf-and dumb. Ha! If the word 'dumb' had any meaning, then its opposite should describe the deaf, who can speak to each other across a crowded room with their eyes.

As Bell gazed into the face of his thin and still-beautiful wife, he struggled to understand what she was telling him.

He resolved to change his ways, and, on the family's return to Washington that fall, he authorized Mabel to arrange several grand parties. His guest list included the scientific men Charles Walcott, Henry Rowland, Samuel Scudder, and Albert Michelson. Many years earlier, Bell had provided Michelson with the funds he needed to measure the speed of the earth relative to the ether. The results of these experiments shook physics. Michelson had shown that the movement of the earth has no effect on the velocity of light in either direction near the earth's surface. A young physicist named Albert Einstein had published a paper in which he depended on Michelson's results to propose that the speed of light is fixed, but the rate at which time passes is conditional.

At one of these evenings, when Michelson was present, Bell played the piano and sang folk songs from his native Scotland. Later, he dropped a scone on the oriental rug, jam side down.

'There's an interesting thing,' he said to Michelson, who was at the time talking with Henry Rowland. 'Why do you suppose it always lands with the jam side down?'

It was during the same evening that he made the acquaintance of the physicist Samuel Pierpont Langley. Bell was already aware of Langley's interest in manned flight. At that time, the press was giving almost daily attention to Langley's experiments with model gliders launched from balloons. Bell himself had made flying toys, following the designs of the Frenchman Alphonse Pénaud.

He told Langley about an observation he had made concerning the lifting power of ice. He happened, he said, to have been walking in Nova Scotia during the winter. By accident, he broke through the ice covering a puddle. When he held a piece of this ice up to the sun, he noticed a translucent fog around it, a fog which was colder than the surrounding air, and which therefore descended away from the sheet of ice, forming a barely-visible jet streaming downward. Now, he asked Langley, would it not be true that if the ice caused the air to move downward, this implied that there would be equal and opposite thrust on the ice upward? While Langley pondered his answer, Bell went on to elaborate his invention. Thin sheets of ice, he said, could be cut from ponds using special high-precision saws. These sheets would then be mounted on a flying machine in lightweight racks like the ones used for making toast in an oven. The machine would take off straight up using its ice-thrusters, and by the time the ice had melted, it would have reached a high altitude. Then it would glide back to earth using conventional wings, exactly as Langley's models did.

Langley thought this idea was preposterous, and said so. He drew a pencil and paper out of his coat and did a calculation of the thrust, based on momentum balance. He showed Bell that the thrust available could not be more than one-millionth of the weight of the ice alone. It is to the credit of both men that they did not fall into a quarrel over this matter or any other in the course of their long friendship.

At Langley's invitation, Bell was present for the first trial of Langley's steam-powered model aeroplane. It was to be catapulted from Langley's houseboat on the Potomac. Bell hired a boy to row him out on the river fifty yards from the shore. The water was dead flat. The sky above was overcast, and therefore nothing on the shore had any colour. As preparations were being made for the flight, the steam leaking from the catapult made Langley's houseboat look and sound like a crab cannery. Bell wore a large box camera around his neck. Even at this time in his life he was heavy. The buttons on his waistcoat were placed under a punishing tension. Since Bell sat in the stern, the bow of the little boat rose out of the water.

Then, with a rush of steam, the model flying machine lifted from the deck of the houseboat and climbed upward at a steep angle. It was borne by two sets of wings, each with a span of nearly twenty feet, one fore and one aft. The propeller flashed as it spun. It sounded like a flying locomotive. It flew directly over Bell's head and then turned inland. The boy at the oars didn't bother to look up. Bell squirmed in his seat and aimed the camera. The picture he took then still exists: it shows the model in flight high above the hills and trees of the Quantico shoreline.

Reflections on Gender and Science

Evelyn Fox Keller

Why are objectivity and reason characterised as male traits and subjectivity and feeling as female? How does this affect the goals and methods of scientific enquiry? This pathbreaking work of feminist theory by the biographer of Nobel Prizewinner Barbara McClintock explores the possibilities that a gender-free science would create for both science and society. **£17.95**

In Her Own Words

Oral Histories of Women Physicians

edited by Regina Markell Morantz, Cynthia Stodola Pomerleau, and Carol Hansen Fenichel

Interviews with three generations of female physicians reveal the formidable obstacles women have faced in finding a place in the male-dominated field of medicine. *Paper* **£9.95**

YALE UNIVERSITY PRESS

13 BEDFORD SQUARE · LONDON WC1B 3JF

Elaine Feinstein
THE BORDER

A story of obsessions and decisions against the backdrop of Europe in flames.

'A stunning novel, ruthlessly brilliant. It has the pace of a thriller and the passion of a love story'
FAY WELDON

'Combines in a remarkable way formal elegance, raw excitement and a profound plangency'
Sunday Times

'An immensely readable book...brilliant controlled and memorable' JANICE ELLIOTT,
Sunday Telegraph

On sale now   Paperback   £2.95

methuen

Cambridge Darkroom
Dales Brewery
Gwydir Street, Cambridge
tel 0223 350725
Tuesday–Saturday 12–6 pm
Admission free

● ● 13 July – 25 August

re-visions

'Fringe interference' in British photography in the 1980s

New work by
Helen Chadwick
Sharon Kivland
Karen Knorr
Mark Lewis
Yve Lomax
Mari Mahr
Olivier Richon

Sponsored by the Gredley Group

ITALO CALVINO
THE LOVES OF
THE TORTOISES

The Loves of the Tortoises

There are two tortoises on the patio: a male and a female. Zlak!Zlak! their shells strike each other. It is the season of their love-making.

The male pushes the female sideways, all around the edge of the paving. The female seems to resist his attack, or at least she opposes a somewhat inert immobility. The male is smaller and more active; he seems younger. He tries repeatedly to mount her, from behind, but the back of her shell is steep and he slides off.

Now he must have succeeded in achieving the right position: he thrusts with rhythmic, cadenced strokes; at every thrust he emits a kind of gasp, almost a cry. The female has her fore-claws flattened against the ground, enabling her to raise her hind part. The male scratches with his fore-claws on her shell, his neck stuck out, his mouth gaping. The problem with these shells is that there's no way to get a hold; and, in fact, the claws can find no purchase.

Now she escapes him, he pursues her. Not that she is faster or particularly determined to run away: to restrain her he gives her some little nips on one leg, always the same one. She does not rebel. Every time she stops, the male tries to mount her; but she takes a little step forward and he topples off, slamming his member on the ground. This member is fairly long, hooked in a way that apparently makes it possible for him to reach her even though the thickness of the shells and their awkward positioning separates them. So there is no telling how many of these attacks achieve their purpose or how many fail, or how many are theatre, play-acting.

It is summer, the patio is bare, except for one green jasmine in a corner. The courtship consists of making so many turns around the little patch of grass, with pursuits and flights and skirmishing not of the claws but of the shells, which strike in a dull clicking. The female tries to find refuge among the stalks of the jasmine; she believes—or wants to make others believe—that she does this to hide; but actually this is the surest way to remain blocked by the male, held immobile with no avenue of escape. Now it is likely that he has managed to introduce his member properly; but this time they are both completely still, silent.

The sensations of the pair of mating tortoises are something Mr Palomar cannot imagine. He observes them with a cold attention, as if they were two machines: two electronic tortoises programmed to mate. What does eros become if there are plates of bone or horny scales in the place of skin? But what we call eros—is it perhaps only a program of our corporeal bodies, more complicated because the memory receives messages from every cell of the skin, from every molecule of our tissues, and multiplies them and combines them with the impulses transmitted by our eyesight and with those aroused by the imagination? The difference lies only in the number of circuits involved: from our receptors billions of wires extend, linked with the computer of feelings, conditionings, the ties between one person and another.... Eros is a program that unfolds in the electronic cluster of the mind, but the mind is also skin: skin touched, seen, remembered. And what about the tortoises, enclosed in their insensitive casing? The poverty of their sensorial stimuli perhaps drives them to a concentrated, intense mental life, leads them to a crystalline inner awareness.... Perhaps the eros of tortoises follows absolute spiritual laws, while we are prisoners of a machinery whose functioning remains unknown to us, prone to clogging up, stalling, exploding in uncontrolled automatisms...

Do the tortoises understand themselves any better? After about ten minutes of mating, the two shells separate. She ahead, he behind, they resume their circling of the grass. Now the male remains more distanced, every now and then he scratches his claws against her shell, he climbs on her for a little, but without much conviction. They go back under the jasmine. He gives her a nip or two on one leg, always in the same place.

The Blackbird's Whistle

Mr Palomar is lucky in one respect: he spends the summer in a place where many birds sing. As he sits in a deck-chair and 'works' (in fact, he is lucky also in another respect: he can say he is working in places and attitudes that would suggest complete repose; or rather, he suffers this handicap: he feels obliged never to stop working, even when lying under the trees on an August morning), the invisible birds among the boughs around him display a repertory of the most varied manifestations of sound; they enfold him in an acoustic space that is irregular, discontinuous, jagged; but thanks to an equilibrium established among the various sounds, none of which outdoes the others in intensity or frequency, all is woven into a homogeneous texture, held together not by harmony but by lightness and transparency. Until the hour of greatest heat, when the fierce horde of insects asserts its absolute domination of the vibrations of the air, systematically filling the dimensions of time and space with the deafening and ceaseless hammering of cicadas.

The birds' song occupies a variable part of Mr Palomar's auditory attention: at times he ignores it as a component of the basic silence, at other times he concentrates on distinguishing, within it, one song from another, grouping them into categories of increasing complexity: punctiform chirps; two-note trills (one note long, one short); brief, vibrato whistling; gurgles, little cascades of notes that pour down, spin out, then stop; twirls of modulation that twist upon themselves, and so on, to extended warbling.

Mr Palomar does not arrive at a less generic classification: he is not one of those people who, on hearing a bird-call, can identify the bird it belongs to. This ignorance makes him feel guilty. The new knowledge the human race is acquiring does not compensate for the knowledge spread only by direct oral transmission: which, once lost, cannot be regained or retransmitted: no book can teach what can be learned only in childhood if you lend an alert ear and eye to the song and flight of birds and if you find someone who knows how to give them a specific name. Rather than the cultivation of precise nomenclature and classification, Palomar had preferred the constant pursuit of a precision unsure in defining the modulating, the shifting, the composite. Today he would make the opposite choice, and following the train of thoughts stirred by the birds' singing, he sees his life as a series of missed opportunities.

Among all the cries of the birds, the blackbird's whistle stands out, unmistakable for any other. The blackbirds arrive in the late afternoon; there are two of them, a couple certainly, perhaps the same couple as last year, as every year at this season. Each afternoon, hearing a whistled summons, on two notes, like the signal of a person wishing to announce his arrival, Mr Palomar raises his head to look around for whoever is calling him. Then he remembers that this is the blackbirds' hour. He soon glimpses them: they walk on the lawn as if their true vocation were to be earth-bound bipeds, and as if they enjoyed establishing analogies with human beings.

The blackbirds' whistle has this special quality: it is identical to a human whistle, the effort of someone not terribly skilled at whistling, but with a good reason for whistling, this once, only this once, with no intention of continuing, a person who does it with a determined, but modest and affable tone, calculated to win the indulgence of anyone who hears him.

After a while the whistle is repeated—by the same blackbird or by its mate—but always as if this were the first time it had occurred to him to whistle; if this is a dialogue, each remark is uttered after long reflection. But is it a dialogue, or does each blackbird whistle for itself and not for the other? And, in whichever case, are these questions and answers (to the whistler or to the mate) or are they confirmations of something that is always the same thing (the bird's own presence, his belonging to this species, this sex, this territory)? Perhaps the value of this single word lies in its being repeated by another whistling beak, in its not being forgotten during the interval of silence.

Or else the whole dialogue consists of one saying to the other 'I am here,' and the length of the pauses adds to the phrase the sense of a 'still,' as if to say: 'I am here still, it is still I.' And what if it is in the pause and not in the whistle that the meaning of the message is contained? If it were in the silence that the blackbirds speak to each other? (In this case the whistle would be a punctuation mark, a formula like 'over and out.') A silence, apparently the same as another silence, could express a hundred different notions; a whistle could too, for that matter; to speak to one another by remaining silent, or by whistling, is always possible; the problem is understanding one another. Or perhaps no one can understand anyone: each blackbird believes that he has put into his whistle a meaning fundamental for him, but only he understands it; the other gives him a reply that has no connection with what he said; it is a dialogue between the deaf, a conversation without head or tail.

But is human dialogue really any different? Mrs Palomar is also in the garden, watering the veronicas. She says, 'There they are,' a pleonastic utterance (if it assumes that her husband is already looking at the blackbirds), or else (if he has not seen them) incomprehensible, but in any event intended to establish her own priority in the observation of the blackbirds (because, in fact, she was the first to discover them and to point out their habits to her husband) and to underline their unfailing appearance, which she has already reported many times.

'Sssh,' Mr Palomar says, apparently to prevent his wife from frightening them by speaking in a loud voice (useless injunction because the blackbirds, husband and wife, are by now accustomed to the presence and voices of Palomars, husband and wife) but actually to contest the wife's precedence, displaying a consideration for the blackbirds far greater than hers.

Then Mrs Palomar says, 'It's dry again, just since yesterday,' meaning the earth in the flowerbed she is watering, a communication in itself superfluous, but meant to show, as she continues speaking and changes the subject, a far greater familiarity and nonchalance with the blackbirds than her husband has. In any case, from these remarks Mr Palomar derives a general picture of tranquility, and he is grateful to his wife for it, because if she confirms the fact that for the moment there is nothing more serious for him to bother about, then he can remain absorbed in his work (or pseudowork or hyperwork). He allows a minute to pass, then he also tries to send a reassuring message, to inform his wife that his work (or infrawork or ultrawork) is proceeding as usual: to this end he emits a series of sighs and grumbles: 'crooked...for all that...repeat...yes, my foot...' utterances that, taken all together, transmit also the message 'I am very busy', in the event that his wife's last remark contained a veiled reproach on the order of 'you could also assume some responsibility for watering the garden.'

The premiss of these verbal exchanges is the idea that a perfect accord between a married pair allows them to understand each other without having to make everything specific and detailed; but this principle is put into practice in very different ways by the two of them: Mrs Palomar expresses herself with complete sentences, though often allusive or sibylline, to test the promptness of her husband's mental associations and the syntony of his thoughts with hers (a thing that does not always work); Mr Palomar, on the other hand, from the mists of his inner monologue allows scattered, articulate sounds to emerge, confident that, if the obviousness of a complete meaning does not emerge at least the chiaroscuro of a mood will.

Mrs Palomar, instead, refuses to receive these grumbles as talk, and to underline her non-participation she says in a low voice, 'Sssh!... You'll frighten them...', applying to her husband the same shushing that he had believed himself entitled to impose on her, and confirming once more her own primacy as far as consideration for the blackbirds goes.

Having scored this point to her advantage, Mrs Palomar goes off. The blackbirds peck on the lawn and no doubt consider the dialogue of the Palomars the equivalent of their own whistles. We might just as well confine ourselves to whistling, he thinks. Here a prospect that is very promising for Mr Palomar's thinking opens out; for him the discrepancy between human behaviour and the rest of the universe has always been a source of anguish. The equal whistle of man and blackbird now seems to him a bridge thrown over the abyss.

If man were to invest in whistling everything he normally entrusts to words, and if the blackbird were to modulate into his whistling all the unspoken truth of his natural condition, then the first step would be taken towards bridging the gap between... between what and what? Nature and culture? Silence and speech? Mr Palomar hopes always that silence contains something more than what language can say. But what if language were really the goal towards which everything in existence tends? Or what if everything that exists were language, and has been since the beginning of time? Here Mr Palomar is again gripped by anguish.

After having listened carefully to the whistle of the blackbird, he tries to repeat it, as faithfully as he can. A puzzled silence follows, as if his message required careful examination; then an identical whistle re-echoes. Mr Palomar does not know if this is a reply to his or the proof that his whistle is so different that the blackbirds are not the least disturbed by it and resume their dialogue as if nothing had happened.

They go on whistling, questioning in their puzzlement, he and the blackbirds.

LEWIS THOMAS
CO-OPERATION FOR
THE BIRDS

Tree swallows are social creatures. Breeding together at close quarters, raising their young within sight of each other, they live together not quite like the members of one family, more like the inhabitants of a row of tenements on the same block. There are social problems. The adults tend to co-operate when predators turn up, ganging up noisily when any alien bird comes by to threaten a nest, but when left to themselves they live the disorderly lives of city folk, each one trying to get ahead of the rest. They compete for nesting space, and, since some living quarters are better than others, there is a tendency towards grabbiness. They know each other as though by name; they are genuine individuals. But they don't necessarily like each other, and they are not what you'd call real friends.

Somehow, despite the internal squabbles and constant competitions, the tree swallow societies manage to get by and survive, year after year. At first glance, it is a puzzle that they can do this, for the communities have the look of instability. All day long, the non-breeder birds, out of season for the time being, are a menace to the successful householders, darting towards their nests, threatening the new nestlings, trying various techniques of eviction. The parents are always on the watch and always under strain, compelled by circumstance to forage out for food and, at the same time, obliged to stay close enough at hand to protect their offspring against vandalism. The non-breeders, driven by the selfishness of their own genes, live in wild anxiety for the housing they will need when their turn at reproduction comes along next season. And, since they are at the moment free of family responsibilities, they can try a break-in whenever they feel like it. They have time on their hands.

But the non-breeders have another reason for getting close to a successful nest: plain curiosity. Having never surveyed such real estate or constructed a household of their own, they need to learn how. Or, at any rate, this seems to be an important part of their intrusive behaviour: they like to come close and look the place over.

Tree sparrows have perfectly effective ways of killing each other if they try hard enough, and sometimes, rarely, they do just that. The nestlings are totally vulnerable both to physical attack and the loss of good providers. At a casual glance, a human observer might conclude that such a system is always on the verge of crashing. One side or the other is bound to win: either the non-breeders will wipe out the new families or the breeders will take over the property, or, as seems to be the approaching norm for *our* species, all parties will go down together in a burst of fury. But it doesn't go that way.

Michael Lombardo, a biologist at Rutgers, has been out in the field studying this situation, and his findings were recently published in *Science.* The observations can be nicely fitted into a new and expanding field of evolutionary theory which attempts to account for the existence of co-operation and altruism among the living things on the earth.

Lombardo's first conclusion, on close and detailed scrutiny over long periods of time, is that the tree sparrow community seems fairly well balanced between random violence and the rule of law. The law is that nobody is allowed to threaten too much or too often, and no one under perceived threat is allowed to recriminate excessively. The birds on opposing sides are surely adversaries, with much at stake, and their behaviour towards each other cannot be called co-operative, but they do exhibit, day to day, a behaviour that can fairly be called restraint. The result is that the majority of breeding nests do survive, the majority of non-breeding birds do learn how nests are built and, with a few nasty accidents from time to time, the whole place works equably.

Some tentative rules for this kind of game were worked out on computer models several years ago, in accordance with the mathematics of game theory. The encounter is of the type known as the 'zero-sum' game, in which animals in competition have more than just the simple option of winning or losing: each side can win or lose a lot but, depending on how the game is played, both sides can consistently win a modest amount—enough to get along on. Last year Robert Axelrod, in his book *The Evolution of Co-operation,* summarized the theory. When two competing organisms encounter each other, they have two obvious choices: to co-operate or betray. 'Betrayed' here means to snatch, and snatching is made easier if the other player, for reasons of his own, makes an effort to co-operate. Hence, if the opponents meet only once in a lifetime, the strategy with the greatest probability of winning is to betray, or at least try to betray. But the game changes if there are to be repeated encounters over the lifetime of both players. In that circumstance, co-operation has a certain reward and is worth a try. Axelrod challenged a large number of computer-game specialists to submit strategies for a pattern of successful social behaviour. A program sent in by Anatol Rapaport of the University of Toronto was the consistent winner. Designated TIT FOR TAT, it was also the simplest: co-operate on the first move, and thereafter copy whatever the other player does.

When played out over a long enough period of time, against other players using different, trickier programs, TIT FOR TAT not only defeats all other strategies, it keeps all the players in the game for indefinite periods of time, with a modest degree of profit shared all round. It responds to grabbiness by a countermove of grabbing, but is immediately forgiving and offers friendship in return for a friendly move. It is, Axelrod asserts, 'nice' behaviour, and it is the pattern governing complex ecosystems, perhaps even the way of the world.

E cologists have long noted a paradox of sorts in the communities they study. They normally contain dominant predators who seem to be stronger and more agile than their competitors, but do not usually achieve total victory over them. Whenever this does happen, however, and one species stands alone amid the dead or devoured, the community as a whole crashes, the victor the biggest loser. There is a logic at work, and TIT FOR TAT may be nature's way of avoiding the death of living systems. Getting along is not only the 'nicest' strategy, it may be in real life the only way to go.

Lombardo's experiments with his tree sparrows are a tentative but promising step towards confirming the theory. He rigged up some stuffed replicas of non-breeding birds (distinguishable from breeders by their plumage colours), and propped them on long sticks in front of the nest boxes of breeders. He counted the number of hostile attacks made against the models over a five-minute period. Then, while the parents were absent, he replaced two nestling birds with two dead ones, and again recorded the number of attacks. As a control, he set up a similar arrangement with other nests in which the live nestlings were not replaced but simply handled and banded.

The outcome was entirely consistent with prediction. During the control periods, when the surrogate adversaries were in place but doing no mischief, only an occasional breeding parent made a casual pass at them; most of the time they were tolerated near the nests. Immediately after the evidence of vandalism, the breeders attacked repeatedly and vigorously, diving at the models and at other live non-breeders in the vicinity, pecking at them and pulling off feathers. Then, a short while later, a second presentation of the dummy antagonists caused no special flurry, as though nothing had occurred. The breeders and non-breeders now behaved normally together, and the community subsided into a reasonably peaceful state again.

The behaviour fitted well with the three stated rules of TIT FOR TAT: one, the breeders were 'nice' to the non-breeders until the act of defection; two, when betrayed, they responded with aggression; and three, they then forgave, maybe forgot.

Robert Axelrod and his biologist colleague W. D. Hamilton have proposed that accomodative inter-living of this sort may be genetically based, having been favoured by natural selection for its advantages in the long survival of complex ecosystems. Survival of the fittest would then take on the meaning of 'fitting in', rather than total victory for one side and unconditional surrender by another. It is a different way of looking at evolution, with little resemblance to the 'red in tooth and claw' view of nature adopted in the last century, and with no connection at all to the social Darwinism extrapolations that were applied in explanations of human behaviour a hundred years ago. It may turn out that tree swallows have come along to a condition of living more advanced than our own, but in the best of worlds we might be able to learn the trick from them or other creatures like them. Dr Lombardo, who did his tree swallow study for his graduate thesis, records in a footnote that the data on bird responses—hovers, swoops, dives, peckings and all—required '488 hours of observation at thirty-nine nest boxes'. There are many worse ways for humans to spend their time.

WILLIAM BROAD
THE SCIENTISTS OF
STAR WARS

Hertz®
It's all part of the service.
HERTZ RENTS AND LEASES FORDS AND OTHER FINE CARS.

In May 1984, I spent a week among a group of young scientists at the Lawrence Livermore National Laboratory, a federal facility for the design of nuclear weapons in a dry valley about forty miles east of San Francisco. Theirs was a world of blue jeans, Coke bottles and top-secret research that took place six and seven days a week, often all night long. Their labours had helped inspire President Reagan's 'Star Wars' speech and were now aimed at bringing his vision to life. Their goal was to channel the power of nuclear explosions into deadly beams that would flash through space to destroy enemy missiles. They worked not only on weapons but on super computers, communication devices and other vital links for the creation of a defensive shield.

Livermore is one of two federal facilities in the United States for the design of nuclear weapons. It makes no production-line warheads. Instead, the weapons are imagined, sketched on blackboards and modelled on computers. Months or years can pass before Livermore decides to build a prototype and ship its parts over the Sierra Nevada mountains for assembly at a government-owned patch of desert in the neighbouring state of Nevada, where it is then exploded underground in a carefully monitored test. If successful, blueprints of the weapon might be distributed to the various factories around the country that make warheads for the nation's bombers, submarines and silos.

The first weapons lab in the United States was Los Alamos, built in the mountains of New Mexico amid the exigencies of World War Two, which, as part of the Manhattan Project, gave birth to the first nuclear weapon. And the other was here, Livermore, built up from an abandoned naval air station in 1952. Today the lab employs nearly 8,000 people and has a budget of more than 800 million dollars a year. These two labs are at the centre of an industry that, in developing, producing, storing and planning for the use of nuclear weapons, involves well over 200,000 people and has an annual budget of more than thirty-five billion dollars. Every day, about eight new warheads roll off the assembly line. And while old weapons are continually being retired, the overall 'stockpile' is steadily increasing. There are currently 26,000 warheads in the American nuclear arsenal. By 1990, there are expected to be 32,000. In a glossy brochure issued during its twenty-fifth anniversary, Livermore claims to have designed nine out of ten of the strategic warheads in the nation's nuclear stockpile.

William Broad

The force behind the founding of Livermore was Edward Teller, a principal developer of the H-bomb, who lobbied passionately in Congress and the Pentagon for a second nuclear lab. Over the years, at Teller's urging, Livermore worked hard to surpass its nuclear rival in New Mexico. And today, Teller's legacy is carried on by a group of scientists headed by forty-two-year-old Lowell Wood. Their weapons, described as a 'third nuclear generation', are much more specialized and precise than the previous two generations, the atomic and hydrogen bombs. In fact *powered* by atomic and hydrogen bombs, third-generation weapons actually begin with the explosive energy at the core and channel it towards targets rather than letting it escape in all directions. The key designs of the group number perhaps half a dozen in all. But the details of only one have slipped through the barrier of government secrecy that surrounds all aspects of nuclear design. This was the invention of twenty-nine-year-old Peter Hagelstein, a nuclear X-ray laser that produces a powerful beam of radiation, the news of which was conveyed by Teller to President Reagan, and which a few months later helped bring about his Star Wars speech. The young inventors of Livermore are now committed to developing weapons that will fire radiation over thousands of miles of space at the speed of light to destroy hundreds of enemy missiles. As the bomb at the core of an X-ray laser-beam battle station explodes, multiple beams will flash out to strike multiple targets before the whole thing consumes itself in a ball of nuclear fire. That, at any rate, is the vision—and one that has won enthusiastic backing in some circles. After President Reagan's speech, a scientific panel headed by former NASA administrator James Fletcher called on the government to spend one and a half billion dollars over six years for research on third-generation nuclear weapons—to evaluate their potential use against enemy missiles in what would be, in effect, a shield that will destroy warheads in the middle and terminal phases of their flight. In all, the five-year plan to investigate merely the feasibility of Star Wars is meant to receive twenty-six billion dollars. If that money materializes, it will make Star Wars the biggest programme of research in the history of Western civilization, an effort dwarfing the Manhattan Project and the Apollo moon programme. Estimates of the cost of actually building a shield have run between two hundred and 1,000 billion dollars—in the worst case, the cost per American household being about $12,000 (£9,500). Parts of the shield might be in place by the 1990s, with a complete shield coming into play some time after the turn of the century—if, of course, Star Wars is deemed feasible.

L owell Wood—the leader of the young scientists and protégé of Edward Teller—let me stay at his house for the length of my visit. The structure sat alone on a high ridge overlooking the Livermore valley and was a rambling two-storey structure made of logs, big enough to accommodate visitors easily, notably young scientists coming to work at the laboratory for a summer who would sometimes stay several weeks. Yet it was not the focus of a lively social life. Wood, a bachelor, spent little time there, and was wedded to his work and to developing a cadre of young scientists.

On my first full day at Livermore, I met Wood in one of the lab's cafeterias, located outside the barbed-wire fence. The large, modern room was empty except for a small group of men in battle fatigues and camouflage hats who had knives and guns strapped to their belts. Wood said they were working under the aegis of the Department of Energy, which was holding exercises to test security procedures at the lab. You could hear bursts from their submachine guns at night, he said, as they tried to take buildings by storm. After lunch we went to the lab itself, the home of his young recruits, entering a long hallway where we were greeted by rock music from someone's office. The walls were covered with maps and posters and photographs and plants. One bushy plant stretched floor to ceiling. I peeked inside a bright office with a sunny window: more plants—huge ferns and philodendrons—and two computer terminals on a cluttered desk. A poster showed the earth suspended in space, LOVE YOUR MOTHER cut in bold letters across its top. The rest of the space was taken up with magnetic tapes, stacks of records and a large stereo system, including turntable, amplifier and headphones.

The offices and hallways were alive with young men in jeans, checked shirts and running shoes—women were nowhere to be seen. There were more than a few beards. Most of Wood's group looked as if they would fit into the engineering or physics departments of any major university in America. The average age of the technical personnel at Los Alamos during World War Two had been twenty-seven, and the average age was probably the same here. There was great activity: individuals came and went, huddled for a few minutes, and then moved on. A paging system came alive every so often.

Wood's group was not universally admired at the lab. Some researchers dismiss it as a clique of brash young scientists who were spoiled and snobbish. Hugh DeWitt, a critic within Livermore who opposes the construction of new weapons, describes them as 'bright young hot-shots who are socially maladjusted. All their time and energy is spent on science. There are no women, no outside interests. They focus on far-out technical projects and extreme defence ideology.'

Roy D. Woodruff, head of the lab's weapons programmes, had a different view: 'They're a unique group, eccentric and extraordinarily bright. Lowell is the leader and, if you will, the guru-adviser. He has been extraordinarily gifted in finding talent, and in bringing it into the laboratory to work on scientific programmes that are second to none.'

Whether praised or ridiculed, the young scientists by their very presence represented a critical victory. A lab brochure by Bruce M. Boatman, *Institutional Plan for 1983-1988*, describes how recruiting for the lab has been inhibited by 'nuclear-freeze ballot initiatives, an increasing number of public demonstrations, some resurgence of anti-weapons groups on college campuses, the media accounts of litigation arising out of early weapons-test programmes, and the general public concern over radiation effects. Some of these factors are transitory, barring further incidents and publicity. Even so, the competition for high-technology personnel will remain strong, and the recruiting for weapons programmes will be particularly difficult.' There is, moreover, an historic prejudice against the lab among the nation's scientists. Livermore was a child of the cold war. The nation was divided and so was opinion on whether another weapons lab was needed. After Livermore came to life, Teller's stormy career and the contempt he inspired in many of the nation's scientists heightened its intellectual isolation. It was not a place automatically sought out by top graduates of the nation's best universities.

Wood led me into a room that appeared to be a kitchen. It had a microwave oven, a refrigerator and an upright freezer. Along one wall, stacked floor to ceiling, were dozens of cases of Coke and Diet Coke in sixteen ounce bottles. On the table with the microwave was a telephone, a popcorn popper and bottles of ketchup, mustard, pickle relish and mayonnaise. The upright freezer was filled with huge tubs of ice cream. A list on the door kept track of how much Coke and ice cream each person consumed.

Cokes in hand, we walked to a small library, where Wood explained what brought young scientists to O Group—Wood's team, devoted to the design of nuclear weapons—and what kept them there. One factor was that Wood was an interviewer for the Hertz Foundation, which gave fellowships to graduate students in the applied sciences. John D. Hertz—a poor immigrant's son made rich by his many business ventures, including Yellow Cab and Hertz car rentals—started the foundation in the 1940s as a way of challenging what he saw as threatening technical advances by the Soviets. Both Wood and Teller were now on the board. The foundation's official address was a post-office box in the city of Livermore. It supported 120 graduate students every year with assets of about fourteen million dollars. The weapons laboratory had twenty-nine Hertz Fellows and was the largest single employer of Hertz alumni. According to a Hertz brochure, the foundation has an 'express interest in fostering the technological strength of America' and 'requires all fellows to morally commit themselves to make their skills and abilities available for the common defense, in the event of national emergency.'

Sometimes in the course of Hertz interviews, Wood said, an extremely talented individual would appear whom he tried to recruit for Livermore. One of the brightest was Rod Hyde. Wood met Hyde in the spring of 1972, when the young engineer was ready, at the age of nineteen, to graduate from the Massachusetts Institute of Technology with a perfect academic record. Soon after, the teenager came to the weapons lab for a summer, mainly to work on the design of a star-ship. He also became a Hertz Fellow and worked on his Ph.D. After joining the lab full time he rose through the ranks and now analysed the feasibility of new ideas in O Group, including those relating to nuclear weapons.

Wood said Rod Hyde was eager to come to the weapons lab because his alternatives were so dismal. 'Kids usually get treated extremely poorly until they get their bachelor's degree,' he said. 'They are considered sub-professionals, not pre-professionals, and are usually unemployable except in minimum-wage jobs serving hamburgers across the counter. In the summers Hyde did agricultural work—stoop labour. The previous summer he had graduated to working at a cannery in rural Oregon—strawberries and beets. After he came here, I asked why he had accepted the position. He said, It was a choice between your bomb factory and a beet cannery! He didn't know what working at the lab was going to involve, except I had told him I wanted him to design a star-ship. He said any kind of star-ship design was preferable to working in a beet cannery.'

I asked Wood if he was ever accused of attracting young students with promises of peaceful research and turning them into bomb-makers.

'They're free, white and twenty-one when they come here, with one or two exceptions. My ability to turn them into bomb-builders and hold them here is obviously almost non-existent. They don't have to make them if they don't want to. They don't have to stay here if they don't want to. There are, in any case, lots of people who do nothing but basic research in O Group, who never set their hands to bomb design or defence work.'

In contrast to Wood, lab administrator Roy Woodruff, one of his supporters, described the situation this way: 'By and large, many of these people eventually work on weapons applications. When they first arrive, they may not have that in mind. But it turns out that they feel more comfortable with the overall ethics after they start looking at what the lab is doing and why. Some of the best and most intellectually sound debates on issues of weapons development and deployment occur right here. These people are well informed. It's not that they see the future any clearer than anybody else, but they've really thought about it. Sometimes I think that people opposed to these activities have not.'

In general, recruits signed up for extended tours: an atmosphere in which the impossible was pursued—where the young were challenged by problems an older generation had already abandoned—kept many of the scientists of O Group from running off towards the lucrative blandishments of Silicon Valley. To some extent they were hooked on the challenge. There was, moreover, tremendous variety. People would tinker on their own projects as well as the guy's across the hall. The lure of the place was becoming evident. The young scientists were engaged in a high-tech free-for-all. It was a remarkable creation that traced its roots to Edward Teller.

My meeting with Edward Teller was brief. He was under no illusions about how formidable the task of developing a defensive shield would be. Nor, for that matter, how formidable were its critics: 'I can tell you that the ideas with which we are now working are greatly superior to what we had ten or more years ago. But, on the other hand, defence is *not* easy.' The *not* lingered.

'The fact that a great many American scientists, perhaps the majority, are against it puzzles me, disturbs me,' Teller continued. 'I believe that my young friend, Lowell Wood, is a first-rate scientist. And I know that he has an extraordinary knack for getting talented young people interested in the topic and making them work hard and willingly on it—not like a chain gang but like a football team. Still, this is a small fraction of the talent there is in America. And almost necessarily it is much less than the talent the Soviets can deploy in the same field. If we had worked during the Second World War in the same way, Hitler would have won.

'A lot of ingenuity is needed. And we just don't have enough talent. Lowell and his friends are doing an incredible amount of work. Nevertheless, the number of our people who could contribute but instead exhaust themselves in fabricating objections is legion. The majority of these people opposed the H-bomb because it was too terrible. Now they oppose defence because it is apt to make a nuclear war less terrible and therefore, they say, more probable. Somehow I don't feel that they can be right both times.'

During our conversation, Teller twice mentioned the H-bomb and its critics. And twice he questioned their judgement, pointing to the reality of the H-bomb and suggesting that now, in the same way, they would be proved wrong about the feasibility of a defensive shield.

The comparison was a little disingenuous: the H-bomb was a single device; strategic defence requires the construction and co-ordinated operation of perhaps thousands of devices, many of them working autonomously in space. Not a few critics had remarked favourably about the physics of the X-ray laser, yet still voiced doubts about the feasibility of defence.

And who would create the defensive system? Remarkably, Teller mentioned only Wood and O Group. It was a stark vision. Here was a man who had been the driving force behind the development of the H-bomb, an invention meant to put the Soviets on the defensive once and for all. But paradoxically, it, like so much else in the arms race, had come back to haunt the United States. Now Teller's intellectual heirs were to make breakthroughs of a similar magnitude, using them to create, once again, a new, safer world where Soviet H-bombs would no longer be a menace. Clearly, O Group—including its Hertz Fellows and alumni—had overcome the intellectual isolation imposed on Teller and his laboratory. In the 1950s Teller was cut off from the intellectual mainstream of American science; he was seen by many to be the 'persecutor' of the 'martyred' J. Robert Oppenheimer.

Scorned by scientific colleagues, Teller began to consort with generals, financiers, industrialists and politicians. The military looked on him as a prophet. Richard M. Nixon, then Vice President and second only to McCarthy as a fervent anti-communist, sought his advice. Nelson Rockefeller became a fast friend. In the 1960s, at Teller's invitation, Ronald Reagan became the first governor of California to visit the Livermore weapons lab.

Sputnik, the Soviet artificial satellite that first circled the earth, quickened Teller's mission. Teller once wrote that the sight of it silently moving across the night sky in 1957 chilled him to the bone. After all, Sputnik signalled the advent of something entirely new in the world of military strategy—bombs from space. If the Soviet Union could loft a satellite, they could launch nuclear warheads as well and land them anywhere in the United States. Bombers could be shot down with conventional weapons. But there was no way to stop what, in effect, would be speeding bullet from space. Teller and other military planners started the formidable job of developing systems of defence against enemy missiles and warheads.

During this critical realignment in Teller's career, a key issue for his weapons lab became where to find young researchers. American universities tended to be dominated by pro-Oppenheimer liberals. It was in the 1950s that Teller had forged a link with the Hertz Foundation. As a board member and interviewer for the fellowship programme, he made sure that many Hertz Fellows ended up at the weapons lab.

On the Hertz board Teller worked with a remarkable spectrum of men who reflected his broadened interests in the wake of the Oppenheimer affair, including Robert Lehman, head of Lehman Brothers investment banking firm; Floyd B. Odlum, the financier who single-handedly backed development of the Atlas missile (the first meant to drop bombs on Russia); and J. Edgar Hoover, director of the Federal Bureau of Investigation. Over the years the Hertz board was joined by other giants of the military and industrial world: General Curtis E. LeMay, head of the Strategic Air Command and chief of staff of the Strategic Air Forces when the first atom bombs were dropped on Hiroshima and Nagasaki; Herman H. Kahn, founder of the Hudson Institute and the nuclear strategist who provoked controversy by asserting that deterrence might fail and that civilization could survive the ensuing nuclear war; Arthur R. Kantrowitz, the physicist who helped develop the first re-entry vehicles for ballistic missiles; Charles Stark Draper, a pioneer of inertial guidance for missiles; and Hans Mark, former Air Force Secretary. In addition, there were a number of New York financiers on the board. Its president was Wilson K. Talley, chairman of the Pentagon's Army Science Board and the only member actually associated with a university, the University of California.

By the 1970s, Teller's role as recruiter had been largely taken over by Wood, who not only interviewed applicants for fellowships but joined the foundation's board with the title 'Coordinator, Fellowship Project'. A Hertz Fellowship was considered something of a plum, although not as much as it had been in the past. The annual stipend for an unmarried graduate student was ten thousand dollars, in addition to a tuition allowance of up to five thousand—still a considerable amount of money in the early seventies.

Except for giving an occasional cash prize to a fellow or a school, the foundation's sole purpose was to award fellowships. Teller and Wood were the key individuals responsible for a bequest of many millions of dollars. Two out of three scientists working in O Group were Hertz Fellows or alumni.

Before visiting Livermore, I had tried to find a description of the third-generation weapons. Details were slim. Their designs and mere existence are some of the federal government's top secrets. Nonetheless, specifics came to light as well as some general characteristics of third-generation weapons.

Third-generation weapons consist of the two previous generations, A-bombs and H-bombs, known respectively as the 'primary' and the 'secondary.' The essential feature of third-generation weapons is that they *focus* the explosive energy of A-

91

bombs and H-bombs through the use of various devices, arrays, metals and other materials. The power of third-generation weaponry is in some cases dictated by the size of its nuclear furnace: the greater the bomb the more powerful the beams. Since the task of defence usually calls for all the punch a beam-weapon can muster, the criterion of power alone suggests that all third-generation weapons start with an H-bomb—which is, by necessity, 'ignited' by an A-bomb. The H-bomb must be fashioned in such a way that its expanding ball of nuclear fire is paced with that of the A-bomb that triggers it, so that all radiation arrives simultaneously at the delicate arrays of energy converters, target trackers and all the other associated hardware of third-generation weapons.

As to the specifics of third-generation weapons, various press accounts and rumours among the community of defence scientists point to four main possibilities out of an untold number that are actually being pursued:

X-RAY LASER: the X-ray laser is the most extensively tested and formidable of all the third-generation ideas, and is also the only one whose details are known publicly. Around its core are long thin metal rods, which when struck by radiation emit powerful bursts of X-rays. What makes the bursts so special is that they are coherent—that is, they are made up of radiation whose waves are all in step with one another. (Regular radiation, such as that from a light bulb, is made up of waves that are jumbled and dissipate quickly in the dark. In contrast, laser light can be made concentrated enough to bounce off the moon and return to earth.) Glowing accounts in the aerospace press, based on a few facts and much technological optimism, report that as many as fifty laser rods might be assembled around a single bomb, meaning that in some scenarios one battle station might be able to hit as many as fifty enemy targets. Since X-rays do not penetrate very far into the earth's atmosphere, these weapons can in theory be used only in the void of space with any effectiveness.

EMP WEAPON: any nuclear bomb detonated high above the atmosphere bathes the area below in a powerful electromagnetic pulse (EMP) that is likely to burn out delicate electronic chips, transistors, computers and power and communication systems. The pulse happens at the speed of light, covering an entire continent. Ever since high-altitude EMP was discovered in 1962 (during a blast that lit up the skies of Hawaii), military planners in the United States have struggled to protect critical systems against its crippling effects.

MICROWAVE WEAPON: similar to EMP bombs, the microwave weapon concentrates the energy of a blast into a narrower band of frequencies of the electromagnetic spectrum to try to knock out enemy missiles. If hit by a sufficiently powerful pulse of energy, the delicate electronics in a missile's navigation system might be upset or ruined. The lure of microwave weapons is that they would better penetrate the earth's atmosphere than X-rays and that a single one might be able to knock out a whole group of missiles as they rose from their silos. The problem is that missiles, too, have long been shielded from electromagnetic attack because of fears about EMP, although much uncertainty surrounds how good this shielding may be. Another drawback is that microwave weapons cannot produce a 'hard kill' in which a missile explodes or drops in its tracks. Rather, it might zoom off course.

PARTICLE BEAMS: X-ray laser, EMP and microwave weapons exploit different types of electromagnetic waves moving at the speed of light. In contrast, another idea is to use a nuclear explosion to accelerate tiny sub-atomic particles—electrons, protons and ions—towards a target. The main problem is actually getting them *to* the target: in space, the path of these charged particles is bent in hard-to-predict ways by the earth's magnetic field. In short, they would penetrate even less far into the atmosphere than X-ray lasers, and therefore they would be of use only to shoot at objects in space.

These four weapon ideas are relatively new, although the concept of *using* specialized nuclear bombs is decades old. At Livermore one of the people behind this early nuclear work, John Nuckolls, told me that there were several reasons why the speculations of the past were today turning into nuclear realities, including the financial support of the Reagan administration, better computers for simulations, a youthful cadre of enthusiastic designers, and the rise of new administrators at Livermore who supported the notion of weapons innovation. The quest for defence is clearly not the only thing that keeps Nuckolls and his colleagues hard at work. In fact, researchers at the weapons lab are often driven as much by curiosity as by the desire to meet specific military needs. Lowell

Wood spoke repeatedly of the intellectual allure: 'Frankly, the offensive game, in addition to its somewhat dubious intent, is awfully easy. There just isn't much challenge there. Success consists of shrinking off an inch here and a pound there or moving the centre of gravity a half an inch forward. It's an engineering problem. Defensive weapons have a real, semi-fundamental challenge to them: in making them work effectively, robustly, and at a very high cost efficiency—against the offence.'

There is also the possibility that these 'weapons of life' will be weapons of aggression. 'There are very few technologies in the history of warfare that have been either totally offensive or totally defensive,' Paul L. Chrzanowski, head of military evaluation and planning at Livermore told me during an earlier visit to Livermore. 'If you can shoot down boosters, it's equally plausible that you could shoot down satellites.'

Teller's creation is known as 'pop-up'; its main requirement: no weapons orbit the earth. Rather, nuclear X-ray lasers and other third-generation weapons would be kept aboard American submarines and shot into space at the first sign of trouble. Rising above the earth's atmosphere, the battle stations would lock their sensors onto the hot flames of Soviet missiles and explode, sending their beams flashing across the heavens at the speed of light.

The rationale for Teller's strategy is the vulnerability of objects in space. Battle stations in orbit would be relatively easy for an enemy to find, track and destroy. Space mines could sneak up on them. Lasers and regular nuclear bombs could knock them out.

'We are not talking about battle stations in space,' Teller told the House Armed Services Committee. 'They are much too vulnerable. We should merely try to have our eyes in space and to maintain them. At the same time, when we notice that there is something amiss, we must be ready with pop-up systems. This involves not putting things in orbit, but putting appropriate objects to high altitudes in a great hurry from the earth's surface. The time available to act, if you take into account how much time you consume in accelerating these objects to high altitude, is counted in seconds—perhaps a hundred seconds.'

Pop-up is more challenging than any defensive system proposed in the past three decades, and requires, beyond the weapons themselves, breakthroughs in rocketry, communications and computers. 'In Livermore we have a magnificent development,' Teller told the committee, 'the S-1 computer project, which for a total multi-year cost of perhaps thirty million dollars, is creating the needed computing hardware. By using these coming super computers, we can make decisions in proper time so that we can orchestrate our defences and we can make sure that we do the best possible job in shielding ourselves from any strategic attack.'

Critics argue that technical breakthroughs are not enough; they insist that pop-up could be foiled easily by a clever enemy and is intrinsically flawed because of the great speed with which it must be deployed. There is no way, they say, that its nuclear weapons could remain under Presidential control.

War by computer is so feared because of the long history of false alerts—the forty-six cent computer chip, for instance, that failed in 1980, setting off alarms and sending B-52 pilots racing for their bombers. After such dramas, the military always explained that humans were in the decision loop, evaluating the information from various sensors and computers. False alerts would always be found out before it was too late, and, indeed, so far they always had. The position of the generals implied a healthy distrust of early-warning technology. Even the ultimate computer, they seemed to be saying, might break down or generate bogus data.

One of the young scientists had told me that a computer error wouldn't matter. 'So what if you deployed defensive armour?' he said. 'Unlike the consequences of unleashing an offensive arsenal, people would not be killed, cities would not be destroyed.' What he said had an element of truth. Yet, as another scientist had pointed out, a defensive system was not always what it seemed. It could be viewed as making offensive weapons 'far more deadly'. A paranoid enemy might misread the deployment of defensive armour in response to a false alert as the first step to something more sinister.

Complex hardware made up only half the computer controversy. The other half was programs—which in their most advanced form started to endow a computer with artificial intelligence. Circuits that operated billions of times faster than the synapses in the human brain were of little use unless the computer had a good program that orchestrated them. It was the difference between a baby's brain and that of an adult—one had circuits, while the other had circuits and some very good 'programs' that translated into such things as skill, compassion, cunning, kindness, and so forth. Good circuits were not enough.

During my third day at Livermore, I met Bruce McWilliams. He was twenty-eight years old but looked younger and was clean shaven. He wore a wedding ring, also a rarity in O Group.

McWilliams was the head of the most ambitious aspect of the S-1 Project—the quest to squeeze the circuitry of a super computer onto a thin silicon wafer. The reason wafer-scale integration is so important is that it would allow information to be processed with incredible speed—a critical requirement for pop-up. A tiny wafer on board a rising X-ray laser could be the battle station's brain—controlling engines and navigation, gathering data from sensors, receiving commands from the ground, pointing laser rods and triggering the nuclear chain reaction that would result in the battle station blowing up and firing its rays at distant targets. As Teller said, it would all have to happen in seconds.

Hundreds of wafers could also be stacked together to form ground-based computers of almost unimaginable power. Before any nuclear X-ray battle stations could be popped into space, an awesome number of steps would have to be taken. Signals from early-warning satellites and from radar stations would have to be processed quickly and double-checked to verify that an attack was underway. The 'threat cloud' would have to be resolved into individual missiles whose trajectories would be plotted. At the same time, computers would have to try to discriminate between real missiles and decoys, after which the data would be assigned and then transmitted to different submarines thousands of miles away, so they could divide up the job of trying to shoot down hundreds and perhaps thousands of Soviet missiles, rising ever more rapidly towards the edge of space. Powerful computers on the ground would be especially critical after the first stages of the battle, when thousands of speeding warheads and decoys might have to be attacked by the second and third tiers of a defensive shield.

No current computer was sufficiently powerful to handle the challenges of pop-up. Military machines and their operators were said to be able to process and verify data from early warning satellites in about two minutes. If the computers in Teller's vision were that slow, pop-up would fail before it ever got off the ground.

On my third day I also met Andy Weisberg, computer whiz, rocket enthusiast and player of nuclear war games.

Tall and gangly, with long black hair and a toothy grin, Weisberg, twenty-nine, was born in New York City and graduated near the top of his class from Stuyvesant, a prestigious science high school in the city. Along with about one hundred of his classmates he went on to study at the Massachusetts Institute of Technology, where he took three degrees—in mechanical engineering, electrical engineering and aeronautics and astronautics. In 1975, at twenty, Weisberg became a Hertz Fellow and started studying at Stanford while working at the weapons lab. He almost single-handedly helped get the wafer project off the ground. He had left O Group in the late 1970s and had recently returned, specifically asking to work on issues related to creating a defensive shield for the nation.

He was currently trying to determine if pop-up would work and if the group's computers would have enought time to perform their complex calculations. He was 'red-teaming it', meaning he was simulating moves the Soviet Union might make to try to outwit a defence. In American military circles, the red team was always the bad guy and the good guy blue. In Andy Weisberg's case, he wrote computer simulations of Soviet rockets, trying to see what the Soviets could do to make them less vulnerable to X-ray lasers and other elements of a shield. Weisberg's work was top secret and quite sophisticated. But it nonetheless bore some resemblance to the 'Missile Command' battles fought by kids in video arcades across the country.

As we talked a loudspeaker in the hall came alive: 'Attention all laboratory personnel. The security department will be holding exercises in a limited area using blank ammunition. These exercises will last until approximately midnight.' The men in battle fatigues from the cafeteria were obviously getting ready to conduct mock raids. Weisberg said that sometimes when he arrived in the morning he would find empty cartridges scattered on the ground.

Although he strongly supported the development of advanced weaponry for defence of the nation, Weisberg, like some of his colleagues, had strong reservations about doing the work himself. 'I have tried over the years to keep my hands clean,' he said. 'I have not entirely succeeded.' He emphasized that his dabblings in weaponry never had anything to do with nuclear bombs. That work he had managed to avoid entirely.

Weisberg described how many of the members of O Group had been recruited and his feelings about those methods. 'Of course you know about the Hertz connection. That's the way most of the manpower has been drafted. The Hertz Foundation concentrated all the applicants. The interviewers combed them even further. And those who were willing to work here were already self-selected for this kind of interest.' Hertz fellows were indeed an elite group. 'I've toyed with the notion that Hertz operates on the model of the child buyer. Here are all these people, after all, with these nice resources picking out the best and the brightest. Let's face it, no one in industry is giving away these kind of scholarships.

'But I really had no qualms once they explained the national defence clause. The Hertz Foundation was a very enlightened way to go through graduate school. They said it was a matter of personal conscience. But I think they did want to find out if defending the country was part of my values. I certainly didn't want to swear that I'd let the government define what constituted a national emergency because they could have defined it as Vietnam. I missed the draft by a year and was profoundly glad about that. Nobody at the time seemed to mind that the prime of American manhood was getting turned into gunship fodder or drug experiments in Southeast Asia.'

Weisberg described what life was like at the weapons lab. The picture he painted was one of remarkable tension between the isolation of the Livermore area and the off-beat attractions of Lowell and the group. Weisberg viewed the situation from a slight remove. He lived in San Francisco and came to the lab only a few days a week.

'There is a real aspect of debate here. Many of the interactions are thinly veiled displays of aggression. It's not just male society, it's a particularly self-selected variant of it. I used to call it ego war. I remember certain evenings sitting around eating popcorn with Rod Hyde and Lowell Wood. Their basic notion of amusement was to set problems for one another that could potentially damage each other's ego, testing the pecking order of who knew most about what.

Nonetheless, whether every position Lowell espouses is right or not, he is a force for innovation. And a scathing critic.

'At any rate, there's not much entertainment at Livermore. With the males around here, you can talk technolese over hamburgers till the cows come home. That's no substitute for a love life. It's not the same thing as an intellectual life. There are sub-societies here in the group, like the people who go to the symphony and the ones who go to rock concerts. There are large dinner groups and movie groups that go into Berkeley. But basically Livermore is no place for a single male to live.'

P eter Hagelstein had never wanted to work on weapons—not in the beginning at least. He wanted to win the Nobel Prize by creating the world's first laboratory X-ray laser, a device that would have no use as a weapon but wide application in biology and medicine. Along the way, however, he got caught in a very different quest, one he had long avoided—the design of nuclear weapons. He did so even though his woman friend objected and threatened to leave him. Amid a bitter break-up and ensuing depression, Hagelstein invented an altogether different kind of X-ray laser, one of enormous power that could be efficiently pumped by a nuclear bomb.

References to Hagelstein's breadth and creativity had come up often in my conversations at the lab. Peter was said to have run marathons in college and been on the swim team. He studied piano and flute. He played violin in a string quartet during his freshman year at MIT, also joining its symphony orchestra and touring with it nationally. He loved French literature. But many people had also commented on Peter's eccentricity. Andy Weisberg, a close friend, had mentioned repeatedly how he was intellectually driven and full of rigour but left himself open to all sorts of mundane problems. 'He's an insomniac in general but especially before important meetings,' Weisberg said. 'He works incredible hours the day before and then can't sleep and shows up looking like a dead fish.'

Another young scientist, Larry West, had been impressed with Hagelstein's ability to concentrate all his energies on a single goal. He recounted how Hagelstein had worked around the clock on computer codes to predict the electron transitions of laboratory X-ray lasers in the 1970s. 'He was working fourteen or fifteen hours a day, night and day, seven days a week.' West added that Hagelstein's meals often consisted of peanut butter sandwiches and a Coke. 'He'd run to the refrigerator, open the bread, slap down some peanut butter, and go right back to the computer terminal. He worked night and day calculating atomic energy levels. There were millions of things he had to do, all of which were very exotic and relied on the most advanced physical theory. He didn't even have a physics background. He learned the most advanced quantum physics by simply reading the technical literature, which was amazing. He worked that way for about seven or eight years.'

When I finally met Peter, he was taller and heavier than I expected, looking like an overgrown choirboy: twenty-nine, with a round unlined face, pale complexion, and silky blond hair. He was withdrawn, cast his gaze downward.

Graduating in 1972 with a National Merit Scholarship, he was quickly accepted by MIT, which offered him a hefty package of financial aid. He took a double load, plus courses during the summer, and after his second year of what is normally a four-year degree was ready to graduate from the Department of Electrical Engineering and Computer Science. In the spring of 1974, he was admitted to MIT's graduate school. Financial aid had paved his way as an undergraduate, but now he worked, first as a research assistant and then as a teaching assistant. Belatedly, Hagelstein began to look through MIT's fellowship file. Hertz stood out as having one of the highest stipends of all.

Hagelstein had an interview with Lowell Wood, and in addition to getting a fellowship was offered a job at the weapons lab for the summer of 1975. Having never heard of the lab, he hesitated at first but eventually accepted.

Did Wood explain the nature of the laboratory? 'He said that in some ways it was like any place else,' Hagelstein answered. 'He said they were working on lasers and laser fusion, which I had never heard of before, and he said there were computer codes out there that were like playing a Wurlitzer organ. It all sounded kind of dreamy.'

At the age of twenty, he drove down Interstate 580 through the Livermore valley toward the weapons lab. What he saw was sharply at odds with the green trees and ponds that had been depicted in a laboratory brochure. 'I got out here at the end of May,' Hagelstein recalled. 'It was close to one hundred degrees and the hills were burned brown. The place looked disgusting. I was driving down the freeway and the sign said the population of Livermore was 35,000. It seemed there were more cows than people.'

At this point, in 1976, Hagelstein was interested only in trying to create a laboratory X-ray laser, an advance that he felt would precipitate a host of biomedical discoveries. The laser's very short wavelength would allow it to 'see' all sorts of biological processes, cell structures, and molecules that previously had been hidden. Moreover, the images would be three-dimensional. Just as lasers at visible wavelengths could take 3-D holographic 'pictures' of large objects such as Coke bottles, X-ray lasers would be able to do the same in the microscopic world of atoms and molecules, revealing the fabric of life. Biologists longed for such pictures. They had already discovered the chemical composition of many biological molecules, and desperately wanted a way to understand how these complex structures fit together in three dimensions, forming membranes and other structures. The pictures would shed light on all sorts of processes, including why cellular machinery went awry in the phenomenon of cancer.

Hagelstein was attracted by the fact that so many scientists had tried and failed to create an X-ray laser over so many decades; its final achievement would spark a world-wide sensation and possibly lead to the Nobel Prize. Indeed, his excitement grew rapidly as he began to understand the scope of the challenge. But the bureaucratic machinery of the weapons lab and the federal government remained cool to the notion of funding any work on a laboratory X-ray laser.

But Hagelstein was not the only individual at Livermore to dream the dream of X-ray lasers. Others had too, and they eventually succeeded in persuading him to join their distinctive efforts. While he had wanted to finesse the experiment, they wanted to use brute force.

The search for the X-ray laser at Livermore had actually got underway in the late 1960s, the pace picking up considerably when Lowell Wood and another scientist named George Chapline later teamed up to pursue it. Chapline, in particular, never stopped pondering the elusive goal, wanting during the mid-1970s to pump an X-ray laser with a power source many billions of times more powerful than the biggest laboratory laser on earth. He wanted to use a nuclear bomb. Such thoughts had occurred to others before. Indeed, for decades the weapons enthusiasts at Livermore had envisioned using nuclear bombs to dig ditches, blast asteroids, create black holes and pump all kinds of exotic beam weapons. But Chapline in 1977 came up with a novel idea for how to go about building a nuclear-pumped X-ray laser. In one of those odd coincidences, that year also marked the appearance of the movie that would eventually become the rallying cry for the work—*Star Wars*.

Chapline's experiment consisted in pounding target material with intense radiation from a bomb with the hope that the material would, with luck, undergo a population inversion and lase at X-ray wavelengths. It would be a 'nuclear' X-ray laser only in the sense that it was pumped by a nuclear bomb. Its atomic nuclei would in no way contribute to the lasing. The explosion took place on 13 September 1978, but the elaborate apparatus of detectors and sensors for measuring the output of the X-ray experiment had broken down. No one knew whether Chapline's innovative idea was a success or a failure.

Throughout 1979, Chapline and the laboratory's main bomb builders interested in the nuclear X-ray laser had been holding regular meetings to discuss it and the impending test. Had they overlooked anything? What were the physics? Was there a better way to try to go about it? Wood and Hagelstein were present at some of those discussions. Hagelstein's input was especially welcome for he had been working all those years on laboratory X-ray lasers and knew the general X-ray laser theoretics better than anybody else at the lab. But his impulse was to resist. He hated bombs. He didn't want to be associated with anything nuclear. This feeling, moreover, was strongly reinforced by a woman he was seeing at the time, Josephine Stein.

Peter and Josie had met at MIT in the early 1970s and had got to know each other while playing together in the symphony. During the summer of 1978, Josie moved from Cambridge to Berkeley to begin work on a master's degree at the University of California. Her boyfriend had recently died in a car crash and she was lonely and depressed. She looked up Peter in nearby Livermore and the two were soon seeing much of each other.

As Josie learned more about the lab and what it did, she began to disparage it. She said bombs were bombs, and would always be agents of death and destruction. She accused Peter and his friends at the lab of ignoring the reality of their work. She told him that Wood and Teller were using him for their own ends. She encouraged him to quit, and to interview at other places for a job.

Hagelstein was sympathetic. He had never liked the notion of working on weapons and had usually managed to do things at the lab that in his own mind had no relation to bombs whatsoever. Now he felt pressure to make some kind of nuclear contribution. He fought it, going out to Bell Laboratories in New Jersey at one point to interview for a job. Throughout 1979, moreover, Josie became more and more militant, at one point joining protesters outside the gates at Livermore.

But despite Hagelstein's aversion to nuclear labours, he accidentally started down a fateful path one day. During the summer of 1979, at one of Chapline's meetings, he let slip with a suggestion that changed the focus of the nuclear X-ray laser programme forever—and may yet change the strategic postures of the superpowers as well.

The day before the meeting, in typical fashion, Hagelstein had been on a binge, working day and night, and arrived at the meeting in his 'dead fish' mode, slightly disoriented and dazed. For years he had pondered how to make X-ray lasers, his mind turning the problem over and over. Now, exhausted from too much work and not enough sleep, his subconscious seemed to take over. He viewed himself from a distance, as if through the wrong end of a telescope. It was the kind of psychological state that comes after an accident or great stress. There was Peter. There was Peter at the meeting with Chapline and Wood and the others. There was Peter saying something that had not been said before, something new in the arcane world of nuclear X-ray lasers.

'I had been up twenty hours,' he recalled. 'It had something to do with being stretched out. The mouth just said it.'

In the days after the meeting, Wood lobbied hard for a test of the approach that Hagelstein had broached. Chapline resisted. In the end, lab officials decided that the impending test of Chapline's nuclear X-ray laser should be modified to include Hagelstein's idea as well, even though making the changes would entail some expense. One bomb would pump two sets of hardware meant to produce an X-ray laser. It was to be a competition—senior physicist versus graduate student.

Wood described Hagelstein's idea as a 'flash of insight'. Hagelstein however was more circumspect. 'It takes five minutes to make a suggestion, and it just happened to be one that hadn't been made before. Then I got my arm twisted to do a detailed calculation. I resisted doing it. There were political pressures like you wouldn't believe.'

He was asked to do much more than scribble for a few minutes on a yellow pad of paper. He was being asked to sit at his computer terminal day after day, pouring his special expertise into the calculation of what might happen when a certain lasing set-up was pumped by a nuclear explosion. The raw material was to be his mammoth computer code, XRASER, which he had written to understand the electron transitions that power all X-ray lasers.

Despite the protests of Josie and his own apprehensions, Peter went ahead and worked on the calculations for the nuclear-pumped X-ray laser. Why? Certainly there were 'political pressures': both Teller and Wood were eager for him to work on what was perhaps the most innovative idea in nuclear weaponry since the H-bomb. Long afterwards, Hagelstein liked to joke about Teller's general influence on people, citing a line out of *Star Wars*: 'The Force has a powerful effect on the weak mind.' Moreover, during the episode Peter read *The Gulag Archipelago,* Solzhenitsyn's three-volume portrait of the nightmares of Soviet concentration camps. During our conversation, Hagelstein said he had read the *Gulag* volumes during this period but insisted that years earlier he had started and dropped them and was in no way naïve about the Soviets, having read much Russian literature and history in high school and college. 'I've got a fairly moody and depressive personality. I read the *Gulag.* I'm afraid I like reading that kind of thing. I don't think the *Gulag* was pivotal. I was depressed that it lifted my spirits.' Perhaps, but others in the group said his reading made a discernible difference in his attitude towards work on nuclear weaponry.

The young scientists of the group remained close friends however, and the friendship even extended to the language they spoke. Classified projects led to classified jokes. After a while, the young scientists began to be cut off from the spontaneity of the outside world. A visitor could engage them in polite conversation, but so much of their world revolved around secret research that free discussions could occur only with other 'Q cleared' people. It was like the Gulag. Stalin's concentration camps were the only place in Russia where people could really criticize the state. Freedom came only in captivity.

During this period, Peter's relationship with Josie began to fall apart. 'At first I tended to agree with her,' Peter had recalled. 'But she was terribly adamant. The more she talked the less sense she made.' Though a parting of the ways was predictable, Peter eventually became very depressed. Of the two, he had been more passionately involved in the relationship. At his lowest moments, after the break-up, the stereo in his office played nothing but requiems by Brahms, Verdi, and Mozart.

Josie went far in the opposite direction. In the months after the break-up, her views of nuclear weaponry and the people who ran the lab deepened and became more pronounced. By remarkable coincidence, she made her views public in a biweekly MIT student newspaper that was dated 3 November 1980, corresponding exactly with the date of Peter's successful nuclear test. Its headline was FELLOWSHIP FOR WORK ON 'HUMAN PROBLEMS' LINKED TO LIVERMORE. It was a detailed account of the recruiting practices of the Hertz Foundation, a picture of Teller in its centre. The understated charge was deception: that the foundation, ostensibly set up to fund graduate education, in truth recruited unsuspecting students to work on bombs. In the article, Josie did not mention Peter by name. But the fact of the article's existence suggested that she had strong feelings about why he had ended up at Livermore. The piece started off by noting that another MIT newspaper had carried ads from the Hertz Foundation meant to bring its fellowship programme to the attention of MIT students. One was reproduced: 'The proposed field of graduate study must be concerned with applications of the physical sciences to human problems, broadly construed.' In the article Josie commented: 'From the information in the announcements, one would never guess that the administration of the fellowship has close ties with the Lawrence Livermore National Laboratory, one of the two national laboratories dedicated to the research and development of nuclear weapons.' She noted Teller's place on the Hertz board, the foundation's address, and the fact that Lowell Wood was both the foundation's chief recruiter and the head of O Group, which 'is largely composed of Hertz Fellows and Hertz alumni.' At the end, she asked whether the competition for Hertz Fellowships was not 'in reality a deceptive campaign to recruit the most capable young technologists to work on nuclear weapons-related projects at Lawrence Livermore Lab? Such a premise would be very difficult to substantiate. However, prospective applicants for the Hertz Fellowship would be well advised to carefully consider the implications of involvement with the foundation and Livermore.'

The underground test itself, code-named 'Dauphin', occurred at the Nevada test site on 14 November 1980. Lowell Wood and George Chapline were there, worrying and fussing and sweating over the details. Peter was not, having stayed behind in Livermore. The test was a success for both devices, although Hagelstein's results were vastly superior. For Peter, the implications of his work on nuclear weapons multiplied in the wake of the successful test, his device rapidly becoming the basis for the nation's nuclear X-ray laser programme and playing a direct role in the genesis of the Star Wars speech. Wood flew back from the Nevada test site. To celebrate, he and Hagelstein and several other members of O Group drove into the heart of downtown Livermore and had ice cream at the Baskin-Robbins 31 Flavors.

'My view of weapons has changed.' Peter recalled. 'Until 1980 or so I didn't want to have anything to do with nuclear anything. Back in those days I thought there was something fundamentally evil about weapons. Now I see it as an interesting physics problem.'

QVEENS
by Pickles

'More bizarre than any fiction'

HUGH DAVID,
THE TIMES EDUCATIONAL SUPPLEMENT

'Fascinating and often brilliant'

MICHAEL TANNER,
THE TIMES LITERARY SUPPLEMENT

'Funny, acute, and very well written'

VICTORIA GLENDINNING,
THE SUNDAY TIMES

'*Queens* is the Sloane Ranger
Handbook for full-time urban
homosexuals — part lampoon,
part vade-mecum'

JOHN RYLE,
LONDON REVIEW OF BOOKS

£8.95 ISBN 0 7043 2439 3

QUARTET BOOKS LIMITED
A member of the Namara Group
27/29 Goodge Street
London W1P 1FD

QUARTET

LETTRE INTERNATIONALE

N° 5 — Eté 1985

LE CINEMA SE MEURT
WOLFRAM SCHÜTTE · WILLIAM ROTHMAN

LES ALLEMANDS
A. RUTH
I. KARLSSON
T. GARTON ASH
V. BRAUN

POÈTES
J. SEIFERT I. ANDRIC
J. GOYTISOLO O. PAZ
C. MILOSZ Z. HERBERT
B. PASTERNAK G. CARDUCCI

ANDRE BRINK ITALO CALVINO
DANILO KIS MARTHE ROBERT

LE PROCES D'EZRA POUND

Le numéro 30 F. Abonnement 100 F, étranger 140 F
14-16, rue des Petits-Hôtels, 75010 Paris (1) 523-48-40.

PRIMO LEVI
CHILDREN OF
THE WIND

It is to be hoped that the Islands of the Wind (Mahui and Kaenunu) will be excluded from the tourist circuit for as long as possible. It would not be easy to develop them, in any case: the soil is so rough that it would be impossible to build an airport, and nothing larger than a rowing-boat can come close to their shores. Water is scarce, in some years totally lacking; the islands have therefore never supported any permanent human settlement. Nevertheless, Polynesian crews have landed there several times, perhaps even in the remote past, and a Japanese detachment stayed for a few months during the last war. The last human vestige to be found on the islands can be traced back to this fleeting presence: on the highest point of Mahui, a modest but steep ridge about one hundred metres high, are the ruins of a dry-stone anti-aircraft bunker. It may never have fired a shot: we have not found a single shell in its vicinity. On Kaenunu we found a whip wedged between two boulders, a vestige of some inexplicable violence.

Today Kaenunu is largely deserted. On Mahui, on the other hand, it is not unusual for anyone with patience and good vision to catch sight of some *atoula*, or more often a *nacunu*, one of the females. If one excludes the well-known cases of certain domestic animals, this is probably the only animal species in which the male and the female have been given different names, a fact that can be explained by the definite sexual dimorphism that characterizes them, and that is certainly unique among mammals. This remarkable species of rodent can only be found on the two islands.

The *atoula*—that is, the males—are as much as half a metre in length and weigh between five and eight kilos. They have grey or brown hair, very short tails, a pointed muzzle furnished with black whiskers, short triangular ears; their belly is naked, pinkish, and barely covered with a sparse down that, as we shall see, is not without its evolutionary significance. The females, which weigh rather more, are longer and sturdier than the males: their movements are swifter and more confident, and according to the Malayan hunters, their senses are also more developed, especially the sense of smell. Their hair is totally different: in all seasons, the *nacunu* wear a gaudy livery of shiny black, streaked with four brownish stripes, two on each side, that cross the flanks from the muzzle and join up near the tail, which is long and thick, and shaded from brown to orange, brilliant red, or purple, according to the age of the animal. While the males are almost invisible on the stony ground where they live, the females on the other hand can be observed from afar, because they are also in the habit of wagging their tails like dogs. The males are torpid and lazy, the females agile and active. Both are mute.

There is no copulation among the *atoula*. In the mating season, which lasts from September to November and coincides with the period of greatest drought, the males climb at sunrise to the top of the ridge, sometimes even into the highest trees, not without some contention for the conquest of the most elevated positions. There they remain all day long without eating or drinking: they turn their backs to the wind, and emit their semen into the wind itself. The semen is made up of a watery fluid that rapidly evaporates in the hot, dry air and spreads on the wind in the form of a cloud of fine dust. Each grain of this dust is a single sperm. We managed to collect some on glass slides spread with oil: the sperm of the *atoula* are different from those of every other animal species, and must rather be equated with the pollen-grains of anemophile plants. They have no caudal filament, and are covered instead with minute hairs, which are branched and bushy so that the sperm can be carried remarkable distances by the wind. On our return journey, we collected some 130 miles from the islands, and to all appearances they were alive and fertile. During seminal emission, the *atoula* stay still, bolt upright on their haunches, with their forelimbs folded, shaken by a light tremor that may have the function of speeding up the evaporation of the seminal fluid from the hairless surface of the belly. When the wind suddenly changes (a frequent event at those latitudes), the spectacle of countless *atoula*, each upright on his eminence, all turning simultaneously in the new direction like the weather vanes formerly placed on rooftops, is quite remarkable. They seem concentrated and tense, and do not react to stimuli: this kind of behaviour is explicable only if one remembers that these animals are not threatened by any predator that would otherwise easily overcome them. Even the Malayan hunters respect them— according to some, because an ancient tradition holds them sacred to Hatola, the wind-god, from whom the *atoula* actually derive their name; according to others, it is simply because at this period their flesh would provoke an unspecified intestinal complaint.

In the season of dissemination, the fixity of the males contrasts with the extreme mobility of the females. Guided by sight and smell, they move quickly and restlessly from one spot to another on the moor; they do not try to approach the males, or climb, as the males do, to the highest places; they seem to be hunting for a position in which they can better be enveloped in the invisible spray of semen, and when they think they have found one, they stop there, spinning voluptuously, but not for more than a few minutes: straight away they dart off with a rapid leap, and resume their dance, up and down on the rocks and the moor. During this period, the entire island swarms with the orange and violet flames of their tails, and the wind is charged with a sharp, musky, stimulating and inebriating odour, which draws all the animals on the island along in an aimless round-dance. The birds fly up screaming, and wheel round in circles, aiming towards the sky like mad things, and then let themselves drop like stones; the jumping mice, which, tiny nimble shadows, can normally be spotted only on moonlit nights, come out of hiding, dazed and incapable in the splendour of the sun, and can be caught with one's hands; even the snakes wriggle out of their dens as if hallucinating, and rise up, coiled on their tails, waving their heads as if in time to a rhythm. During the brief nights that interrupted the days, even we experienced unquiet slumbers, crammed with multicoloured and indecipherable dreams. We have not managed to establish whether the smell that pervades the island emanates directly from the males or whether it is secreted by the inguinal glands of the *nacunu*.

Their pregnancy lasts about thirty-five days; delivery and lactation are unremarkable; the nests, built of twigs in the shelter of a rock, are prepared by the males, and lined on the inside with musk, leaves, and sometimes with sand: every male prepares more than one. Approaching delivery, each female chooses her own nest, examining several with attention and hesitation, but without dispute. The 'children of the wind', born between five and eight to a litter, are tiny but precocious: only a few hours after delivery they go out into the sun: the males learn at once to turn their backs to the wind like their fathers, and the females, although still lacking their livery, show themselves off in a comic parody of their mothers' dance. After only five months, *atoula* and *nacunu* are sexually mature and already live in separate herds, waiting for the next windy season to prepare their remote and airy nuptials.

Translated from the Italian by Simon Rees and Antonio Tanca

two firsts from Penguin

*Winner of the David Higham Prize and
the 1984 Whitbread Award for a First Novel*

A PARISH OF RICH WOMEN

A CONTEMPORARY THRILLER
James Buchan

*'Horror and pity shimmer through James
Buchan's brisk style'— The Times*

£2.95

*Published for the first time in the UK,
the beguiling debut novel by the acclaimed
author of Heat and Dust*

TO WHOM SHE WILL

Ruth Prawer Jhabvala

*Evoking the India of the early 1950s, a
beautifully told, richly comic tale of young love..*

£3.95

GRANTA

JOHN BERGER
BORIS

Sometimes to refute a single sentence it is necessary to tell a life story.

In our village, as in many villages in the world at that time, there was a souvenir shop. The shop was in a converted farm house which had been built four or five generations earlier, on the road up to the mountain. You could buy there skiers in bottles, mountain flowers under glass, plates decorated with gentians, miniature cow bells, plastic spinning wheels, carved spoons, chamois leather, sheepskins, clockwork marmots, goat horns, cassettes, maps of Europe, knives with wooden handles, gloves, T-shirts, films, key rings, sunglasses, imitation butter-churns, my books.

The woman who owned the shop served in it. She was by then in her early forties. Blond, smiling but with sharp eyes, she was buxom with small feet and slender ankles. The young in the village nick-named her the Goose—for reasons that are not part of this story. Her real name was Marie-Jeanne. Earlier, before Marie-Jeanne and her husband came to the village, the house belonged to Boris. It was from him that they inherited it.

Now I come to the sentence that I want to refute.

Boris died, said Marc, leaning one Sunday morning against the wall that twists (like the last letter of the alphabet) through our hamlet, Boris died like one of his own sheep, neglected and starving. What he did to his cattle finally happened to him: he died like one of his own animals.

Boris was the third of four brothers. The eldest was killed in the War, the second by an avalanche and the youngest emigrated. Even as a child Boris was distinguished by his brute strength. The other children at school feared him a little and at the same time teased him. They had spotted his weakness. To challenge most boys you bet that they couldn't lift a sack of seventy kilograms. Boris could lift seventy kilograms with ease. To challenge Boris you bet him that he couldn't make a whistle out of a branch of an ash tree.

During the summer, after the cuckoos had fallen silent, all the boys had ash whistles, some even had flutes with eight holes. Having found and cut down the little branch of wood, straight and of the right diameter, you put it in your mouth to moisten it with your tongue, then tapped on it, all round, briskly but not too hard with the wooden handle of your pocket knife. This tapping separated the bark from the wood so that you could pull the white wood out, like an arm from a sleeve. Finally you carved the mouth piece and reinserted it into the bark. The whole process took a quarter of an hour.

Boris put the little branch into his mouth as if he was going to devour the tree of life itself. And his difficulty was that he had invariably struck too hard with his knife handle, so that he had damaged the bark. His whole body went tense. He would try again. He would cut another branch and when it came to tapping it, either he would hit too hard, or, with the concentrated effort of holding himself back, his arm wouldn't move at all.

Come on, Boris, play us some music! they teased him.

When he was fully grown, his hands were unusually big and his blue eyes were set in sockets which looked as though they were meant for eyes as large as those of a calf. It was as if, at the moment of his conception, every one of his cells had been instructed to grow large; but his spine, femur, tibia, fibula had played truant. As a result, he was of average height but his features and extremities were like those of a giant.

One morning in the alpage, years ago, I woke up to find all the pastures white. One cannot really talk of the first snow of the year at an altitude of 1600 metres, because often it snows every month, but this was the first snow which was not going to disappear until the following year, and it was falling in large flakes.

Towards midday there was a knock on the door. I opened it. Beyond, almost indistinguishable from the snow, were thirty sheep, silent, snow on their necks. In the doorway stood Boris.

He came in and went over to the stove to thaw out. It was one of those tall stoves for wood, standing free in the centre of the room like a post of warmth. The jacket over his gigantic shoulders was white as a mountain.

For a quarter of an hour he stood there silent, drinking from the glass of gnole, holding his huge hands over the stove. The damp patch on the floorboards around him was growing larger.

At last he spoke in his rasping voice. His voice, whatever the words, spoke of a kind of neglect. Its hinges were off, its windows broken, and yet, there was a defiance in it, as if, like a prospector living in a broken-down shack, it knew where there was gold.

In the night, he said, I saw it was snowing. And I knew my sheep were up by the peak. The less there is to eat, the higher they climb. I drove up here before it was light and I set out. It was crazy to climb by myself. Yet who would come with me? I couldn't see the path for the snow. If I'd lost my foothold, there was nothing, nothing at all, to stop me till I reached the church-yard below. For five hours since daybreak I have been playing against death.

His eyes in their deep sockets interrogated me to check whether I had understood what he was saying. Not his words, but what lay behind them. Boris liked to remain mysterious. He believed that the unsaid favoured him. And yet, despite himself, he dreamed of being understood.

Standing there with the puddle of melted snow at his feet, he was not in the least like the good shepherd who had just risked his life for his flock. St John the Baptist, who crowned the Lamb with flowers, was the very opposite of Boris. Boris neglected his sheep. Each year he sheared them too late and they suffered from the heat. Each summer he omitted to pare their hooves and they went lame. They looked like a flock of beggars in grey wool, Boris's sheep. If he had risked his life that day on the mountain, it wasn't for their sake, but for the sake of their market price.

His parents had been poor, and from the age of twenty Boris boasted of the money he was going to make one day. He was going to make *big* money—according to the instructions received at his conception and inscribed in every cell of his body.

At market he bought cattle that nobody else would buy, and he bought at the end of the day, offering a price which twelve hours earlier would have appeared derisory. I see him, taciturn beside the big-boned animals, pinching their flesh with one of his immense thumbs, dressed in khaki and wearing an American army cap.

He believed that time would bring him nothing: and that his cunning must bring him everything. When he was selling he never named his price. 'You can't insult me,' he said, 'just tell me what you want to offer.' Then he waited, his blue, deep-set eyes already on the brink of the derision with which he was going to greet the price named.

He is looking at me now, with the same expression. I told you once, he says, that I had enough poems in my head to fill a book, do you remember? Now you are writing the story of my life. You can do that because it's finished. When I was still alive, what did you do? Once you brought me a packet of cigarettes whilst I was grazing the sheep above the factory.

I say nothing. I go on writing.

The uncle of all cattle dealers once told me: 'A ram like Boris is best eaten as meat.'

Boris's plan was simple: to buy thin and sell fat. What he sometimes underestimated was the work and time necessary between the two. He willed the thin cattle to become fat, but their flesh, unlike his own, was not always obedient to his will. And their bodies, at the moment of conception, had not received the same instructions.

He grazed his sheep on every scrap of common land and often on land which wasn't common. In the winter he was obliged to buy extra hay, and he promised to pay for it with lambs in the spring. He never paid. Yet he survived. And his herd grew bigger: in his heyday he owned a hundred and fifty sheep. He drove a Land Rover which he had recuperated from a ravine. He had a shepherd whom he had recuperated from an alcoholic's clinic. Nobody trusted Boris, nobody resisted him.

The story of his advancement spread. So too did the stories of his negligence—his unpaid debts, his sheep eating off land which belonged to other people. They were considered a scourge, Boris's sheep, as if they were a troop of wild boar. And often, like the Devil's own, his flock left and arrived by night.

In the Republican Lyre, the café opposite the church, there was sometimes something of the Devil about Boris too. He stood at the bar—he never sat down—surrounded by the young from several villages: the young who foresaw initiatives beyond the comprehension of their cautious yet wily parents, the young who dreamed of leisure and foreign women.

You should go to Canada, Boris was saying, that's where the future belongs. Here, as soon as you do something of your own, you're mistrusted. Canada is big, and when you have something big, you have something generous!

He paid for his round of drinks with a fifty thousand note, which he placed on the counter with his wooden-handled knife on top of it, so that it wouldn't blow away.

Here, he continued, nothing is ever forgiven! Not this side of death. And, as for the other side, they leave it to the curé. Have you ever seen anyone laughing for pleasure here?

And at that moment, as though he, the Devil, had ordered it, the door of the café opened and a couple came in, the woman roaring with laughter. They were strangers, both of them. The man wore a weekend suit and pointed shoes, and the woman, who, like her companion, was about thirty, had blond hair and wore a fur coat. One of the young men looked out through the window and saw their car parked opposite. It had Lyons number plates. Boris stared at them. The man said something and the woman laughed again. She laughed shamelessly, like a cock crowing.

Do you know them?

Boris shook his head.

Shortly afterwards he pocketed his knife, proffered the fifty thousand note, insisted upon paying for the two coffees the couple from Lyons were drinking, and left, without so much as another glance in their or anybody else's direction.

When the strangers got up to pay, the patronne simply said: It's already been settled.

Who by?

By the man who left five minutes ago.

The one in khaki? asked the blond. The patronne nodded.

We are looking for a house to rent, furnished if possible, said the man. Do you happen to know of any in the village?

For a week or a month? queried the patronne.

No, for the whole year round.

You want to settle here? asked one of the youths, incredulous.

My husband has a job in A——, the blond explained. He's a driving instructor.

The couple found a house. And one Tuesday morning, just before Easter, Boris drew up in his Land Rover and hammered on the door. It was opened by the blond, still wearing her dressing gown.

I've a present for you both, he said.

My husband, unfortunately, has just gone to work.

I know. I watched him leave. Wait!

He opened the back of the Land Rover and returned with a lamb in his arms.

This is the present.

Is it asleep?

No, slaughtered.

The blond threw her head back and laughed. What should we do with a slaughtered lamb? she sighed, wiping her mouth with her sleeve.

Roast it!

It still has its wool on. We don't know how to do such things and Gérard hates the sight of blood.

I'll prepare it for you.

It was you who bought us the coffee wasn't it?

Boris shrugged his shoulders. He was holding the lamb by its hind legs, its muzzle a few inches from the ground. The blond was wearing mules of artificial leopard skin.

Come in then, she said.

All this was observed by the neighbours.

The hind legs of the lamb were tied together and he hung it like a jacket on the back of the kitchen door. When he arrived, the blond had been drinking a bowl of coffee which was still on the table. In the kitchen there was the smell of coffee, of soap powder and of her. She had the smell of a buxom, plump body without a trace of the smell of work. Work has the smell of vinegar. He put out a hand to touch her hips as she passed between the table and the stove. Once again she laughed, this time quietly. Later he was to recall this first morning that he found himself in her kitchen, as if it were something he had swallowed, as if his tongue had never forgotten the taste of her mouth when she first bent down to kiss him.

Every time he visited her, he brought her a present; the lamb was only the first. Once he came with his tractor and trailer and on the trailer was a side-board. He never disguised his visits. He made them in full daylight before the eyes of his neighbours who noticed that each time, after about half an hour, the blond closed the shutters of the bedroom window.

And if one day her husband should come back unexpectedly? asked one of the neighbours.

God Forbid! Boris would be capable of picking him up and throwing him over the roof.

Yet he must have his suspicions?

Who?

The husband.

It's clear you've never lived in a big town.

Why do you say that?

The husband knows. If you'd lived in a big town, you'd know that the husband knows.

Then why doesn't he put his foot down, he can't be that cowardly?

One day the husband will come back, at a time agreed upon with his wife, and Boris will still be there, and the husband will say: What will you have as an aperitif, a pastis?

And he'll put poison in it?

No, black pepper! To excite him further.

Boris had been married at the age of twenty-five. His wife left him after one month. They were later divorced. His wife, who was not from the valley, never accused him of anything. She simply said, quietly, that she couldn't live with him. And once she added: perhaps another woman could.

The blond gave Boris the nickname of 'Little Humpback'.

My back is as straight as yours.

I didn't say it wasn't.

Then why—

It's what I like to call you.

Little Humpback, she said one day, do you ski?

When could I have learned?

You buy the skis and I'll teach you.

I'm too old to start, he said.

You're a champion in bed, you could be a champion on the ski slopes!

He pulled her towards him and covered her face and mouth with his huge hand.

This too he was to remember later when he thought about their two lives and the differences between them.

One day he arrived at the house carrying a washing machine on his shoulders. Another day he came with a wall-hanging, as large as a rug, on which were depicted, in bright velvet colours, two horses on a mountainside.

At that time Boris owned two horses. He'd bought them on the spur of the moment because he liked the look of them and he'd beaten down their price. In the spring I had to deliver a third horse to him. It was early morning and the snow had melted the week before. He was asleep in his bed and I woke him. Above his bed was a Madonna and a photograph of the blond. We took a bale of hay and went out to the field. There I let the horse go. After a long winter confined to the stable, she leapt and galloped between the trees. Boris was staring at her with his huge hands open and his eyes fixed. Ah Freedom! he said. He said it in neither a whisper nor a shout. He simply pronounced it as if it were the name of the horse.

The blond hung the tapestry on the wall in the bedroom. One Sunday afternoon, when Gérard was lying on the bed watching television, he nodded at the tapestry where the horses' manes were combed by the wind as if by a hairdresser and the horses' coats gleamed like polished shoes and the snow between the pine trees was as white as a wedding dress, and he said:

It's the only one of his presents I could do without.

I like horses, she said.

Horses! He made a whinnying noise.

Your trouble is that horses scare you!

Horses! The only thing to be said about a picture—and that's a picture even if it is made out of cotton—

Velvet!

—same thing, the only thing to be said about that picture there—is that in a picture horses don't shit.

She laughed, her shoulders and bosom shaking.

Have you talked to him about the house yet? Gérard asked.

How difficult it is to prevent certain stories becoming a simple moral demonstration! As if there were never any hesitations, as if life didn't wrap itself like a rag round the sharpest blade!

One midday, the following June, Boris arrived at the blond's house, covered in sweat. His face, with his hawk-nose and his cheekbones like pebbles, looked as if he had just plunged it into a water trough. He entered the kitchen and kissed her as he usually did, but this time without a word. Then he went to the sink and put his head under the tap. She offered him a towel which he refused. The water from his hair was running down his neck to the inside of the shirt. She asked him whether he wanted to eat; he nodded. He followed her with his eyes wherever she went, not sentimentally like a dog, nor suspiciously, but as though from a great distance.

Are you ill? she asked him abruptly as she put down his plate on the table.

I have never been ill, he replied.

Then what is the matter?

By way of reply he pulled her towards him and thrust his head, still wet, against her breast. The pain she felt was not in her chest but in her spine. Yet she did not struggle and she placed her plump white hand on the hard head. For how long did she stand there in front of his chair? For how long was his face fitted into her breast like a gun into its case lined with velvet? On the night when Boris died alone, stretched out on the floor with his three black dogs, it seemed to him that his face had been fitted into her breast ever since he first set eyes on her.

Afterwards he did not want to eat what was on his plate.

Come on, Humpback, take your boots off and we'll go to bed.

He shook his head.

What's the matter with you? she screeched. You sit there, you say nothing, you eat nothing, you do nothing, you're good for nothing!

He got to his feet and walked towards the door. For the first time she noticed he was limping.

What's the matter with your foot?

He did not reply.

For Christ's sake have you hurt your foot?

It's broken.

How?

I overturned the tractor on the slope above the house. I was flung off and the fender crushed my foot.

Did you call the doctor?

I came here.

Where's the jeep?

I can't drive, the ankle is blocked.

She started to untie the boots. She began with the unhurt foot. He said nothing. The second boot was a different matter. His whole body went rigid when she began to unlace it. His sock was drenched in blood and the foot was too swollen for her to remove the boot.

She started to snivel. He, now that the boot no longer gave his foot support, could not stand up. Her head hanging, her hands limp by her side, she sat on the kitchen floor at his feet, sobbing inconsolably.

His foot had eleven fractures. The doctor refused to believe that he had walked the four kilometres from his farm to the blond's. He said it was categorically impossible. The blond had driven Boris down to the surgery, and, according to the doctor, she had been at Boris's house all morning but for some reason didn't want to admit it. This is why, according to the doctor, the two of them had invented the implausible story of his walking four kilometres. The doctor, however, was wrong and the blond knew it. Of all the many times that Boris visited her, this was the only one which she never once mentioned to Gérard. And when, later, she heard the news of Boris's death, she immediately asked whether he was wearing boots when they found him.

No, was the surprising reply, he was barefoot.

B oris, when young, had inherited three houses, but all of them, by the standards of the towns, were in a pitiable condition. In the house with the largest barn he himself lived. There was electricity but no water. The house was below the road and the passer-by could look down its chimney. It was in this house that the three black dogs howled all night when he died.

The second house, the one he always referred to as the Mother's house, was the best situated of the three and he had long-term plans for selling it to a Parisian—when the day and the Parisian arrived.

In the third house, which was no more than a cabin at the foot of the mountain, Edmond, the shepherd, slept when he could. Edmond was a thin man with the eyes of a hermit. His experience had led him to believe that nearly all those who walked on two legs belonged to a species named Misunderstanding. He received from Boris no regular salary but occasional presents and his keep.

One spring evening, Boris went up to the house under the mountain, taking with him a cheese and a smoked side of bacon.

You're not often at home now! was how Edmond greeted him.

Why do you say that?

I have eyes. I notice when the Land Rover passes.

And you know where I go?

Edmond deemed the question unworthy of a reply, he simply fixed his unavailing eyes on Boris.

I'd like to marry her, said Boris.

But you can't, said Edmond.

She would be willing.

Are you sure?

Boris answered by smashing his right fist into his left palm. Edmond said nothing.

How many lambs? asked Boris.

Thirty-three. She is from the city isn't she?

Her father is a butcher in Lyons.

Why hasn't she any children?

Not every ram has balls, you should know that. She'll have a child of mine.

How long have you been going with her?

Eighteen months.

Edmond raised his eyebrows. City women are not the same, he said, and I ought to know. I've seen enough. They're not built the same way. They don't have the same shit and they don't have the same blood. They don't smell the same either. They don't smell of stables and onions and vinegar, they smell of something else. And that something else is dangerous. They have perfect eyelashes, they have unscratched legs without varicose veins, they have shoes with soles as thin as pancakes, they have hands white and smooth as peeled potatoes and when you smell their smell, it fills you with a god-forsaken longing. You want to breathe them to their dregs, you want to squeeze them like lemons until there is not a drop or a pip left. And shall I tell you what they smell of? Their smell is the smell of money. They calculate everything for money. They are not built like our mothers, these women.

You can leave my mother out of it.

Be careful, said Edmond, your blond will strip you of everything. Then she'll throw you aside like a plucked chicken.

With a slow blow to the face Boris knocked the shepherd over. He lay spread-eagled on the ground.

Nothing stirred. The dog licked Edmond's forehead.

Only somebody who has seen a battlefield, can imagine the full indifference of the stars above the shepherd spread-eagled on the ground. It is in face of this indifference that we seek love.

Tomorrow I will buy her a shawl, whispered Boris, and without a glance behind him, took the road back to the village.

Next morning the police came to warn him that his sheep were a public danger, for they were encumbering the motorway. Edmond, the shepherd, had disappeared and he was not seen again until after Boris's death.

The month of August was the month of Boris's triumph. Or is glory a better term? For he was too happy, too self-absorbed, to see himself as a victor who had triumphed over others. It had become clear to him that the instructions inscribed at the moment of his conception had involved more than the size of his bones, the thickness of his skull or the power of his will. He was destined, at the age of forty, to be recognized.

The hay had been brought in, his barn was full, his sheep were grazing high in the mountains, without a shepherd but God would preserve them, and every evening he sat on the terrace of the Republican Lyre overlooking the village square, with the blond in a summer dress, her shoulders bare, her feet in high-heeled silver sandals, and, until nightfall, the pair of them were the colour-television picture of the village.

Offer drinks to every table, he said, leaning back in his chair, and if they ask what's happened, tell them that Boris is buying horses!

Humpback, not every night, you can't afford it!

Every night! My balls are swollen.

He placed one of his immense hands on the bosom of her red polka-dot dress.

His energy made her laugh.

It's true about the horses, he said, I'm going to breed horses—for you! Breed riding horses that we'll sell to the idiots who come for weekends.

What should I do with horses? she asked, I can't ride.

If you have a child of mine—

Yes, Humpback.

I'll teach the child to ride, he said. A child of ours will have your looks and my pride.

The last word he had never uttered before concerning himself.

If we have a child, she whispered, the house where we live now is too small. We'd need at least another room.

And how many months have we got to sort out the question of a house? asked Boris with his cattle-dealer's canniness.

I don't know, Humpback, perhaps eight.

A bottle of champagne, Boris shouted, pour out glasses for everybody.

Are you still buying horses? asked Marc, who, with his pipe and blue overalls, is the sceptic of the Republican Lyre, the perennial instructor about the idiocy of the world.

That's none of your business, retorted Boris; I'm buying drinks.

I'll be tipsy, said the blond.

I'll get you some nuts.

On the counter of the Republican Lyre is a machine where you put in a franc and a child's handful of peanuts comes out. Boris fed coin after coin into the machine and asked for a soup plate.

When the men standing at the bar raised their glasses of champagne and nodded towards Boris, they were each toasting the blond: and each was picturing himself in Boris's place, some with envy, and all with that odd nostalgia which everyone feels for what they know they will never live.

Beside Marc stood Jean who had once been a long-distance lorry-driver. Now he kept rabbits with his wife and was seventy. Jean was in the middle of a story.

Guy was pissed out of his mind, Jean was saying; Guy slumped down on to the floor and lay there flat out, as if he were dead. Jean paused and looked at the faces around the bar to emphasize the impasse. What should we do with him? It was then that Patrick had his brainwave. Bring him round to my place, said Patrick. They got Guy into the car and they drove him up to Patrick's place. Bring him in here, lay him on the work bench, said Patrick. Now slip off his trousers.

The blond started to laugh.

You're not going to harm him? Slip off his trousers I tell you. Now his socks. There he lay on the work bench, as naked as we'll all be when the Great Holiday starts. What now? He's broken his leg, announced Patrick. Don't be daft. We're going to make him believe he broke his leg, Patrick explained. Why should he believe it? Wait and see. Patrick mixed up a bathful of plaster and, as professionally as you'd expect from Patrick, he plastered Guy's leg from the ankle to half-way up the thigh. Jean paused to look round at his listeners. On the way home in the car Guy came round. Don't worry, mate, said Patrick, you broke your leg, but it's not bad, we took you to the hospital and they've set it in plaster and they said you could have it off in a week, it's not a bad fracture. Guy looked down at his leg and the tears ran down his cheeks. What a cunt I am! he went on repeating. What a cunt I am!

The blond broke out into laughter, her head flung back, her chest out, her red-spotted dress stretched tight.

What happened afterwards, she asked, her mouth still open.

He was a week off work, watching the telly, with his leg up on a chair!

Boris put the back of his hand against her throat—for fear that the palm was too calloused—and there he could feel the laughter which began between her hips, gushing up to her mouth. Systematically he moved the back of his immense hand up and down the blond's throat.

Jean, the lorry-driver who now kept rabbits, watched this action, fascinated, as if it were more improbable than the story he had just told.

I couldn't believe it, he recounted to the habitués of the Republican Lyre later that night: there was Boris, over there, bone-headed Boris caressing the blond like she was a sitting-up squirrel, and feeding her nuts from a soup plate. And what do you think he does when the husband comes in? He stands up, holds out his hand to the husband and announces: What do you want to drink? A white wine with cassis? I'm taking her to the ball tonight, Boris says. We shan't be back till morning.

The ball was in the next village. All night it seemed to Boris that the earth was moving past the plough of its own volition.

Once they stopped dancing to drink. He beer, and she lemonade.

I will give you the Mother's house, he said.

Why do you call it that?

My mother inherited it from my father.

And if one day you want to sell it?

How can I sell it if I've given it to you?

Gérard will never believe it.

About our child?

No. About the house, he won't agree to move in, unless it's certain.

Leave Gérard! Come and live with me.

No Humpback, I'm not made for preparing mash for chickens.

Once again, by way of reply, Boris thrust his massive head against her breast. His face fitted into her breast like a gun into its case lined with velvet. For how long was his face buried between her breasts? When he raised it he said: I'll give you the house formally, I'll see the notary, it'll be yours, yours not his, and then it'll go to our child. Do you want to dance again?

Yes, Humpback.

They danced until the white dress with red polka-dots was stained with both their sweats, until there was no music left, until her blond hair smelled of his cows.

Years later, people asked: how was it possible that Boris, who never gave anything away in his life, Boris, who would cheat his own grandmother, Boris, who never kept his word, how was it that he gave the house to the blond? And the answer, which was an admission of the mystery, was always the same: a passion is a passion.

Women did not ask the same question. It was obvious to them that, given the right moment and circumstances, any man may be manipulated. There was no mystery. And perhaps it was for this reason that the women felt a little more pity for Boris than the men.

As for Boris, he never asked himself: Why did I give her the house? He never regretted this decision, although—and here all the commentators are right—it was unlike any other he had ever taken. He regretted nothing. Regrets force one to relive the past, and, until the end, he was waiting.

The flowers which grew in the mountains had brighter, more intense colours than the same flowers growing on the plain; a similar principle applied to thunderstorms. Lightning in the mountains did not just fork, it danced in circles; the thunder did not just clap, it echoed. And sometimes the echoes were still echoing when the next clap came, so that the bellowing became continuous. All this was due to the metal deposits in the rocks. During a storm, the hardiest shepherd asked himself: What in God's name am I doing here? And next morning, when it was light, he might find signs of the visitations of which, fortunately, he had been largely ignorant the night before: holes in the earth, burned grass, smoking trees, dead cattle. At the end of the month of August there was such a thunderstorm.

Some of Boris's sheep were grazing just below the Rock of St Antoine on the far slopes facing east. When sheep are frightened they climb, looking to heaven to save them; and so Boris's sheep moved up to the screes by the rock, and there they huddled together under the rain. Sixty sheep, each one resting his drenched head on the oily drenched rump or shoulders of his neighbour. When the lightning lit up the mountain—and everything appeared so clear and so close that the moment seemed endless—the sixty animals looked like a single giant sheepskin coat. There were even two sleeves, each consisting of half-a-dozen sheep, who were hemmed in along two narrow corridors of grass between the rising rocks. From this giant coat, during each lightning flash, a hundred or more eyes, glistening like brown coal, peered out in fear. They were right to be frightened. The storm centre was approaching. The next forked lightning struck the heart of the coat and the entire flock was killed. Most of them had their jaws and forelegs broken by the shock of the electrical discharge, received in the head and earthed through their thin bony legs.

In the space of one night Boris lost three million francs.

It was I, thirty-six hours later, who first noticed the crows circling in the sky. Something was dead there, but I didn't know what. Somebody told Boris and the next day he went up to the Rock of St Antoine. There he found the giant sheepskin coat, discarded, cold, covered with flies. The carcasses were too far from any road. The only thing he could do was to burn them where they were.

He fetched petrol and diesel oil and started to make a pyre, dragging the carcasses down the two sleeves and throwing them one on top of another. He started the fire with an old tyre. Thick smoke rose above the peak, and with it the smell of burned animal flesh. It takes very little to turn a mountain into a corner of hell. From time to time Boris consoled himself by thinking of the blond. Later he would laugh with her. Later, his face pressed against her, he would forget the shame of this scene. But more than these promises which he made to himself, it was the simple fact of her existence which encouraged him.

By now everybody in the village knew what had happened to Boris's sheep. No one blamed Boris outright—how could they? Yet there were those who hinted that a man couldn't lose so many animals at one go unless, in some way, he deserved it. Boris neglected his cattle. Boris did not pay his debts. Boris was having it off with a married woman. Providence was delivering him a warning.

They say Boris is burning his sheep, said the blond, you can see the smoke over the mountain.

Why don't we go and watch? suggested Gérard.

She made the excuse of a headache.

Come on, he said, it's a Saturday afternoon and the mountain air will clear your head. I've never seen a man burning sixty sheep.

I don't want to go.

What's niggling you?

I'm worried.

You think he could change his mind about the house now? He'll certainly be short of money.

It's not a flock of sheep that's going to make him change his mind about the house.

We shouldn't count our chickens—

Only one thing could make him go back on his word about the house.

If you stopped seeing him?

Not exactly.

What then?

Nothing.

Has he mentioned the house recently?

Do you know what he calls it? He calls it the Mother's house.

Why?

She shrugged her shoulders.

Come on, said Gérard.

Gérard and his wife drove up the mountain to where the road stopped. From there, having locked the car, they continued on foot. Suddenly she screamed as a grouse flew up from under her feet.

I thought it was a baby! she cried.

You must have drunk too much. How can a baby fly?

That's what I thought, I'm telling you.

Can you see the smoke? Gérard asked.

What is it that's hissing?

His sheep cooking! said Gérard.

Don't be funny.

Grasshoppers.

Can you smell anything?

No.

I wouldn't like to be up here in a storm, she said.

He wasn't here often either.

It's all very well for you to talk, you've never lifted a shovel in your life, she said.

That's because I'm not stupid.

No. Nobody could call you that. And he's stupid, Boris is stupid, stupid, stupid!

He was encouraging the fire with fuel, whose blue flames chased the slower yellow ones. He picked up a sheep by its legs, and swung it back and forth, before flinging it high into the air so that it landed on top of the pyre, where, for a few minutes longer, it was still recognizable as an animal. The tear-stains on his cheek were from tears provoked by the heat, and, when the wind turned, by the acrid smoke. Every few minutes he picked up another carcass, swung it to gain a momentum, and hurled it into the air. The boy, who had never been able to tap the ash-bark gently enough, had become the man who could burn his own herd single-handed.

Gérard and the blond stopped within fifty yards of the blaze. The heat, the stench and something unknown prevented them approaching further. This unknown united the two of them: wordlessly they were agreed about it. They raised their hands to protect their eyes. Fires and gigantic waterfalls have one thing in common. There is spray torn off the cascade by the wind, there are the flames: there is the rock-face dripping and visibly eroding, there is the breaking up of what is being burned: there is the roar of the water, there is the terrible chatter of the fire. Yet at the centre of both fire and waterfall there is an ungainsayable calm. And it is this calm which is catastrophic.

Look at him, whispered Gérard.

Three million he's lost, poor sod! murmured the blond.

Why are you so sure he isn't insured?

I know, she hissed, that's why. I know.

Boris, his back to the fire, was bent over his haversack drinking from a bottle of water. Having drunk, he poured water on to his face and his black arms. Its freshness made him think of how he would strip in the kitchen this evening and wash before going to visit the blond.

When Boris turned back towards the fire he saw them. Immediately a gust of smoke hid them from view. Not for a moment, however, did he ask himself whether he had been mistaken. He would recognize her instantly whatever she was doing, anywhere. He would recognize her in any country in the world in any decade of her life.

The wind veered and he saw them again. She stood there, Gérard's arm draped over her shoulders. It was impossible that they had not seen him and yet she made no sign. They were only fifty yards away. They were staring straight at him. And yet she made no sign.

If he walked into the fire would she cry out? Still holding the bottle, he walked upright, straight—like a soldier going to receive a medal—towards the fire. The wind changed again and they disappeared.

The next time the smoke cleared the couple were nowhere to be seen.

Contrary to what he had told himself earlier, Boris did not come down that night. He stayed by the fire. The flames had abated, his sheep were ashes, yet the rocks were still oven-hot and the embers, like his rage, changed colour in the wind.

Huddled under the rock, the Milky Way trailing its veil towards the south, he considered his position. Debts were warnings of the ultimate truth, they were signs, not yet insistent, of the final inhospitality of life on this earth. After midnight the wind dropped, and the rancid smell, clinging to the scree, was no longer wafted away; it filled the silence, as does the smell of cordite when the sound of the last shot has died away. On this inhospitable earth he had found, at the age of forty-one, a shelter. The blond was like a place: one where the law of inhospitality did not apply. He could take this place anywhere with him, and it was enough for him to think of her, for him to approach it. How then was it possible that she had come up the mountain on the day of his loss and not said a word to him? How was it possible that on this rock, far above the village, where even the church bells were inaudible, she should have come as close as fifty yards and not made a sign? He stirred the embers with his boot. He knew the answer to the question and it was elementary. He pissed into the fire and on the stones his urine turned into steam. It was elementary. She had come to watch him out of curiosity.

Before he saw her, he was telling himself that, after all, he had only lost half his sheep. As soon as he saw her with his own eyes, and she made no sign to him, his rage joined that of the fire: he and the fire, they would burn the whole world together, everything, sheep, livestock, houses, furniture, forests, cities. She had come out of curiosity to watch his humiliation.

All night he hated her. Just after sunrise, when it was coldest, his hatred reached its zenith. And so, four days later he was asking himself: could she have had another reason for coming up to the Rock of St Antoine?

B oris decided to remain in the mountains. If he went down to the village, everyone would stare at him to see how he had taken his loss. They would ask him if he was insured, just in order to hear him say No. This would give them pleasure. If he went down he might start breaking things, the windows of the mayor's office, the glasses on the counter of the Republican Lyre, Gérard's face, the nose of the first man to put an arm round the blond's waist. The rest of his sheep were near Peniel, where there was a chalet he could sleep in. Until the snow came, he would stay there with his remaining sheep. Like that, he would be on the spot to bring them down for the winter. If she had really come to see him for another reason, she would come again.

A week passed. He had little to do. In the afternoons he lay on the grass, gazed up at the sky, occasionally gave an order to one of the dogs to turn some sheep, idly watched the valleys below. Each day the valleys appeared further away. At night he was obliged to light a fire in the chalet; there was no chimney but there was a hole in the roof. His physical energy was undiminished, but he stopped plotting and stopped desiring. On the mountainside opposite the chalet was a colony of marmots. He heard the marmot on guard whistle whenever one of his dogs approached the colony. In the early morning he saw them preparing for the winter and their long sleep. They lifted clumps of grass with roots attached, and carried them, as if they were flowers, to their underground hide-out. Like widows, he told himself, like widows.

One night, when the stars were as bright as in the spring, his anger returned to galvanize him. So they think Boris is finished, he muttered to the dogs, but they are fucking well wrong. Boris is only at the beginning. He slept with his fist in his mouth, and that night he dreamed.

The following afternoon he was lying on his back looking up at the sky, when suddenly he rolled over on to his stomach in order to look down the track which led through the forest to the tarred road. His hearing had become almost as acute as that of his dogs. He saw her walking towards him. She was wearing a white dress and blue sandals, around her neck a string of beads like pearls.

How are you, Humpback?

So you've come at last!

You disappeared! You disappeared! She opened her arms to embrace him. You disappeared and so I said to myself: I'll go and find Humpback, and here I am.

She stepped back to look at him. He had a beard, his hair was tangled, his skin was dirty and his blue eyes, staring, were focused a little too far away.

How did you get here? he asked.

I left the car at the chalet below.

Where the old lady is?

There's nobody there now, and the windows are boarded up.

They must have taken the cows down, he said, what date is it?

September 30th.

What did you come for, when I was burning the sheep?

How do you mean?

You came up to the Rock of St Antoine with your husband.

No.

The day I was burning the sheep, I saw you.

It must have been somebody else.

I'd never mistake another woman for you.

I was very sorry to hear about what happened to your sheep, Boris.

Grandma used to say that dreams turned the truth upside down. Last night I dreamed we had a daughter, so in life it'll be a son.

Humpback, I'm not pregnant.

Is that true?

I don't want to lie to you.

Why did you come to spy on me? If you're telling the truth, tell it.

I didn't want to.

Why didn't you come over and speak to me?

I was frightened.

Of me?

No, Humpback, of what you were doing.

I was doing what had to be done, no more. Then I was going to come and visit you.

I was waiting for you, she said.

No, you weren't. You had seen what you wanted to see.

I've come now.

If he's conceived today, he'll be born in June, he said.

He took her arm and led her towards the crooked chalet whose wood had been blackened by the sun. He pushed open the door with his foot. The room was large enough for four or five goats. On the earth floor were blankets. The window, no larger than a small transistor radio, was grey and opaque with dust. There was a cylinder of gas and a gas-ring, on which he placed a black saucepan with coffee in it.

I'll give you whatever you want, he said.

He stood there in the half light, his immense hands open. Behind him on the floor was a heap of old clothes, among which she recognized his American army cap and a red shirt which she had once ironed for him. In the far corner something scuffled and a lame lamb hobbled towards the door where a dog lay. The floor of beaten earth smelled of dust, animals and coffee grounds. Taking the saucepan off the gas, he turned down the flame, and its hissing stopped. The silence which followed was unlike any in the valley below.

If it's a boy, I'll buy him a horse—

Ignoring the bowl of coffee he was holding out to her, without waiting for the end of his sentence, her eyes bulging, she fled. He went to the door and watched her running, stumbling downhill. Occasionally she looked over her shoulder as if she thought she were being pursued. He did not stir from the doorway and she did not stop running.

In the evening it began to snow, tentatively and softly. Having brought all three dogs into the chalet, Boris bolted the door, as he never usually did, lay down beside the animals and tried to sleep, his fist in his mouth. The next morning, beneath the white pine trees and through the frozen brambles and puddles of water, he drove his flock of miserable grey sheep towards the road which led down to the village.

When Corneille the cattle dealer drew up in his lorry before Boris's house and walked with the slow strides of the fat man he was, through the snow to tap on the kitchen window, Boris was not surprised; he knew why Corneille had come. He swore at his dogs who were barking, threatened them with being salted and smoked if they were not quieter, and opened the door. Corneille, his hat tilted towards the back of his head, sat down on a chair.

It's a long time since we've seen you, said Corneille. You weren't even at the Fair of the Cold. How are things?

Quiet, replied Boris.

Do you know they are closing the abattoir at Saint-Denis. Everything has to be taken to A——— now.

I hadn't heard.

More and more inspections, more and more government officials. There's no room for skill anymore.

Skill! That's one way of naming it!

You've never been short of that sort of skill yourself, said Corneille. There I take my hat off to you!

In fact he kept his hat on and turned up the collar of his overcoat. The kitchen was cold and bare, as if it had shed its leaves like the beech trees outside, its leaves of small comfort.

I'll say this much, continued Corneille, nobody can teach me a new trick, I know them all, but there's not one I could teach you either. All right, you've suffered bad luck—and not only last month up on the mountain, the poor bugger Boris we said, how's he going to get out of this one—you've suffered bad luck, and you've never had enough liquid cash.

From his right-hand overcoat pocket he drew out a wad of fifty-thousand notes and placed them on the edge of the table. One of the dogs sniffed his hand. Fuck off! said Corneille, pushing the dog with one of his immense thighs, the overcoat draped over it so that it advanced like a wall.

I'm telling you, Boris, you could buy the hindlegs off a goat and sell them to a horse! And I mean that as a compliment.

What do you want?

Aren't you going to offer me a glass? It's not very warm in your kitchen.

Gnole or red wine?

A little gnole then. It has less effect on Old King Cole.

So they say.

I hear you swept her off her feet, said Corneille, and the husband under the carpet!

Boris said nothing but poured from the bottle.

Not everyone could do that, said Corneille, that takes some Old King Cole!

Do you think so? What are you showing me your money for?

To do a deal, Boris. A straight deal, for once, because I know I can't trim you.

Do you know how you count, Corneille? You count one, two, three, six, nine, twenty.

The two men laughed. The cold rose up like mist from the stone floor. They emptied the little glasses in one go.

The winter's going to be long, said Corneille, the snow has come to stay. A good five months of snow in store for us. That's my prediction and your uncle Corneille knows his winters.

Boris refilled the glasses.

The price of hay is going to be three hundred a bale before Lent. How was your hay this year?

Happy!

Not your woman, my friend, your hay.

Happy, Boris repeated.

I see your horses are still out, said Corneille.

You have sharp eyes.

I'm getting old. Old King Cole is no longer the colt he once was. They tell me she's beautiful, with real class.

What do you want?

I've come to buy.

Do you know, said Boris, what the trees say when the axe comes into the forest?

Corneille tossed back his glass, without replying.

When the axe comes into the forest, the trees say: Look! The handle is one of us!

That's why I know I can't trim you, said Corneille.

How do you know I want to sell? Boris asked.

Any man in your position would want to sell. Everything depends upon the offer, and I'm going to mention a figure that will astound you.

Astound me!

Three million!

What are you buying for that? Hay?

Your happy hay! said Corneille, taking off his hat and replacing it further back on his head. No, I'm willing to buy everything you have on four legs.

Did you say ten million, Corneille?

Boris stared indifferently through the window at the snow.

Irrespective of their condition, my friend. I'm buying blind. Four million.

I've no interest in selling.

So be it, said Corneille. He leaned with his elbows on the table, like a cow getting up from the stable floor, rump first, forelegs second. Finally he was upright. He placed his hand over the pile of bank notes, as if they were a screaming mouth.

I heard of your troubles, he said very softly in the voice that people use in a sick room. I have a soft spot for you, and so I said to myself, this is a time when he needs his friends and I can help him out. Five million.

You can have the horses for that.

Corneille stood with his hand gagging the pile of money.

If you take my offer, if you have no animals during the winter, my friend, you can sell your hay, you can repair the roof of your barn and when the spring comes, you'll have more than enough to buy a new flock. Five million.

Take everything, said Boris. As you say, it's going to be a long winter. Take everything and leave the money on the table. Six million.

I don't even know how many sheep I'm buying, muttered Corneille.

On this earth, Corneille, we never know what we're buying. Perhaps there's another planet where all deals are straight. All I know is that here the earth is peopled by those whom God threw out as flawed.

Five and a-half, said Corneille.

Six.

Corneille lifted his hand from the pile and shook Boris's hand.

Six it is. Count it.

Boris counted the notes.

If you want a tip from a very old King Cole, Corneille spoke evenly and slowly, if you want a tip, don't spend it all on her.

For that you'll have to wait and see, Corneille, just as I am going to do.

There followed the correspondence between Boris and the blond. This consisted of two letters. The first, with the postmark of October 30th, was from him:

> My darling,
> I have the money for our fares to Canada. I am waiting
> for you—   always your Boris.

The second, dated November 1st, was from her:

> Dearest Humpback,
> In another life I might come—in this one forgive Marie-
> Jeanne.

There were no longer any sheep to feed. The horses had gone from the snow-covered orchard. When the lorry had come to fetch them, there was half a bale of hay lying on the snow and Boris had thrown it into the lorry after his horses. On one small point Marc was right when he said that Boris died like one of his own beasts. Not having to feed his animals gave him the idea of not feeding himself.

In the icy trough in the yard he lay down a bottle of champagne, ready to serve cold. The water detached the label and after a week it floated to the surface. When the police opened the kitchen cupboard, they found a large jar of cherries in *eau-de-vie* with a ribbon round it, and a box of After Eight chocolates, open but untouched. Most curious of all, on the kitchen floor beneath the curtainless windows, they found a confectioner's cardboard box with golden edges, and inside it were rose-pink sugared almonds such as are sometimes distributed to guests and friends after a baptism. On the floor too were blankets, dog-shit and wet newspapers. But the dogs had not touched the sugared nuts.

In the house during the unceasing period of waiting he did not listen to the sounds which came from outside. His hearing was as unimpaired as is mine now, registering the noise of my pen on the paper—a noise which resembles that of a mouse at night earnestly eating what its little pointed muzzle has discovered between its paws. His hearing was unimpaired, but his indifference was such that the crow of a neighbour's cock, the sound of a car climbing the road from which one looks down on to the chimney of his house, the shouts of children, the drill of a chain-saw cutting in the forest beyond the river, the klaxon of the postman's van—all these sounds became nameless, containing no message, emptier, far emptier than silence.

If he was waiting and if he never lost for one moment, either awake or asleep, the image of what he was waiting for—the breast into which his face at last fitted—he no longer knew from where it would come. There was no path along which he could look. His heart was still under his left ribs, he still broke the bread into pieces for the dogs with his right hand, holding the loaf in his left, the sun in the late afternoon still went down behind the same mountain, but there were no longer any directions. The dogs knew how he was lost.

This is why he slept on the floor, why he never changed a garment, why he stopped talking to the dogs and only pulled them towards him or pushed them away with his fist.

In the barn when he climbed a ladder, he forgot the rope, and, looking down at the hay, he saw horses foaling. Yet considering his hunger, he had very few hallucinations. When he took off his boots to walk in the snow, he knew what he was doing.

One sunny day towards the end of December, he walked barefoot through the snow of the orchard in the direction of the stream, which marks the boundary of the village. It was there that he first saw the trees which had no snow on them.

The trees form a copse which I would be able to see now from the window, if it were not night. It is roughly triangular, with a linden tree at its apex. There is also a large oak. The other trees are ash, beech, sycamore. From where Boris was standing the sycamore was on the left. Despite the December afternoon sunlight, the interior of the copse looked dark and impenetrable. The fact that none of the trees was covered in snow, appeared to him to be improbable but welcome.

He stood surveying the trees as he might have surveyed his sheep. It was there that he would find what he awaited. And his discovery of the place of arrival was itself a promise that his waiting would be rewarded. He walked slowly back to the house but the copse was still before his eyes. The night fell but he could still see the trees. In his sleep he approached them.

The next day he walked again through the orchard towards the stream. And, arms folded across his chest, he studied the copse. There was a clearing. It was less dark between the trees. In that clearing she would appear.

She had lost her name—as the champagne bottle which he was keeping for her arrival had lost its label. Her name was forgotten, but everything else about her his passion had preserved.

During the last days of the year, the clearing in the copse grew larger and larger. There was space and light around every tree. The more he suffered from pains in his body, the more certain he was that the moment of her arrival was approaching. On the second of January in the evening he entered the copse.

During the night of the second, Boris's neighbours heard his three dogs howling. Early next morning they tried the kitchen door which was locked on the inside. Through the window they saw Boris's body on the floor, his head flung back, his mouth open. Nobody dared break in through the window for fear of the dogs, savagely bewailing the life that had ended.

SWALLOW

ABACUS

From the internationally acclaimed author of
ARARAT and THE WHITE HOTEL

SWALLOW
D. M. Thomas

'Richly enjoyable'
MAIL ON SUNDAY

The superb successor to ARARAT

D. M. Thomas
Booker Prize shortlisted for the *THE WHITE HOTEL*

'Brilliant and shockingly funny'. GUARDIAN

'Richly enjoyable'. DAILY MAIL

ABACUS

TIM O'BRIEN
QUANTUM JUMPS

The hole snorts and says, *Do it.*
It's a smug, self-satisfied voice. Constant chatter all night long—*Star light, star bright! Shut me up with dynamite!*
Below, in their hammocks, Bobbi and Melinda sleep beautifully, and the backyard shimmers with the lights of Christmas, and here, at last, I've come up against the edge of an imposing question: What now? Three hours till daylight. Soon, I realize, it will be time for absolutes.

Chasm! Spasm!

The hole releases a steamy, insinuating laugh, then coughs and belches. I can smell its breath.

I lie back and watch the lights.

Certain truths appear. I love my wife. I loved her before I knew her, and I love her now, and I will not let her go. I'm committed. I believe in fidelity. I will not be separated. One thing in my life will last and keep lasting and last forever. Love is absolute.

What I need now is silence, but the hole has a mind of its own: *Here's a good one.... Jack be nimble! Jack be slick! Jack me off with a dynamite stick!*

I shake my head: 'I'm not interested.'

The hole snickers.

Oh, yeah, you're interested. I'm the mouthpiece, you're the brains. Now and never. Do it.

I'm wired. I'm hot. But I know the difference between life and death. When the hole hoots and says, *Home, sweet hole,* I don't respond, not even a shrug. I get to my feet and do some exercises. A clear, calm night, but there's a dynamic moving through the dark. I'm at wits' end; I can't think beyond black and white. In a time of relativity, I wonder, how does one achieve absolutes? Separate, Bobbi said. She was gracious about it. She smiled and said she loved me. But then she said separate—she needed space—what does space mean?—and later there was a poem called *Space Walk*—walk on air, walk away—but I can't be relative about it. I won't let it happen. Trouble is, what now? I want to nail our hearts together. I want no space between us. I want wholeness, without separation. I want it all, now and forever.

The question is simple. In this age, at this late hour, how do I make a happy ending?

The odds, I know, are poison.

It's a real world and it's dangerous. Science takes no prisoners; the atom forecloses; there are no epilogues. Here, at the rim of the hole, I can see what I'm up against. Oceans boiling, cities in ash. I can *see* it. A Titan II missile: ten feet in diameter, 103 feet tall, 330,000 pounds of launch weight, a flight range exceeding 6,000 miles, two engines, five megatons of no-bullshit firepower. It's out there. It's deep in the Kansas soil—you can touch it, man to metal—you can walk the underground corridors and press your fingers against the cool, damp technology. There it is. Just look: the whirring exhaust fans, bright lights, no shadows, the chrome launch console, the red box with its two silver keys, the coffee pot, the photographs of loved ones, the clocks and computers and holstered pistols, the crew-cut missileers in their spit-shined boots and SAC-blue uniforms and daredevil scarves. It is in fact there. And here's how it happens. Topside, it's a hot Kansas day. A record-buster—roasting heat. It's witch weather. A freaky black atmosphere and high winds and high voltage. Just look and say the words: Nuclear war. Kansas is the creeps. Tornado country, ghost country. Say it: Nuclear war. Look at it: black-eyed susans and sunflowers staring at you from roadside ditches, vast fields of wheat, the sun and soil. And it happens. There's lightning now, huge neon Zs, a violet virga, and then the sky divides itself into two perfect halves—one hemisphere bruised and ugly, the other bright like summer—and the crease opens up like a smile over that Titan silo. This is it. A sudden wind comes up. It's hard to stand, but you lean against the wind. You ponder the hemispheres. You see a small plot of land enclosed by barbed wire; you see a cow grazing; you see a farmer on his tractor; you see a little boy circling under a pop fly; you see a parked Air Force truck and a tiny white outbuilding and a stencilled sign that reads: DEADLY FORCE AUTHORIZED. You consider running. You hear thunder. You watch a 700-ton concrete lid blow itself sideways; you say, 'Oh!'; you see a woman run for the telephone; you see the Titan rising through orange and yellow gases—there's still that wind and that Kansas sun and that grazing cow—and you gawk and rub your eyes—not disbelief, not now, it's belief—and you stand there and listen to the thunder and track the missile as it climbs into that strange smiling crease in the sky, and then, briefly, you ask yourself the simple question: Where on earth is the happy ending?

Kansas is burning. All things are finite.

'Love,' I say feebly.

The hole finds this amusing.

I am all there is, it says. *Keyhole, rathole, asshole, eyehole, hellhole, loophole, knothole, manhole, peephole, foxhole, armhole, sinkhole, cubbyhole, pothole, wormhole, buttonhole, water hole, bullet hole, air hole, black hole, hidey-hole.... I am that I am. I am that which nearly was but never will be, and that which never was but always will be. I am the unwritten masterpiece, I am the square root of infinity. I am one hand clapping. I am what happened to the dinosaurs. I am the ovens at Auschwitz, the Bermuda Triangle, the Lost Tribes, the Flying Dutchman, the Missing Link. I am Lee Harvey Oswald's secret contact in Moscow. I am the anonymous tipster. I am Captain Kidd's treasure. I am the uncaused cause, the unnamed source, the unindicted co-conspirator, the unknown soldier, the untold misery, the unmarked grave. I am, in modesty, Neverness. I am the be-all and end-all. I am you, of course. I am your inside-out—your Ace in the Hole.*

There's a sharp grinding sound. Rock slides against rock, a perilous shifting.

Go on, do it. Dynamite.

'No,' I say.

Light the fuse! What's to lose? Like a time capsule, except we dispense with time. It's absolute! Nothing dies, everything rhymes. Every syllable. The cat's meow and the dog's yip-yip—a perfect rhyme. Never rhymes with always, rich rhymes with poor, madness rhymes with gladness and sadness and badness.... I could go on forever.

'Lunatic,' I say.

Can't have sorrow without tomorrow.

'Crazy!'

The hole laughs and sings: *Oh, I got plenty o' nuttin', an' nuttin's plenty fo' me.*

I shut it out. I squat down and fold my hands and wait. For what, I don't know. A miracle, I suppose, or some saving grace.

I'm not myself.

It's a feathery hither-and-thither sensation, like riding music, slipping up and down the scales of my own life. A balmy night in

May—May 1958—and I grab my pillow and run for the basement and crawl under the ping-pong table and lie there face up. I hear my father calling out my name. I smell the dank, sweet-sour odour of mildew, the concrete walls and basement moisture. 'Easy, now,' my father says. He takes me in his arms and says, 'Just a dream, cowboy, just a bad, bad dream.' But he's wrong. It's beyond dreaming. It's right here and it's real.

Balls to the wall! the hole yells. *Off your ass, yo-yo!*

The Christmas lights sparkle all around me.

There's no other way.

Reluctantly, I move to the tool shed. I bend down and lift a crate and hoist it to my shoulder. There's a queer sense of standing a few steps outside myself, a non-participant.

I carry the explosives across the yard.

Just the mechanics.

I use a pickaxe to chisel out three notches along the rim of the hole. I study the angles. I lay in the charges, crimp the caps, wire it up, test the firing device. I'm careful. I concentrate on each task as it comes.

When the surface work is done, I set in the ladder and climb down and prepare three more charges against the base of the north wall.

Dark down here—I stumble. I drop a blasting cap and jump back, then I spend five minutes searching for it on my hands and knees. *Pitiful,* the hole says, or maybe I say it, or both of us together: *All thumbs, no nerve. Fire and ice—poetic justice!*

I find the blasting cap.

An omen, I think. Then I wonder: Do we find the omens or do the omens find us?

Riddles!

I won't be rushed. I work slowly, at my own pace.

The hole seems to press in closer, and there's a foul, clammy smell that makes me wheeze as I wedge in the last stick of dynamite and lean down to hook up the firing device. I feel queasy. It's partly the stench, partly my own misgivings. No hurry, I tell myself, just follow the sequence—attach the copper wires, turn the screws, make sure it's a solid connection.

Done.

And what now?

I kneel at Melinda's hammock. She sleeps with a thumb at the edge of her mouth, her tongue taut against the lower front teeth, her expression frank and serious. I stroke her hair. I want to cry but I can't; I want to rescue her but I don't know how. There are no survivors. When it happens, the proteins dissolve and the codes are lost and there is only the endless rhyme. I feel some remorse, and even grief, but the emotions are like ice, I can't get a grip on them.

What's wrong with me? Why am I alone? Why is there no panic? Why aren't governments being toppled? Why aren't we in the streets? Why do we tolerate our own extinction? Why do our politicians put warnings on cigarette packs and not on their own foreheads? Why don't we scream it? Nuclear war!

I love my daughter, I love my wife. It's permanent. Gently, with love, I smooth the blankets around Melinda's neck and shoulders, kissing her, surrendering to a moment of intimacy, then I turn and go to Bobbi and stoop down and put my arms around her and say, 'I love you.' I rock the hammock. I'm frightened but I keep the vigil, just waiting, cradling the firing device, watching for the first frail light of dawn.

Once, I drift off.

There's a fluttering in the darkness, like wings, and I snap awake and jerk my finger from the yellow button.

I lock my hands together.

So much can go wrong. Madness or malfunction, simple evil, an instant of overwhelming curiosity. Like a child with a chemistry set, and the instructions say, 'Never mix X with Y,' but the kid starts wondering, *What if?* He's human. He has to know. And so one day... Curiosity, that's all. A noble instinct. A craving for secrets..... So one day the kid creeps to his room and opens up his chemistry set and cautiously sprinkles out a little X and a little Y, just to *know*, and it's the discovery of a lifetime, there are no more hypotheses, knowledge becomes perfect and absolute, and again there's that simple question: A happy ending?

If you can imagine it, I remind myself, it can happen.

But imagine this: Nuclear war.

A dark movie theatre and you're eating buttered popcorn and

someone shouts, 'Nuclear war!'

You laugh.

But this: 'Fire!'

Drop the popcorn and run. It's a stampede.

And then again this: 'Nuclear war!'

Shrug? Shake your head? A joke, you think?

Imagine the surprise.

In the dark I hear someone chuckling, which startles me, but it's just the hole. *T minus nine,* it says softly. *Like falling off a log. We'll all dream the same sweet dream—pure metaphor, that's all it is. Push the button.* Its voice is smooth and mellow. It recites nursery rhymes. It tells stories from the Bible, as if reminiscing, adding and subtracting here and there. *Amen,* it says. *T minus eight, the century's late.*

I try not to listen.

I watch the night reorganize itself, the movements of stars and shadows. The patterns tend towards stasis.

God knows, I don't want it this way. Folded in forever like the fossils. I don't want it but I can see it, as always, the imprints in rock, the wall shadows at Hiroshima, leaves and grass and the Statue of Liberty and Bobbi's diaphragm. Here, she can't leave me. The fossils don't move. Crack open a rock and she'll be curled around me. Her smile will be gold and granite. Immutable, metamorphic, welded forever by the stresses of our age. We will become the planet. We will become the world as it should be. We will be faithful. We will lace through the mountains like seams of ore, married like the elements...

Jackass! the hole says. *Very pretty, very stupid! Push the fucking button!*

It scares me. I'm tempted.

I put down the firing device and stand and try to shake out the brain waves. I'm capable of atrocity. Lucid, entirely practical, I feel both powerful and powerless, like the stars. I make myself move. I circle the floor of the hole, feeling my way, but also not feeling—which is what scares me—then I sit down and check the safety on the firing device and stare at the walls and look for signs in the darkness. I see myself crawling under barbed wire. Flares and tracers. The terrible things man will do to man. I see the wreck of the

Thresher. I see my father dying. He won't stop, he's a professional, he keeps dying. I hear sonar. I hear Melinda yelling, 'Daddy!' I hear Bobbi's warm blond voice, scanning itself, free verse on the brink of blank. She needs space, she tells me. She pins *Space Walk* to my pillow. There's a transworld look in her eyes when she sees my rage, when I take a scissors to her diaphragm, when I burn the poem, when I tell her no one's leaving. I see her sleeping. It's after midnight, and I kiss my wife's cheek and quietly slide out of bed. No lights, no alarm. Blue jeans and a flannel shirt, then out to the backyard, where I pick a spot near the tool shed and begin digging. I won't permit separation. It's final. Am I crazy? Maybe, maybe not, but I see black flashes against a chrome sky, scalps in a punch bowl, mass going to energy. Everything is combustible. Faith burns. Trust burns. Everything burns to nothing and even nothing burns. There are no footprints—the footprints burn. There are no messages in bottles, because the bottles burn, and there is no posterity, because posterity burns. Cement and steel, it all burns. The state of Kansas, the forests, the Great Lakes, the certificates of birth and death, every written word, every sonnet, every love letter. Graphite burns. Churches burn. Memory burns, and with it the past, all that ever was. The reasons for burning burn. Flags burn. Liberty and sovereignty and the Bill of Rights and the American way. It just burns. And when there is nothing, there is nothing worth dying for, and when there is nothing worth dying for, there is only nothing.

The hole makes a sound of assent.

Nothing.

The night seems to stretch out like elastic. Melinda turns in her sleep and looks at me with half-opened eyes. 'Hey, there,' I whisper, and she nods, then tucks her chin down and sleeps.

If I could, I would save her life.

I let myself sway with the night. Bobbi's breathing. The influences of the moon.

'Oh, Lord,' I say, but I don't know what to ask for.

I smell daylight coming.

The hole says, *Now and never.*

I lift the firing device. It's light in my hands, or seems light, box-shaped, an aluminum casing with a small plastic safety catch and a yellow button. The copper wires wind off towards the north wall. All it takes is a touch. Not even courage, bare volition. It occurs to me that I'm not immune to curiosity—so easy. I think about my father, my mother, and it's the simple desire to discover if the dead are ever truly dead.

In the absence of hope, what can we hope for?

Does love last forever?

Are there any absolutes?

I want to know what the hole knows. The hole is where faith should be. The hole is what we have when imagination fails.

'Hey,' Melinda says.

Something moves inside me.

'Hey—'

She makes a languid, woozy motion with her arm. After a moment she sits up in the hammock, rubs her nose, turns her head slightly to one side, and looks at me without recognition.

I feel unsteady.

There's a sudden compression when she says, 'Daddy?' Enormous pressure, it's too much for me. I place the firing device at my feet and get down on my hands and knees and practise deep breathing. The hole, it seems, is in my heart.

'Daddy?' Melinda says.

'Here, angel.'

'Where? How'd I get down in this…. God, it's dark. Where's Mommy?'

'Mommy's fine.'

'Yeah, but—' She stops and touches her flannel nightgown. Her eyes wander. She looks at the granite walls, then up at the Christmas lights, then down at me, then at the firing device. There isn't enough light to make out her expression, but I can easily imagine it. 'Man oh man,' she says, 'what's going on?'

It isn't a question, though. She knows.

Her eyes, if I could see them, would be blue and full of wisdom. Drawing conclusions, perhaps. Maybe a little frightened.

I'm still on my hands and knees. The squeeze is on.

No dignity in it, but I don't trust myself to stand.

Melinda stares at me.

'Daddy,' she says, 'what's happening?'

I keep smiling. I want to go to her but I can't manage it; I make a queer crabbing motion, knees and knuckles. It's a balance problem. I'm embarrassed when I feel myself slipping—I can't get traction.

The hole cackles.

Dynamite!

Melinda seems startled. I'm smiling at her—it's all love—but she recoils and hugs herself and says, 'What?'

'Nothing, baby.'

'I *heard* you.'

'Nothing.'

'That *word*,' she says,' I *heard* it. You *said* it, I *heard* you! I can't *believe* this.'

She's wide awake now.

Quickly, she gets out of the hammock and takes a step towards me and stops and glances at Bobbi and then steps backward. All I can do is smile. She takes another step backward.

There's silence while she makes the connections.

'Get up,' she says sternly.

'In a second.'

'Daddy.'

'One second, princess.'

She puts a thumb against the edge of her mouth.

'No,' she says, 'I don't *want* a second. I want *out*. This hole, God, it smells like…. Let me out!'

'Melinda—'

'Out!' she shouts.

I can see her eyes now. She glares at me, then spins around and moves to a wall and hits it with her fist. 'Now,' she screams, 'I want *out!*' The Christmas lights give her face a splotchy blue and red tint. She kicks the wall. 'Now!' she screams. Her eyes keep roving—quick, jerky movements of the head, up and down.

When she spots the dynamite, I pretend it's not what it is. It's not evil, I think. Not murder, not sorrow.

'Oh, wow,' she grunts.

With her left hand, gingerly, she reaches out and nudges one of the copper blasting caps.

Reality impinges.

'Baby, don't,' I say.

It's a discovery for both of us. Melinda wipes her hand and turns and looks at me. I can't explain it. Just the sadness of discovery, the dynamite and the wiring and the blasting caps, and when she looks at me—not accusing, only knowing—there is nothing that can be said or done. She bites down on her lip. She wants to cry, I know. Her tongue makes a light clicking noise against her teeth.

I'm helpless. I'm aware of the night's pure harmonics, but I can't make myself move.

I watch her trace the wires back to the firing device. Stooping, she inspects the plastic safety catch; she clutches her nightgown at the throat. Not murder, I remind myself. There is no evil in it, no rancour or shame, and we are all innocent and unsullied and sane. Even so, I suck in my breath when she finds the yellow button.

'God,' she says.

And she knows.

Now, at this instant, we share the knowledge that there is no mercy between fathers and daughters. We will kill for our children. Our children will kill for us. We will kill for families. And above all we will kill for love, as men have always killed. Crimes of passion. As terrorists kill. As soldiers kill for love of honour and love of country. Just love. And when there is no love, there is nothing worth dying for, only nothing, and Melinda knows this.

She picks up the firing device.

'I don't care what,' she says, 'I'm not afraid of you. I'm just not.'

'I know that.'

'I'm *not*.'

'Fine, then,' I tell her. 'But be careful, okay? Be extra careful.'

'Don't move, Daddy.'

'I won't.'

'Stay right there,' she says. 'You better not even move, because…. You better not.'

'Careful, baby. Extra super careful.'

'I mean it. You better *not*.'

She carries the firing device to the far side of the hole, near Bobbi's hammock. I do the calculations. Five or six paces between us, maybe four seconds. Hard to be sure. Would my legs work? What about the shock? All the imponderables.

'Sweetheart,' I say, very softly, 'I wish you'd—'

'Don't move.'

'No, I'm not moving.'

'If you do, though, I might—you know—I *might*. Just stay there. Just be nice, don't scare me.'

A gallant little girl. And smart. She keeps her eyes on me. We both know. She reaches out and shakes Bobbi's arm.

'What's wrong?' she says. 'How come Mommy won't wake up?'

Again I smile. 'Just can't, I guess. Maybe—I don't know —maybe Mommy forgot how.'

'Forgot?' Melinda says. She makes a motion with her shoulders. 'That's stupid. Not even funny. It's almost.... How'd I get down here in the first place? Just dumped me in, I suppose.'

'I carried you, baby. Both of you.'

'You could've dropped me, though.'

'I didn't.'

'Yeah, but I mean—' Suddenly, almost falling, she sits down and clamps her arms around the firing device. 'I don't *mean* that!' she yells. But she doesn't cry; she doesn't dare. She measures the distance between us. One hand flutters up to her ear, as if to brush away an irritation, then she flicks her thumb against the safety catch. 'I mean *this* thing. I mean, *why?* I always thought you sort of loved me.'

'I do,' I say. 'I do love you.'

'Okay, but I mean, how come you almost tried to blow me up? You did, didn't you?'

'Never.'

'You *did!*'

'No way. Never. Careful, now.'

For a moment she's on the verge of crying. She puts a finger near the button.

'Scared?' she asks.

'You bet I am.'

'Don't move, then. Better be real scared.'

'I am,' I say. 'I'm scared.'

She runs a hand across her forehead. I know what she's going through, I've been there myself.

'Don't think I'm chicken,' Melinda says, 'because I'm not. And if something bad happened, I bet you'd be so goddamn sorry you couldn't believe it.'

She makes a small, incongruous fist and holds it over the firing device and screams, 'Goddamn!'

There is nothing I can do.

'Goddamn!' she cries, and the hole laughs and says, *No survivors!* and Melinda yells, 'Stop it!'

We sit facing each other from opposite sides of the hole. She's crying now; I can see her shouders shaking. 'Daddy, please!' she says. 'Let's get *out* of here!' And if I could, I would do it. I would take her in my arms and be calm and gentle and find safety by saving. God, yes, I would. 'A joke,' I'd say, 'just a big silly joke,' then I'd carry her up the ladder, and Bobbi, too, both of them, one in each arm, and I'd laugh and say, 'What a joke.' I'd be a hero. I'd do magic. I'd lead them into the house and brew up some hot chocolate and talk about the different kinds of spin you can put on a ping-pong ball. And the world would be stable. The balance of power would hold. A believer, a man of whole cloth, I would believe what cannot be believed. The power of love, the continuing creation—it cannot be believed—and I would therefore believe. If you're sane, the world cannot end, the dead do not die, the bombs are not real.

Am I crazy?

I am not.

To live is to lose everything, which is crazy, but I choose it anyway, which is sane. It's the force of passion. It's what we have.

When I get to my feet, Melinda whimpers and says, 'Stay *away* from me.' But I'm willing to risk it. I'm a believer. The first step is absolute. 'Daddy,' she says, 'you better not!' But I have to. I cross the hole and kneel down and lift the firing device from her lap and hold her tight while she cries. I touch her skin. It's only love, I know, but it's a kind of miracle.

At daylight we climb the ladder.

And that, too, is easy.

I hustle Melinda into the house, turn on the shower, test the temperature, and tell her to hop in.

She looks at me through the steam. She nearly smiles, but doesn't.

'I'm a grown-up *girl*,' she says. 'You can't just stand there and *watch.*'

'No, I guess I can't.'

'God. What a father.'

'Right,' I say.

I close the bathroom door, listen for a moment, then return to the hole. It's a fine summer morning. I take Bobbi from the hammock, holding her as if we're dancing, and when she opens her eyes, the hole seems to laugh and whisper, *One more clown in the screwy cavalcade. Hickory dickory hope.*

It doesn't matter.

I'm a realist. Nothing's real.

Bobbi goes first, up the ladder, I follow behind with the firing device. I turn off the Christmas lights. The sky at this hour is purple going to blue. The mountains are firm and silent. There are morning birds in the trees, and the grass is a pale dusty green, and I love my wife. She leans against me. For some time we stand together in the backyard, and later I lead her into the house and make coffee and sit with her at the kitchen table. There is little to say. I ask how much space she needs; I ask if we could stay together a while longer. Bobbi touches my hand. Her eyes, I notice, don't quite focus. Her voice, when she says anything's possible, comes from elsewhere. She's thinking of other worlds. But she does smile. She lets me love. In her heart, I suppose, there's a lyric forming, but even that doesn't matter.

I have a last piece of business.

Outside, I pick up the firing device and take shelter behind the tool shed. Nuclear war, it's a hoax. A belly laugh in the epic comedy. I flip up the safety catch, crouch low, look at the sky, and put my finger against the yellow button.

I know the ending.

One day it will happen.

One day we will see flashes, all of us.

One day my daughter will die. One day, I know, my wife will leave me. It will be autumn, perhaps, and the trees will be in colour, and she will kiss me in my sleep and tuck a poem in my pocket, and the world will surely end.

I know this, but I believe otherwise.

Because there is also this day, which will be hot and bright. We will spend the afternoon in bed. I'll install the air-conditioner and we'll undress and lie on the cotton sheets and talk quietly and feel the coolness. The day will pass. And when night comes I will sleep the dense narcotic sleep of my species. I will dream the dreams that suppose awakening. I will trust the seasons. I will keep Bobbi in my arms for as long as she will stay. I will obey my vows. I will stop smoking. I will have hobbies. I will firm up my golf game and invest wisely and adhere to the conventions of decency and good grace. I will find forgetfulness. Happily, without hesitation, I will take my place in the procession from church to grave, believing what cannot be believed, that all things are renewable, that the human spirit is undefeated and infinite, always. I will be a patient husband. I will endure. I will live my life in the conviction that when it finally happens—when we hear that midnight whine, when Kansas burns, when what is done is undone, when fail-safe fails, when deterrence no longer deters, when the jig is at last up—yes, even then I will hold to a steadfast orthodoxy, confident to the end that E will somehow not quite equal mc^2, that it's a cunning metaphor, that the terminal equation will somehow not quite balance.

Psychic Survival in Troubled Times
THE MINIMAL SELF
Christopher Lasch
Original, penetrating analysis of modern social and political life by the author of **The Culture of Narcissism.** The future seems uncertain in the face of the overwhelming threats posed by war, crime and chronic economic decline. People retreat from long-term commitments. They become defensive, shrinking to their minimal selves. Christopher Lasch proposes provocative solutions in this lucid social essay.

Hardback £8.95 Paperback £2.95 Published 7 June

PICADOR

A painfully funny account of disorganisation and despair in the post war British rag trade.
SOMETHING WHOLESALE
My Life and Times in the Rag Trade
Eric Newby
The family business is Lane and Newby, Wholesale Costumiers and Mantle Manufacturers. The trade is peopled by impossible amazons running absurd accounts. Chaos is given free reign by Newby Senior, who is marvellously eccentric. Into this slips Eric.

Paperback £2.50 Published 7 June

PICADOR

'A brilliant theological fantasy... profound and comic'
New York Review of Books
THE WANDERING JEW
Stefan Heym

Stefan Heym undermines the authorised version of the story of the Wandering Jew, irreverently, ironically and philosophically. Luther, Lucifer, God and Man jostle each other on a journey conceived by German genius.

Hardback £8.95 Paperback £3.50 Published 4 April

PICADOR

'...full of intrigue and counterpoint, an artful and welcome fiction. Polyphonic.' Le Monde
MAÍRA
Darcy Ribeiro
The rape of the Amazon and its people is explained through a magical mix of powerful Christian allegory, capitalism and the inequality of cultural pluralism. Part mystery, part anthropology; a novel that is expertly executed.

Hardback £8.95 Paperback £3.50 Published 3 May

PICADOR

Mary Gordon
The Imagination
of Disaster

I am aware of my own inadequacies, of course, but if this happens, no one will be adequate: to be adequate requires a prior act of the imagination, and this is impossible. We are armed; they are armed; someone will take the terrible, the unimaginable vengeful step. And so we think in images of all that we have known to be the worst. We think of cold, of heat, of heaviness. But that is not it; that does not begin to be it. A mother thinks: how will I carry my children, what will I feed them? But this is not it, this is not it. There will be no place to carry them, food itself will be dangerous. We cannot prepare ourselves; we have known nothing of the kind.

But some days I think: I should prepare, I should do only what is difficult. I think: I will teach myself to use a gun. I hide behind the curtain and when the mailman comes I try to imagine his right temple in the gun sight as he goes down the sidewalk. How sure one must be to pull the trigger, even to kill for one's own children, for their food, their water, perhaps even poison. The imagination is of no use.

The imagination is of no use. When I run two miles a day, I make myself run faster, farther, make myself feel nauseated, make myself go on despite my burning ribs. In case this one day will be a helpful memory, a useful sensation. Of endurance and of pain. My daughter comes and asks my help in making clay animals. On days like this, I want to say: no, no clay animals, we'll dig, we'll practise digging, once your father was a soldier, he will teach you to use a gun. But of course I cannot do this; I cannot pervert her life so that she will be ready for the disaster. There is no readiness; there is no death in life.

My baby son is crying. Will it be harder for males or females? Will they capture boy children to wander in roving gangs? Will my son, asleep now in his crib, wander the abashed landscape, killing other boys for garbage? Will my daughter root among the grain stalks, glistening with danger, for the one kernel of safe nourishment? Ought I to train them for capitulation? I croon to him; I rock him, watch the gold sun strike a maple, turn it golder. My daughter comes into the room, still in her long nightgown. Half an hour ago, I left her to dress herself. She hasn't succeeded; she's used the time to play with my lipstick. It is all over her face, her hands, her arms. Inside her belly is another tiny belly, empty. Will she have the chance to fill herself with a child, as I have filled myself with her and with her brother? On days like this I worry: if she can't dress herself in half an hour, if she cannot obey me in an instant, like the crack of a whip, will she perish? She can charm anyone. Will there be a place for charm after the disaster? What will be its face?

When the babysitter comes, I get into my car. She can make my daughter obey in an instant; she can put my son to sleep without rocking him, or feeding him, or patting him in his crib. On days like this I think I should leave them to her and never come back, for I will probably not survive and with her they will have a greater chance of surviving.

To calm myself I read poetry. When it comes, will the words of 'To His Coy Mistress' comfort me, distract me as I wait to hear the news of the death of everything? I want to memorize long poems in case we must spend months in hiding underground. I will memorise 'Lycidas', although I don't like Milton. I will memorize it because of what Virginia Woolf said: 'Milton is a comfort because he is nothing like our life.' At that moment, when we are waiting for the news of utter death, what we will need is something that is nothing like our life.

I come home, and begin making dinner. I have purposely bought a tough cut of meat; I will simmer it for hours. As if that were an experience that would be helpful; as if that were the nature of it: afterwards only tough cuts of meat. I pretend I am cooking on a paraffin stove in a basement. But I cannot restrain myself from using herbs; my own weakness makes me weep. When it comes, there will be no herbs, or spices, no beautiful vegetables like the vegetables that sit on my table in a wooden bowl: an eggplant, yellow squash, tomatoes, a red pepper and some leeks. The solid innocence of my vegetables! When it comes, there will be no innocence. When it comes, there will be no safety. Even the roots hidden deep in the earth of forests will be the food of danger. There will be nothing whose history will be dear. I could weep for my furniture. The earth will be abashed; the furniture will stand out, balked and shameful in the ruin of everything that was our lives.

We have invited friends to dinner. My friend and I talk about our children. I think of her after the disaster; I try to imagine how she will look. I see her standing with a knife; her legs are knotted and blue veins stick out of them like bruised grapes. She is wearing a filthy shirt; her front teeth are missing; her thick black hair is falling out. I will have to kill her to keep her from entering our shelter. If she enters it she will kill us with her knife or the broken glass in her pocket. Kill us for the food we hide which may, even as we take it in, be killing us. Kill us for the life of her own children.

We are sitting on the floor. I want to turn to my friend and say: I do not want to have to kill you. But they have not had my imagination of disaster, and there can be no death in the midst of life. We talk about the autumn; this year we'll walk more in the country, we agree. We kiss our friends good night. We love them like family since our own family we do not love. Good night, good night, we say, we love you. Good night, I think, I pray I do not have to kill you for my children's food.

My husband puts on red pyjamas. I do not speak of my imagination of disaster. He takes my nightgown off and I see us embracing in the full-length mirror. We are, for now, human, beautiful. We go to bed. He swims above me, digging in. I climb and meet him, strike and fall away. Because we have done this, two more of us breathe in the next room, bathed and perfect as arithmetic.

I think: Perhaps I should kill us all now and save us from the degradation of disaster. Perhaps I should kill us while we are whole and dignified and full of our sane beauty. I do not want to be one of the survivors; I am willing to die with my civilization. I have said to my husband: Let us put aside some pills, so that when the disaster strikes we may lie down together, holding each other's hands and die before the whole earth is abashed. But no, he says, I will not let you do that, we must fight. Someone will survive, he says, why not us? Why not our children?

Because the earth will be abashed, I tell him. Because our furniture will stand out shamed among the glistening poisoned objects. Because we cannot imagine it; because imagination is inadequate; because for this disaster, there is no imagination.

But because of this I may be wrong. We live with death, the stone in the belly, the terror on the road alone. People have lived with it, always. But we live knowing not only that we will die, that we may suffer, but that all that we hold dear will finish; that there will be no more familiar. That the death we fear we cannot even imagine, it will not be the distinguished thing, it will not be the face of dream, or even nightmare. For we cannot dream the poisoned earth abashed, empty of all we know.

DAVID MAMET
THE BRIDGE

It occurred to him that the warning the world would end in fire next time referred, of course, to nuclear war; and that it would happen in his lifetime, before the millennium and the announced return of Christ. He repressed an impulse to find a Bible and read it. He dreamed that night of nuclear war.

In his dream he was standing on a bridge. The bridge spanned a river; beyond the furthest bank was a lake. He saw vague lighted delta shapes above him in the haze. He'd never seen shapes like them, and he knew that they were bombers. He did not hear the bombs fall, but, all of a sudden, the sky had changed colour—to orange—and the people around him were all dead. Except one couple.

They were Italian. She had her head underneath his sweater, and he was comforting her. On the bridge he saw the water down below begin to bubble and to rise. He knew that, also, there would be a tidal wave coming from the lake. He feared the water from the river, which was boiling hot, would reach him before the cool water from the lake.

The river kept rising, and he was filled with great remorse. All of a sudden the hot water from the river came up in a rush and, at once, the lake beyond became a wall of cool and saving water twenty storeys tall, and sped towards him. He was scalded and was thrown up in the tidal wave which turned the hot to warm and then to cool. He thought if he could only hold his breath—although it seemed impossible—he would be all right. If he could only hold his breath until the wave had settled.

He rose up inside the tidal wave. It became cool. He thought again, it would be impossible to hold his breath as long as was required of him. And then he felt the water grow less dense, and his head broke the surface at the moment that he woke up. He was frightened for a while—a moment—then he realized that it had been a dream.

But he was haunted by the images. Of the two lovers on the bridge—she had her head beneath her lover's sweater like a kitten, and he was comforting her. And of the delta-shaped lights of the bombers cutting through the haze in echelon. He was depressed and toyed with the idea of allowing the fantasy of the dream to give birth to and explain his rational, waking depression.

Surely the world *was* going to end. And probably in fire—in nuclear destruction, by mistake, or at the hands of madmen. Surely Christ predicted conflagration and surely again, He set it just before the second coming, before the millennium, before the year 2000. Could these things be true? Could writings in the Bible contain all of time? And why not? Who else had explained the misery in the world, and the lack of any ethical or moral betterment during two thousand years? Suppose it was all predetermined and we *were* to perish in a fire. How upsetting that would be.

How megalomaniacal, though, to take on oneself all the burden of the world. To be visited in dreams by visions of the future. What was he supposed to do? Proclaim his terror in the streets? Proclaim his love and his desire to protect his fellows from the horror which they were about to wreak upon themselves? What was rationally expected of him?

He did feel so alone, though, in his dream, upon the bridge. Not that the fellow with the girl felt less alone—he knew not—or that she did. And he was, finally, glad to have been alone there. In the water, too; regretting no one, but regretting all.

'What have we done?' he thought, feeling alone like someone insane—thinking, bemused: 'Isn't it strange that this is how a *crazy* person acts! I'll bet if I saw someone acting this way I would think they were insane. And yet, *I'm* not!' He felt this for society inside his dream. 'What have we done?' And, further, 'Why?' and, if it all had been predicted in the Bible, to what purpose? He thought that since man had been endowed with consciousness the thought of *purpose* must suppose *benevolence*: predicted and predetermined, the holocaust must have a purpose. And so what of the intervening twenty hundred years?

What of the suffering in them? It must have counted for nothing, and human life, again, was worthless. Then what, in the name of God, was going on here? If he were to die before the holocaust, he thought, what meaning would it have? And would it not then *be* the holocaust?

The room was full of lines. He did not want to get up. He wanted to stay in bed. It was daylight outside, and lines made by the space between the window frame and shade were thrown upon the walls and ceiling, and they shifted when the wind blew. It comforted him for a moment. He wondered why, and saw that it brought him back to his childhood. He would lie in bed at night and hear the cars and then see lines from their bright lights projected, crawling up the wall and on the ceiling from venetian blinds.

He did not want to leave the bed. He thought that he could lie in bed all day. When he found out the time, then he could plan how long he'd have to lie in bed before his body started to get tired and he, once again, could go to sleep. He knew that if he slept again he would wake up in the middle of the night, and feel disoriented. He'd know there was nothing he could do. He could dress and go out, but where would he go?

What could he do then, in the middle of the night? When he had slept enough for two days but was tired still? He could get up and look at television in the other room. He could look through the bookcase to see if there might be something there he meant to read, but he knew that there would not be. And, if there were, he'd only take it and get back in bed. That would not be correct. That would be monstrous, in the middle of the night he would not have really left his bed for one whole day. He was not sick.

At four a.m. there would be nothing he'd want to do. He would be empty of desire to find a thing to do. He'd just feel a longing to be, once again, asleep and—more—not to have woken up. He wondered how his dreams would change as he slept more and was awake less. The shade blew and the air inside his room smelled sweet.

Outside, he thought, out there are people with no con-sciousness of themselves. Breathing cool air in their chests—like bulldogs—sleek and healthy. Glad to be about the business they're on. 'If only,' he thought, 'Oh, if only I were one of them! I hate this bed. I Hate this Bed,' he thought, 'I hate the things which keep me in an infant state. I do not need them. I grow tired of myself.' He felt superior and calm. His room seemed cleaner. It seemed very clear. And quiet. He thought of his dream.

'If I were there upon the bridge and could dream a time of quiet—without knowledge of our end by nuclear destruction, and it was inside this room, what would I put here? Clean sheets and a cool young girl. A day of work before last night, a bath and sleep. I would awake this morning happy. Like a labourer of some sort. Having moved things yesterday. Or made them, or put them together. Or solved problems. I would wake without self-consciousness—except the knowledge of my body—feeling like a bulldog, sleek and powerful. And, today, I would look forward to what?' He searched for what he thought he might find exciting in the coming day.

'It would,' he thought, 'be morning, and there'd be something for breakfast, for I wouldn't have eaten anything the day before—a snack at lunch, but no dinner at all, because I'd fallen into bed exhausted.

'When I woke (the shade flapped in the breeze and woke me, one *flap*, like a sharp guncrack) I sat up in the bed. I was alone. The girl came in dressed in white cotton. She had dark skin, dark hair, and looked at me devoid of want. Only politeness in her glance. 'What did I want?' To exercise! I'd leap down from the bed and pull on shorts and run along the beach outside . . . .'

There was no beach outside, and he shifted his reverie of exercise to fencing with a fencing master on the roof for three-quarters of an hour. In his fantasy he'd learned to fence: he was accomplished at it, and it gave him satisfaction both corporeal and aesthetic. After fencing he'd come down and shower, eat, and make love to the girl if he felt moved to do so—or perhaps he would insult her—he would cut her.

Then he'd leave. He would get out. He would leave the apartment, and he would not say goodbye to her, for after all . . . He tried to think 'After all . . . what?' And could not. But everything would end if he went back to sleep. 'What if . . .' he thought, 'what if there were something that I'd forgotten, and which would occur to me? A monstrous thing I'd done which I'd forgotten. Which I'd buried. Which, if I remembered, would force me to kill myself?' He used a word or combination of words or ideograms—some combination of 'to force', or 'to allow', in thinking of his suicide. What if: what if he'd killed someone—what if he'd killed his son? (If he had had a son, and killed him.) If he could not tell his wife. He'd killed her in his passion when he told her of the accident.

When he confessed. (If he had had a wife she'd surely love his son.) Or what if he came home and found her dead? She'd been terribly mutilated, and he could not bear to live in a world where such things went on. So . . . . No. If he had gone to sleep and woke up to remember that his wife was dead it would mean that she was still in the living-room—dead—or else that he had thrown her down, in which case someone would have heard her fall into the alley, or they would have found her in the daylight. That she had been all night dead there in the living-room was also unacceptable. The very idea of her presence would destroy the iffy nature of the fantasy. It would be clear and proveable what had occurred, and he could not, then, toy with his own psychological imbalance, which was teasing him with guilt—with memory.

But what if, he thought, it was *her* son by a former marriage, and he'd come in to find that the father (her ex-husband) was there and had murdered his son and ex-wife and left? Aha! No one had seen him entering the building, nor would see him leaving. The ex-husband had been out of town for years, and would not be considered the culprit.

He. *He* would be blamed! He'd been asleep on the couch and woke to find that they were dead. His neighbours would remember the fight they had had the other week in the grocery. He'd surely be convicted of the murder. And why not? Was he not, he thought, in some way guilty of their deaths? In what way? Well, perhaps, if he had been more *loving* . . . . No. Could that stop the ex-husband's coming in the middle of the night to kill?

What if he had not really been asleep? Yes. That was it! What if he had not been asleep—if he'd been *partially* asleep and heard—with one part of his mind—the door. And *knew* he'd heard her tentatively say, 'Hello?' He heard the thwacks the heavy knife made and he knew that they were dying in there, but he told himself that it was all a dream. He could have saved them. If he had been braver. Did he have a choice? That is what he thought. He did not, finally, he did not *know* that there was murder in the next room.

A nd it *could* have been a dream. And even now it still could be a dream. It could go either way. It might come to him that this fantasy was but a millisecond long and just his mind's way of staving off the realization that he had killed, or had looked on and condoned murder. No. He saw himself upon the witness stand, his life in the balance. 'Can you *say*,' they asked him, 'Can you truly *say* that you were totally asleep during the time the murderer was in the next room?'

He smelled salt air and he turned and saw, far below him, waves. And heard the giant motors of the ship. He felt the throb. He was up on the flight-deck of an aircraft carrier. He looked and, far away, at the horizon, he saw orange balls. Huge orange balls, evenly spaced. He knew that they were protective devices, and were linked together—though he could not see the links.

The Complete Tales of Nikolai Gogol
Volumes 1 and 2
Edited by LEONARD J. KENT
Translation by Constance Garnett, revised by Leonard J. Kent

These two volumes at last bring together all of Gogol's fiction (with the exception of his novel *Dead Souls*) in paperback. In Volume 1 there is *Evenings on a Farm Near Dikanka,* the early Ukranian folktales which first brought Gogol fame, as well as 'Nevsky Prospekt' and 'Diary of a Madman'. Volume 2 includes Gogol's *Migorod* stories, 'The Nose', 'The Coach', 'The Portrait', and the most influential of his Petersburg stories, 'The Overcoat.'

Leonard J. Kent's skilful new edition of Gogol's fiction includes helpful notes which are often the first annotations in English, and provides an introduction which steers the correct middle course between making Gogol an irresponsible artist of the grotesque and proving him a documentary historian of backward Russia. It will undoubtedly increase Gogol's reputation as the most original, imaginative and exuberant of all Russian writers and establish him as the greatest humorist among a rather solemn crowd!

Volume 1: £9.50   Paperback   262pp   0-226-30068-4
Volume 2: £9.50   Paperback   352pp   0-226-30069-2

THE UNIVERSITY OF CHICAGO PRESS
126 Buckingham Palace Road London SW1W 9SD

Q. What do the following writers have in common?

Angela Carter
Norman Lewis
Paul Theroux
Colin Thubron
JG Ballard
Tariq Ali
Salman Rushdie
William Boyd
Raymond Carver
Kazuo Ishiguro
G Cabrera Infante

A. They have all written for

LONDON'S BIGGEST SELLING WEEKLY GUIDE.
TimeOut
FROM ANY NEWSAGENT.

DARRYL PINCKNEY
ENGLAND,
WHOSE ENGLAND?

There was, I thought, nothing I did not know about white people. After all, I was a Hoosier, born and raised, like a chicken, in Indianapolis, Indiana. My birthright of invisibility made me an observer, not a participant. I concluded that I was stranded in a land of rednecks, hillbillies and crackers who, rich or poor, ranked high on the list of the enemies of promise. A leading businessman once confessed to my father: 'I used to think all you people were lazy. Now I understand. It's sickle cell.'

I made up my mind to leave the 'All-American City' to the Americans. I leapt, it seemed, in a single afternoon, from Edward Eggleston's *The Hoosier Schoolmaster* to Josephine Tey's *The Daughter of Time*. I found my true homeland in a world of dreams, and right in the middle of the American heartland I suffered from a volatile and obsessive love—England.

Indianapolis was an unlikely soil for the growth of this passion. Perhaps I adored England because I imagined it as the opposite of America. Perhaps all that mattered was that it was not America. No, my family was not Jamaican, not Trinidadian, not Barbadian— just black. As a child in the sixties, I, abysmally absorbent, in need of rescue, devised my secret strategies of compensation and retribution. One day, I told myself, I would be better than what I was, someone baptized and recreated in the flood of British freedom. I would, one fine day, float in a barge triumphantly up the Thames, and then America would be sorry for having despised me. The books, the images of that far country, were readily available. So, as my grandfather used to say, no need to force a door that stands wide open.

Automobiles were the sacred cows of Indianapolis, the 'Crossroads of America', so proud of its multiplying links of smooth interstate highway. The miracle of speed brought out the pioneer spirit and there seemed to be more car dealerships than churches. The used-car lots on the fringes of town had something of the atmosphere of revivalist tents, decorated, as they were, with placards and strings of yellow bulbs. Each asphalt fiefdom was presided over by a sallow man whose style recalled that of an evangelist. Come forward, brethren, and accept this Ford Mustang. It was at an automobile show that I had my first battle with a white. The dogma of those days held that American cars were superior to all others. One patriotic, chubby kid punched me in the nose when I sounded off too vehemently about how a Stingray couldn't compare with a Jag. I was disgraced, but I took comfort in having had the chance to behold, before my father dragged me away, a classic Silver Cloud. Mounted on a pedestal, protected from the mob by a ring of velvet rope, it was more magnificent than the Pièta I had seen at the World's Fair from a conveyor belt that moved the whispering crowd in one door and out another.

The television in the living room was a crystal ball that revealed scenes of the life to come. I violated curfew and slipped out of bed to watch *Saturday Night, Sunday Morning.* A spokesman for the local station apologized in case Albert Finney had offended the morals of the viewers. Of course I missed the point of these films. *The Loneliness of the Long-Distance Runner*, even *The L-Shaped Room*, might as well have been *Topper*. The high comedies and low romances, the gloomy mysteries and adaptations from Dickens— they sent out to me, rocking in the glow of the television screen, one message: *In England's green and pleasant land.*

My bicycle became a motorcycle and the girl with thick braids who hung on to the back seat for dear life was Rita Tushingham. I wanted to be a Ted, but my mother wouldn't hear of pointed shoes. I hoped to be a Rocker one Halloween, but my mother wouldn't dress me in dirty denims and leather jacket under any circumstances. She proved just as adamant against Mods and Carnaby Street. London, she declared, would have to swing without me. I slicked down my hair with grease when my parents were out; dangled, at the proper angle, a candy cigarette from my lip; squinted; said 'bloody', 'bloke', and 'quid' a lot. I wasn't sure what a quid was.

I sailed in my make-believe from reign to reign, but the other black kids weren't pleased with these fantasies. My War of the Roses ended in anarchy because no one bothered to keep straight who was Yorkist and who Lancastrian. I transposed scenes of empire building from R. J. Minney's *No. 10 Downing Street: A House in History* to the backyard and alley, but my playmates, bored, went away. Sometimes I played 'England' in exquisite solitude. I dug a deep ditch at the side of the house, filled it with water and launched tiny plastic ships against the Armada. Another day the battle at Trafalgar raged loud and long. I was prevented from ever again doing my duty after the hose I left unattended caused the sunless sea to overflow and drown the seedlings in a neighbour's garden.

Once I got in big trouble for dusting my mother's wig with talcum powder in order to open Parliament. My prized possession was a splintered cane that sheathed a rusted sword. I scavenged for other accessories: my father's cummerbund, which I wore as a sash across my chest, together with my mother's brooch as the Garter; and, to top if off, a satin burgundy comforter as my coronation robes. I sat in a chair in the dining-room and my dog swore an oath of fealty by licking a cereal-box ring. I had put away these unsatisfactory props by the time I rose one bracing January dawn to watch the broadcast of Churchill's state funeral.

All along I had been receiving tidings of great joy from the transistor radio I held to my ear under the covers. My head rang with the prophecies of the Mersey Sound. The few cents of my allowance went in tribute to the Beatles the moment they flashed their hair in front of Ed Sullivan's cameras. The whirring 45s and long-playing albums contained the magic of fetishes. The posters plastered on my walls and the bubble-gum cards glued into my scrapbook were icons. I did not neglect Cilla Black, the Animals, the Yardbirds, Gerry and the Pacemakers or the Rolling Stones, the lesser saints of 'the British Invasion'. I venerated them too and had no tolerance for the Dave Clark Five, Freddy and the Dreamers or Herman's Hermits, the false idols. The mounting issues of *Tiger Beat* and *Melody Maker* were gospel.

The Beatles, by some miracle, performed at the Indiana State Fair and eclipsed forever the beauty of the roller coaster, the haunted house, the shooting gallery, the stock car races, the cows lowing in stalls of manure and straw. I could not see the stars of *A Hard Day's Night*, so far were they from the tier where I jumped up and down. I could not hear them above the roar. Some girls were hit by the holy spirit and collapsed, others threatened to throw themselves from the railings. One sweating teen hoisted me over the barricade and I ran around in circles. Policemen and paramedics panicked at the power of the rude songs. *Beware! Beware!*

Exhausted and soaked, strangers embraced strangers. Long after the amplifiers had been switched off and the hissing lights dismantled, I thought about that paradise of equality among the faithful. A heavy-set kid on the block said that I had made up the whole thing, that I would never have been allowed in the auditorium. When I showed him my ticket-stub, he said that I had picked it out of the gutter. He teased me for wanting hair like John Lennon's. He claimed the Beatles had said that they would never let a black kid like me even spit on their boots.

I knew this kid's reputation. His shaved, brown head made him appear sinister beyond his years. I knew his father was something of a gangster, that his mother drank gin and then fell asleep on top of her hi-fi to let the beat of the blues pulse through her. I didn't care. He won, but only after a struggle that surprised him. He never messed with me again. When my family, free at last, moved to the outskirts of town, I had learned to hide my feelings.

We moved to a suburb of creeks and houses hidden behind phalanxes of apple trees, yellow poplar, paper birch. Evidently some of our new neighbours were not appeased by the old Steinway under which the moving men grunted. Vandals decapitated the mailbox while we slept, crept up the drive and slashed tyres. Across the road from us flourished a segregated country club. My parents were welcomed at its gates only on election day when the clubhouse doubled as a polling station. Golfers who poked in our yard with driving irons for wayward balls I regarded as poachers, and, to me when I walked about in a Castle Howard vein, the manicured green of the drowsy links was simply a lucky backdrop, as if the move from the city, from the black neighbourhood, had been nothing more than the transplanting of slips from a pot to the open air.

I remember one Memorial Day weekend when I forgot where I was. Memorial Day was a dangerous holiday, the time of the Indianapolis 500, because a mood of boom-town excess overtook the citizens. The tradition on Memorial Day was to raise hell, and hell rose from the patios, picnic grounds and back roads, from the campers, pick-up trucks and station wagons. And sometimes hell was pulling up next to a lone black and aiming a shotgun through the window.

Beer bottles littered the state parks, condoms peeked up like water moccasins in the reservoirs above the limestone dams, from which teenagers with hair like thistle-down rode on frisbees to choruses of cowboy whoops. Hell also rose from the speedway where thousands armed with binoculars, devilled eggs and liquor watched drivers careen around the track in snarling machines. Sometimes there was the hell of sensational crack-ups that sent tyres and twisted metal flying amid great balls of orange fire.

It was May, hot, my parents were away, the woman who looked after me had nodded off, and I, dressed in a beret from the British Fez Company and a cape, escaped. I carried my passport, David Cecil's *The Young Melbourne*, and followed the fence tatted with barbed wire alongside the country club to a lane that led to a goldfish pond. I heard through the hedges a cheerful commotion; saw, in the distance, red-vested waiters balancing trays of melon; and, all places being in my mind one country, I rushed to strike a noble pose.

I swept into the clearing. Two blue-haired matrons gasped and left behind half-moons of lipstick on long-stemmed glasses. They alerted some of the other guests who then took a few steps in my direction. I pretended to be absorbed in the book that dampened in my hands. But something was wrong with the performance. My audience had disappeared. What to do? Exit, stage left.

Soon a patrol car was behind me in the road. I heard a honk and a wave of recklessness rushed through me like a drug that closes the gaps between synapses. The horn sounded again. I waved like a gentleman out for a stroll. The patrol car drew alongside and a deputy demanded to see some identification. Confusion made me dumb, and they, looking me up and down, took this dumbness for defiance. They accused me of trespassing, but I knew better. I was different and therefore need not abide by the rules of that classic encounter—cop confronts black boy.

'You live hereabouts?'

'I dare say.'

'Hey. We're not done here.'

'Yes, but I am, you see.'

'Sweet Jesus.' They got out of the car.

I ran and knocked down a spaniel yelping on a chain in a

neighbour's yard. My cape snagged on a bush I tried to clear. The fall knocked the wind out of me. One deputy tried to make me lie still, the other retrieved my beret. My lungs filled and I hollered. The housekeeper exploded across the yard, reared back on her slippers and unleashed a hail of abuse that beat down the deputies' attempts to explain what had happened. She told them it was nobody's business if I dressed up like Batman. The racket we set up lured curious neighbours, made motorists slow down. The deputies apologized and backed away. I was led to the house through a gauntlet of tender hands, and it was then that I began to suspect that the coward is the man who does not know how much he can get away with.

My new school was miles away and the yellow bus meandered past drained swimming pools, abandoned roadside greenhouses and weedy tennis courts. It was not considered a trauma for a black student to travel to a white school. Those were the days before court-ordered busing. It didn't matter that the seat beside me stayed vacant. My new classmates knew about baseball, batting averages, the won-lost records of legendary pitchers, and I knew the names of Queen Victoria's nine children, nineteen grandchildren, and thirty-seven great-grandchildren who spread, like termites, from the House of Saxe-Coburg-Gotha.

It was a thrill for me to go with my father to the one news-stand downtown that sold papers from 'out of state'. I loaded up on week-old tabloids, the *Illustrated London News, The Times*. I searched church flea-markets for relics such as *Maids of Honour, The Fair Ladies of Hampton Court, The New Elizabethans, The Poems and Drawings of Lady Diana Bridgeman*. Most fathers, when they came home, were greeted by the reassuring sounds of whistling sprinklers, basketballs bouncing off garage doors or the grind of power mowers. But my father, one twilight, was met by the sight of his son, meditating on the fireflies, arrayed in a frilled shirt and patent leather shoes with brass buckles. Arranged around me were mottled Macmillan Pocket Classics of Bacon and Pope, a lime-green volume of the Sonnets, paperback anthologies—not that I understood any of them or could pronounce Pepys correctly. The books I carted out were ornaments.

One of my first efforts was entitled 'Stanzas—Written in Dejection, Near Indianapolis'. I refashioned my handwriting to make it resemble the script on the dustjacket of *Lord Hervey's Memoirs* and the holographs of poets reproduced in textbooks. My parents didn't even want to talk about going to Britain for the Investiture. Their indulgence had its limits: my mother smashed to bits *Folksongs of Britain*, a record I played over and over.

I could hardly keep still when elderly relatives, having heard through the family grapevine about my 'hobby', thought to entertain me with recollections of Paul Robeson and Florence Mills on the London stage, of Hutch with the *café-au-lait* voice, of Nancy Cunard hunting for dark meat or parading one May Day in red rags designed by Chanel. A great uncle who had toured with Noble Sissle in the thirties was appalled. He tried to set me straight about the Palladium, the Dorchester, Ciro's, Café de Paris. He, who had been presented to the Prince of Wales and had seen the lobby of the British North, had nothing good to say about any of it. The only memory that gave him pleasure was that of Jack Hylton's orchestra, whose brass section executed passages that were difficult even for strings.

I ignored the drift of his reminiscences. The times and the Flying Scotsman had changed. If he had had trouble finding a room or friends to show him the town, then the blame was his. He had not served the proper apprenticeship. But I was going to be happy, happier than the dapper black steward in *Redburn* who walked unmolested with a good-looking Englishwoman on his arm.

My Anglophilia was something like haemophilia—that is, I was easily bruised by facts and so stayed away from them. I used the names of Granville Sharp and Wilberforce like disinfectants, but I didn't believe that slavery and racism had anything to do with me. I was Ignatio Sancho under the protection of the Duke of Montagu, Julius Soubise fencing for the wild Duchess of Queensberry. I, who couldn't wait to grow up and burn my draft card, refused to talk about Africa or Ireland. What was there I would not do? All vows demand that a part of the self must die.

And when—my Lord, what a morning—I was given a ticket as a high school graduation present, it was like being paroled. I was allowed to pack without parental supervision and my father, with his unerring sense of occasion, palmed prophylactics into my kit.

That was 1971, a year, as I later learned, during which more blacks left the United Kingdom than entered it.

    I had never been on such a large jet, and most of the sleepless crossing I was under the impression that the jumbo's wing, so far out in space, was the edge of Greenland. The first thing I saw when I entered the terminal was Godfrey Cambridge, who was being interviewed on a moving travellator. Reporters wagged microphones in his face and tried not to fall backwards. The big time, I, seventeen years old, thought as I hopped from foot to foot at customs. On the bus from Heathrow I poked my nose in a discussion a family was having about how to get to an aunt's place. I recited the tube stations from Finchley Road to Wembley Park, and I did so through my teeth, in a fake British accent.

'Have you lived here before?'

'Sort of,' I piped.

The London that dominated my imagination was quaint, colourful, odorless, clean. I was not prepared for the size, the noise, the diesel fumes, the traffic, the heat, the merciless grey. A taxi deposited me at a musty hotel squeezed into Great Cumberland Place. Arabs billowed in and out of the lift. The woman at the desk fondled a ring of keys. There was no record of my reservation. She wobbled away on high heels. I told the man behind me that I was going to talk about Heath at Speaker's Corner. The woman returned, a smile seeped through her mask of powder and mascara. I was in a hurry and didn't mind carrying my own bags.

I circled like a moth around Piccadilly and watched the characters change as the sun went down. A plump girl wrapped in a vinyl jacket of leather spots approached me under a marquee. I had heard about prostitutes. She was pissed that I did not want to do business. In the middle of my explaining that it was nothing personal, she bristled and grabbed my crotch. I jumped back and bumped against someone. I didn't see him, but I smelled his patchouli oil, felt his deft fingers at my waist. The hooker bounced out of sight. The phantom was also gone and I realized that I had been relieved of a wad of what had been, until that instant, like play money from a board game.

I searched for the theives and ended up in The Mall. The first bobby I saw was busy giving a carload of sullen Africans a piece of his mind. The manager at the hotel was sorry, but there was nothing anyone could do: London was not what it used to be. I agreed and, though determined to stay awake for the anthem, succumbed to fatigue during 'The First Churchills'.

Not too much money had been pinched, but I still had to find cheaper accommodation. It was a dream come true—combing the back pages, closing the door of the red booth, pushing a coin in the slot on cue. I was eager to start over, to leave the hotel in Great Cumberland Place. I had detected a weird vibe from the management, which was confirmed when the woman with the jangling keys informed me that some guests had complained about my snoring in the lounge. She wondered why I had bothered to take a room if I insisted on sprawling across a sofa in public. I checked out in a huff and got charged for an additional day. The taxi driver said that I had been dinged and that I should go back and stand up for myself. The woman behind the desk curled her finger and I followed her to one of the rooms where she pointed to a notice that gave the official hour of check-out. I appealed, as a student, for sympathy. She said it was not her fault if I had not yet learned to read. The taxi was waiting, the meter running.

The hotel in Lexham Gardens was so austere that it looked as if it had been stripped. Retired Swedes had muffled conversations over motor coach schedules, Belgian couples on strict budgets barked for extra jam at breakfast. Such an odd collection of transients shuffled through the dim halls that I never ventured to the loo until all was quiet. The narrow windows were dark with soot, marks in the frayed carpet indicated where the wardrobe had once stood. The seediness struck me as romantic.

If only I had known some of the testimony against Earl's Court, the sanctuary of many a colonial pilgrim, I would not have felt that my anglophilia brought me any special privileges. I strutted towards the Cromwell Road like the first person on an uncharted coast. Blacks were expected to exchange greetings of solidarity in the snack bars and on the streets to show that we were united, one family. I looked away from the fists raised in salute and walked on.

Some days the only words I spoke outside the hotel were at the counter of a Wimpy Bar. It got harder and harder to be enthusiastic

185

about what there was to see from Richmond to Abbey Road to Greenwich. Londoners were either all on holiday or hiding out. It was the height of the tourist season. Those knots of club members in bermuda shorts and fishing caps, hunched over boxed lunches, with cameras banging around their necks, had at least each other for company. Americans whom I found on the Embankment, their backs to Somerset House, did not respond to what I thought were arresting opening lines—how Elizabeth Tudor had raised procrastination to a high art, how Lucille Ball had had her stomach pumped after shooting a television show that called for a swim in the river. Every day began with a stubborn sense of renewal, of possibility, and every night unravelled in defeat.

Waiters and barmen laboured under a peculiar myopia. A sort of film came down over their eyes that made me the last served in Mayfair. In one bustling establishment I waited until closing for my first taste of stout, too embarrassed to speak out. I spent my evenings after that in a Pakistani dive. Urdu wafted like steam from the portholes of the kitchen. Men swatted the tables with towels and stared, like me, into the sultry street. It was there that I learned to linger, smoke and drink.

I sat up late with the young Argentine manager of my hotel and his Czech wife. They did what they could to distract me from my anxiety, but they were too burdened with immigration worries to adopt me. It was painful to pass under a window and hear music. Strangers at corner tables, on Underground platforms, on traffic islands dispensed morsels of advice like alms and hurried away. One night, just to talk to someone, I asked for directions from the Old Bill who had a jolly voice. He looked over my shoulder and muttered that what he'd really like to show me was the way back to the jungle.

During the day I kept on the move, stayed ahead of my thoughts. The nights were hard. Then I saw an advertisement for a friendship society. I put on my navy-blue suit, imagined a venerable structure crawling with alumni of the British Club in Shanghai drinking whisky neat and found, instead, an obscure door, a flight of crooked steps, and a run-down loft where Asians in paisley shirts milled about, annoyed that there was no hiding place from the bright lights overhead. They were there to perfect their English under the tutelage of a clerkly type whoose sleeves were held up by rubber bands and whose very pores seemed to ooze a false warmth. He guarded the bowl of watery pink punch and glanced at me suspiciously, as if I had invaded his turf or meant to upstage him. He assigned us places around a scarred table and I took my turn reading from Agatha Christie's 'Ten Little Niggers'.

One day I went window shopping in King's Road. Frantic at the cost of the presents I wanted for my family, I collided with a Dutch boy and fruit spilled from his backpack. Ton was my age and also in London for the first time. We wandered around and by the time we sat over furry peaches in the drizzle of St George's Park, I had made a friend. Ton was amused by my disappointment that nothing was as it had been pictured in the brochures. He had unlimited energy and he knew his Pevsner. Every morning we went on exhausting excursions. We took in art nouveau bronzes at one end of town and the bust of Marx at the other. Ton even taught me how to hitchhike, a risky practice for blacks where I came from.

London was, for Ton, a vast open air theatre, from the fascists and spiritualists competing on the boxes to the girls who chatted us up outside the Roundhouse in the belief that through the heart of every guy coursed the blood of a punter. For Ton—clever, attractive, bold—these encounters were commonplace. But for me, his sidekick, sharing a game of darts or a meal in a posh restaurant, they were exotic, crucial. It was as though Ton had lifted a stone to let a novice make a study of the swarm beneath.

I placed Ton like an interpreter between the populace and me, and through him met some of the strange souls young travellers don't mind listening to. A musicologist not only claimed to be a warlock but said he was in touch with the ghosts that haunted the catacombs below the Mason's Arms. A dowager took a fancy to Ton and nearly cried as she recalled those who had dined with her in Upper Berkeley Street in the good old days. A mime who performed under Marble Arch picked the Liberty Bell mushrooms that dotted the parks after muggy evenings and gave them to Ton to distribute at a party in Well Walk, after which Hampstead dissolved in a million shimmering particles.

One morning Ton and I were to meet in Trafalgar Square for

another vigorous outing. I paced with the assembly of pigeons around the slippery pavement. I started off, certain that I had been late, towards the Tower of London, thinking I could catch him. I ran back, sure that I was early, hoping Ton had been behind me all the while. On Ludgate Hill I almost got in a brawl for springing on a fellow who looked like Ton from the back. I sat in Trafalgar long after most of the crowd had dispersed: I could not afford to lose Ton. He lodged somewhere in Maida Vale, and I looked for him for three days in the bed and breakfasts before I gave up.

I decided not to get soppy, in honour of Ton. I scrubbed until I glowed and called the grandmother of a classmate back home whose family had asked me to pick up some parcels from her. She asked me to tea. I arrived at a block of ugly modern flats. The doorman made me wait on the sidewalk. He returned with two packages. He said the lady was indisposed, for which she was sorry, but she was most grateful for the trouble I was going to take to carry her packages three thousand miles. He plopped the packages on the brick ledge. They were heavy, he said, and he didn't envy me.

The bus from Camden was thick with passengers. On one side I got a whiff of something like liver and onion, on the other hair-cream and perfume.

'I think I'm going to be sick,' I exhaled.

A burly man elbowed a path to the platform. I stumbled after him.

'I'm sick,' I repeated.

'Fuzzy-wuzzy,' I thought I heard.

I stepped down, the conductor rang the bell, the bus lurched forward, and I tumbled out with the packages. I will never forget the leer on the conductor's face when I looked up from the dust.

The crushed packages I buried in a dustbin, the gash on my chin I cleaned with my shaking hands. The next morning I left in a stupor for Southampton. The train wheels chanted *will you, won't you, will you, won't you,* and where Vespasian's legions had struck the sand I called it quits. In the waiting-room, across from the cola machine, a toddler popped up and tugged at my hair. His mother slapped him. The ferry moaned into the Channel. So much for the dance.

I wish I could say that I shaped up in college, that Manhattan helped me to get over the Royal Borough of Kensington and Chelsea, in the way it is said that the only release from one love is to find another. I wish I could say that when my heart skipped a beat in stanza class it was solely for the feminine rhymes of Sidney, for the sprung rhythm of Hopkins.

A graduate student, Oliver, ferocious about the dignity of his Twansa heritage, took a specialist interest in my case. Oliver's trek from a township near Johannesburg to a life of seminars and subsidy had been complicated, violent. His stories of listening to tapes of banned books, of an uncle who had lost an eye to the *sjambok*, of cousins lost to tuberculosis, were the proper rebuke to my misplaced loathing. He knew Britain well, and when I trotted out lines in the back room of a bar near campus to show that I had crossed over to the hip—'Hell is a city much like London', (Exhibit A), or 'London defies the imagination and breaks the heart' (Exhibit B)—he hinted that I had culled my slogans from compromised sources.

'Man, they're all in on it,' Oliver said in answer to my distinction between Boers and English liberals. 'Rio Tinto Zinc, Courtaulds, Leyland, Imperial Chemical, Unilever, Barclays,' he counted on his large fingers. 'Helicopters, tanks, armoured cars. Not just Americans selling that thing there.' He sucked his teeth.

Oliver introduced me to the Malcolm X Lounge, a campus meeting place that also functioned as a clinic for the treatment of 'Eurocentrism'. A long reading list was prescribed. Political acts were also considered therapeutic. I did not need a committee to know that there was something exorcistic about my yelling in front of the UN to protest against apartheid or Ian Smith.

The consciousness-raising sessions were going well until the night of a debate on Amin and Obote. I showed up drunk and didn't mean to sing so loudly:

There were three niggers of Chiceraboo—
Pacifico, Bang-bang, Popchop—who
Exclaimed one terribly sultry day
'Oh, let's be kings in a humble way.'

I was denounced as a provocateur and the group voted to kick me out. Oliver washed his hands of me, refused to come to the phone when I called to say that I was sorry.

I went back to London in 1978 on something like a dare. I wasn't doing much with my life other than calling people abroad with the help of the corporate credit card numbers that the Yippies had stolen and published. One black friend from school, Bargetta, said that she was nicely set up in Muswell Hill and that a break from Manhattan would do me a world of good. She assured me that generations of families on the dole had set the youth on fire. I trusted Bargetta; she had led the way to Steel Pulse, the Clash, Big Youth, Linton Kwesi Johnson. I knew all about Enoch Powell, Notting Hill and Brixton. I was not in danger of being taken in again.

London, what I saw of it, was putty, brass and paint. The colour of the bank notes had changed. The sus laws had polluted Santayana's Eden of eccentricity, heresy and individuality. For the poor, one metropolis is much like another. Bargetta and I spent most of our time looking for a place to stay. Her flat in Muswell Hill had fallen through.

'I didn't know,' Bargetta said in a sleazy caff, 'I had my pictures up on the wall and this agent came and said "You can't live here." Just like that. I should have known. The wanker.'

We slagged about, ligged when we could. I attached myself like a barnacle to Bargetta, in the way I had hidden behind Ton seven years earlier. Bargetta consulted *Time Out*, dressed up for appointments, but when she appeared she was invariably told that the flat in question had just been rented. I had a round trip ticket and didn't much care what happened. A shrewd drifter, she took up with a young man who claimed to be so well connected that she dubbed him Hyphen-Hyphen. We settled with him in Aristotle Road.

Hyphen-Hyphen, with his mane of Pre-Raphaelite hair, had the heedlessness of the well-born and a certain smugness about racial matters. It was, he said, because of material determinism that the elderly whom he visited in his work for the GLC screamed about black bastards and wogs. He hung out in smoky shebeens and considered himself something of an expert on Black Britannia. He

190

did not really think that blacks like Bargetta and me were the genuine article because we were not sufficiently oppressed. Bargetta was enraged that in one place in Ladbrook Grove Hyphen-Hyphen calmly drank his Red Stripe Beer while the Jamaican clientele ridiculed her headgear and made unpleasant suggestions about how she, the 'Yankee skiff', had earned the ninety pounds for her air fare.

Behind Hyphen-Hyphen lived a lunatic. He was called Rosie because he sold flowers at Clapham North Station, though he pretended that he was in charge of several important warehouses and properties. Rosie waged a daily campaign against racial pollution. He even hated Aussies. His campaign took the form of throwing things at likely offenders. A steel band rehearsed across the road from him and he fell upon the band's window with a hammer. The police were summoned and Hyphen-Hyphen appointed himself mediator.

'The monkeys started it!' Rosie screamed through his tusk-like whiskers.

'He has a problem getting on with blacks,' Hyphen-Hyphen confided.

'Who doesn't? an officer replied.

Bargetta accepted a no-strings-attached invitation from a Rasta in Islington. The house was condemned; there was no hot water. The Rasta was a part-time lorry driver, but everyone else in the warren of rooms seemed to do nothing but sit on bare mattresses and smoke black hash. One afternoon Bargetta and I, down to our last pack of cigarettes, were watching *Kojak* in the front room. A brick crashed through the window and we were sprayed with glass.

'Not again,' Bargetta sighed. She shook glass from her sleeve, took a drag from her cigarette. The Rasta barrelled outside. Bargetta turned her attention back to *Kojak*. The argument outside drowned the sound of gunfire from the telly. I tried to stay as cool as Bargetta.

'That's my brother!' The Rasta ran through the room to the telephone. 'I'm going to kill him!' I noticed that his accent had become less Rasta-like. Evidently the Rasta's brother was taking revenge for having been burned by the Rasta in a business transaction of an unspecified nature. The Rasta ranted into the mouthpiece and his brother decided to go for broke: two more bricks in quick succession flew through the window and it collapsed completely in the English June.

Some of the residents gathered around the Rasta and tried to yank the telephone away. Apparently, an enormous quantity of various drugs was stashed throughout the house. The cry went up that the police were coming, and people who had not moved from their mattresses in days vaulted the banister, stampeded out of the front door, banged out of the back door.

Bargetta scooped up our few belongings. 'It's sliding time.' We heard the siren and froze.

'Look what my friggin' brother did,' the Rasta wailed. He was asked to go to the station to make out a complaint. They looked at us and we dug for our passports.

'I'm an American student,' Bargetta said. 'I'm going home. I don't want to go to the station. I don't know what this is about.'

The Rasta climbed into the police car. Bargetta picked up her dry-cleaning and I followed her to the tube station where we stayed the night. We were not alone. Other youths called it home that evening. The talk stopped, as if a plug had been pulled, when a gang of skinheads wearing National Front badges circled around us like sharks. Bargetta feigned sleep. 'For this,' she whispered, 'we could have gone to Mississippi.'

The strange thing was that I never understood how conventional, even philistine, my Anglophilia was. Even after I got a card from Bargetta saying that she was finished with London forever, those old feelings surfaced from time to time, like a viral strain that becomes manifest after its supposed eradication. When I came across the Brits one found everywhere in Manhattan, I slid into a vestal masochism not unlike that of the little black boy in the lines of Blake.

Messages in bottles floated towards me. There was the journalist who rejoiced in the Militant tendency and the tactics of the Bengalis in the Brick Lane Area; the historian musing over the fate of the *real* Sebastian Flyte; a miller who had sat in the Brixton Ritzy only to hear that the Cocteau Festival had been cancelled owing to armed insurrection in the streets. Even Sid Vicious, looking milk-fed and wasted, fainting on the steps of a punk club, or the weirdo in a coffee shop with stacks of *Soldier of Fortune* who relived for the waitress the excitement of Paki-bashing in Southall held, for me, a kind of fascination.

When I mock American students who have picked up accents after a summer at Oxford, as if they had found something nifty at Crolla's boutique in Bond Street, I have only to think of myself on the job. I work as a secretary, am often asked to dial numbers in England, and fall into the most ludicrous Masterpiece Theatre voice as soon as someone gets on the line.

I heard myself speaking with this voice in a nightmare not long ago, and the fear that I had become a ventriloquist's dummy woke me. For a moment I didn't know where I was. The squeaking of the radiator sounded like the birds back home. On the floor, among the debris, was a coupon from a socialist organization asking for donations to the strike fund for the British miners, and a letter from Ton. He remembered, after we missed meeting in Trafalgar Square that summer in 1971, my last name and my home town, and incredibly I got his letter.

It was Sunday. I headed to the office to put in some overtime. Keen, fitful gusts had scraped the Manhattan streets clean. I was alone on the bus for several blocks and it pleased me to think the driver might suggest that we just keep going, that we drive south to a warm place where new identities and plausible histories awaited us in the locker of some border town depot.

The canyons of midtown were nearly deserted. Ahead of me trudged a solitary bag lady, one of the homeless, an unfortunate who, perhaps, had been discharged from a mental ward or a city agency to sink in some corner of the city. She was enormous. She wore a blonde wig braided into two upturned pigtails which, given her bulk, the shaggy layers of thin coats, made her resemble a water buffalo. I paused at the doors of the office building to watch her and she stopped too. Her face was discoloured like the trunk of an ailing sycamore. She stooped to look into the eyes of a forlorn jack-o'-lantern that was perched on a heap of garbage in front of a restaurant.

'What's the matter, baby?' she crooned. 'It'll be all right.' She freed a hand to caress the pumpkin. 'Beg pardon. Didn't mean to bother your privateness.'

A taxi pulled up and a woman swathed in fur scooted out. The bag lady bore down on her. 'A quarter for your sins!' The woman in fur darted towards the building and pushed by me into the revolving doors. I could feel the cold on her coat, her matching hat. 'You're going to be holy one day for sure!' the bag lady called out in the wind.

The man on watch in the lobby asked the woman to sign in. She said that she had come to collect her nephew and would be but a few minutes. She was either English or faking it. Her consonants were so precisely enunciated that it sounded like a succession of small pillboxes snapping shut. The man turned down his radio and said she had to sign in. She told him to ring her nephew's office. He said that was impossible. I edged around her, signed in, and walked into the elevator. The woman stood her ground and argued. She reminded me of the customers who, not knowing the difference between tepid and boiling water, demand constant attention at the misnamed high teas so popular at the glitzy new hotels in town.

Procedure was procedure. She relented, tore off a glove, snatched up the pen, then tossed it across the desk. She clicked towards the elevator, stopped dead, and gave me a look like that of the virginal daughters in the old films about the savagery of the Mau Mau.

'The next one will do.'

The door rattled and I rode up alone, wondering how I could arrive back where I started.

For things will all be over then
Between the Queen and me.

Ryszard
Kapuściński
Warsaw Diary

The December 1982 edition of the monthly magazine *Odra* publishes an account by Emil Górski of the death of the Polish writer Bruno Schulz. On 19 November 1942, Schulz was shot in the street by a Gestapo soldier. The soldier was named Gunter and killed Schulz for no other reason than to annoy his rival in the Gestapo, a man named Landau, for whom Schulz then worked. Gunter knew a number of things: that Schulz was drawing Landau's portrait, that he was painting frescoes in Landau's flat, that Schulz was, in short, an artist. Górski writes that Schulz was killed by a Gestapo man, a fascist, but that description—fascist—defines Gunter so narrowly that the essence of the problem escapes us.

Before Gunter had the opportunity of becoming a fascist he was a mobster, obtuse and brutal. Schulz was killed not simply by a fascist but first by a wild and vicious thug—a member of the mob. If there is no mob, there is no fascism: it is impossible. The mob is the carrier of contempt, unrestrained force, baseness, the will to destroy. Even if fascism as a political movement disappears, its manifestations remain—if the mob remains.

History as class struggle? As a struggle of systems? Agreed: but history is equally the struggle between culture and the mob, between humanity and bestiality.

Models of consumerism are disseminated with greater ease than those of labour. The model, an existence of affluence and excess, is conveyed to us everywhere—constantly—by television, radio, newspapers and magazines. But the images we see belong to a world of consuming, not producing. We observe the results—the products—of labour, not the labour itself. Thus the naïve belief that it is possible to have the benefits of consumerism, at its highest possible level, without the labour and the efficient organization to achieve it. This way of thinking (or non-thinking) is the source of a number of our frustrations and forms of social neuroses. Herbert Marcuse's definition of revolution is appropriate: 'The revolt of a population injected with needs they are unable to satisfy.'

Marx believed that the increase of capital results in wealth accumulated at one extreme of society, while depriving more and more the other. Among developed countries this vision has not materialized; but among humanity as a whole, it has been verified in a world in which wealth accumulates at the extreme of the rich nations, depriving the poor ones that sink further and further into poverty.

They accuse him of having changed. But is the change to be condemned? How has he changed? They accuse him of having lined his pockets; now they reproach him because he doesn't. They have lost a partner; hence their anger. The morality of a criminal gang: solidarity through the practice of corruption. The moment you stop you ask to be condemned by those whom you have revealed by your act of refusal. The longer you stay with the gang, the more powerfully you feel you are condemned to remain with it. You may want to leave, but first face the question: will the other side accept me? What force keeps us from leaving? The fear less of the gang's revenge, than that we will not be accepted by those outside it.

Cynicism. We perpetrate abuses as though perpetrated by others. We achieve our goal by the most direct route—even by destroying those in the way. A contemptible treatment of values and principles. I rule that I am above the others; it is therefore, lawful for me to break the law.

Jean Guitton writes in his *Diary* that 'pessimism arises from perceiving things on a small scale, including a small time-scale.' His observation recalls Teilhard de Chardin—that optimism derives from considering existence from a larger perspective—a cosmic one.

A limited mobility is a feature of tribal society. Your place in the community is determined absolutely. The result is not progress or development, but balance, stability, the hierarchy, a strong sense of separateness, a division between us and them—a division characterized by an antagonism in which *they* are the adversary and the external world is therefore hostile, a trap.

A crime: the higher the level at which it is committed, the greater the likelihood it will be seen as not a crime but a necessary manoeuvre of politics.

A. believes that a man may undergo several reincarnations during his life. He was a monster and is now an angel, was a swine and is now a dove. He may not remember his previous life, or perhaps may want to forget about it completely. He dies and is resurrected, falls and rises again, vanishes and lives once more—so different, so unlike the man he had once been.

In *The Resurrection* Tolstoy writes: 'Suppose we had to solve the following psychological problem: how to make the people of our time, Christians, humanitarians—in other words, good people—perpetrate the most awful villainies without feeling a sense of guilt? There is only one possibility: make them satraps, prison governors, officers and policemen. That is, they would have to be convinced, first, that there is an institution called government service that treats people as objects, as deserving no humane brotherly treatment, and second that government service should be organized so that the responsibility for the outcome of treating people in this way will not fall on any one individual. These are the only conditions under which it is possible in our time to perpetrate the cruelties I have witnessed today.

Our world is one of states: one is identified chiefly by the state to which he belongs—*then* follows the division by race, class and religion.

An example of the absurdities created by the thinking of state bureaucracies: that Colombia refused visas to Polish missionaries, claiming they were communists because of their passports.

What does it mean to be closer to nature? To be away from the factories, fumes, polluted water and overcrowded streets. But also to be away from the baseness, from the mendacity and its spokesmen, from those wanting to humiliate and destroy you.

Bribery is a means to an end; it is also a way of securing a respite from the ceaseless fretting, effort and tension that characterize every one of our attempts to acquire goods, rights, certificates and relief. Bribery is a port where we rest before venturing out again into a sea of worry and anxiety. It is also a form of contact, the germ of a perverse, subterranean commonwealth created by the criminal pact itself.

Progress is not a historical necessity: it is a possibility, often an impossibility.

'One could say,' Mariano Aguirre writes in *El Pais*, 'that the Third World War has already occurred.' Between 1945 and 1983, there have been 140 wars in the Third World, from which twenty-five million people have died, and from which millions have joined the exodus of refugees. 'Given that 300 million people live in poverty, that 500 million are under-nourished, that 1,300 million have incomes below the subsistence level, the arms race in the Third World becomes an act of force, even though a single shot may not have been fired.'

Aguirre points, almost accidentally, to the relation between the arms race and totalitarian power. The totalitarian system is 'welcome' in a country characterized by low productivity, enabling it to divert its greatest resources to armaments at the expense of raising the population's standard of living. We tend to believe that if the expenditure on armaments is restricted, there will be more money to feed the people. We should believe instead that by restricting the development of armaments, there will be more democracy.

In self-defence we duplicate reality: we act, imagining the alibi that will protect us from persecution and punishment. The time and energy we devote to imagining alibis often seem to be more than we give to thinking about our own actions. We imagine and create fictions that drain more of our strength than our actual productive work. We invent constantly and instinctively ever-new alibis, until the lie becomes our form of thought, and, protecting us, ceases to be seen as evil.

Recalling his time in the concentration camp, Professor Pigoń offers a guide for survival: 'Do not admit doubt or defeat; hide in the most inpenetrable thicket; endure like a stone on the ground. No one will shift me!' Endure like a stone on the ground: how powerful and splendid!

Each time inflation rises it weakens morale, destroying our belief in the permanence of things, removing our faith in the future. Deprived of that faith, we are without responsibilities to ourselves and others. Inflation is not only a phenomenon of economics; it is equally a problem of ethics, a disease that attacks and destroys culture.

How can we understand the past and recreate it? The problem is not merely the paucity of sources: it is also the poverty of our imagination. How can we imagine people without our experience of the inventions of communication—electricity, aeroplanes, telephones, cinema—how are we to represent their view of the world, their understanding of time and space? In Poland we lack the means of knowing either the future or the past. Our minds are grounded in a single time: the present—but even here we move gingerly and clumsily.

A Latin proverb: *violenta non durant*—violence is short-lived. Nadezhda Mandelstam has a similar thought: terror is not constant in its intensity. It moves in waves like a tide.

The difference between colonialism and neo-colonialism, between the traditional and the modern forms of subjugating weaker states, lies in a new idea of domination and a new form of dependence. In the past we accepted the theory that the best protector of the nation is the state, which must therefore be maintained and strengthened at all costs. Today, we accept that neo-colonialism is different. In neo-colonialism, the state, arising from a formerly dependent territory, is *formally* independent. But *in reality* the neo-colonial state is governed by classes (élites) already sold out to foreign interests. The population perceives the state not as a power protecting the nation—serving its values, developing its material and spiritual resources—but as an oppressor.

The real object of the larger country today is not to occupy and liquidate the dependent *state*, but to weaken and deprive the *nation* inhabiting it—the nation being a source of threat and a defender of liberty. Today it is not the dependent states that are imperilled, but the nations, which the dominant powers—with the help of these very dependent states—seek to break up and decimate. Thus, the aim of the larger country: to strengthen the state of the conquered and subdued!

C ancer—the pathologists' verdict? The more primitive the cells in the new plasma, the more aggressive. It is the relationship between the primitive, the aggressive and the mobster: the mobster is active—fanatical and insistent; he is an indefatigable force, an evil attacking relentlessly.

A long involvement with politics deforms and corrupts the mind. Politics is characterized by its expansiveness and its greed to control, embrace, penetrate and occupy everything it touches: it destroys, in the way a drug destroys.

The system aims at a ceaseless, unswerving and pervasive control. Everyone watches everyone else, rummaging in their papers, their handbags, their refrigerators. Is there anyone who has never been controlled or controlled others? The philosophy behind this is pessimistic in the extreme, even fatalistic. It assumes that by definition man is evil, directing his energy into anti-social acts that are malicious and unethical. To save him one must watch him—constantly. Thus, this penetrating and indefatigable over-seeing is actually an expression of the magnanimity of those who have him in their care, a never-ending act of grace.

In 'Our Spiritual Needs', an article published in 1912 in *Tygodnik Polski* (*Polish Weekly*), Stefan Czarnowski writes that the struggle for a nation's future is decided not by economics but culture. Czarnowski argues that our neighbours know this and that therefore 'both in the provinces controlled by the Hohenzollerns and in those ruled by the Russians, our spiritual development is being constricted, decisively and systematically.'

Czarnowski continues: 'The principle adopted by our romantic poets of strengthening the spiritual might of the nation was not just a mystico-romantic illusion. It derived from their supreme grasp of the essence of social phenomena in general and of the existential condition of the Polish nation in particular.' He recalls Finland as a nation that has maintained its independence owing to the fact that 'during the last one hundred years the citizens of this little country have worked tenaciously to strengthen their culture.'

Everyone discusses politics here. But is this really discussion? Is it a rational disagreement? No. They make declarations and elaborate decisive opinions. Each one says his bit with feeling and fury. And then they disperse, irritated, shaken and indignant.

A scenario: a *coup d' état*. It takes place at dawn; the city is sleeping. A tank and only one tank—the country is small, the army limited and badly equipped—and two lorries of soldiers stop outside the television station. A drowsy sentry in his box by the gate. It is dark and the main building is empty. Gradually the technicians, engineers, camera and lighting men arrive. They are bewildered and frightened. The building comes alive. There is activity in the corridors and the studio. At dawn the announcer reads the first communiqués and directives of the new rulers.

The palace during the same hours. No one now takes any notice of the President. Messengers cross the city informing ministers that the President awaits them—some arrive, some don't. In the palace the atmosphere is one of nervousness, fear, imminent apocalypse. An appeal is rushed to the nation, reminding it of the sole legal authority. But the appeal remains a scrap of paper, unknown to anyone outside the palace: the television and radio as well as the editorial offices of the country's sole newspaper are now in the hands of the conspirators. The President and his entourage, placed outside the sphere of action, have ceased to exist. The conspirators have established their headquarters in the television building from which they now issue their decrees and commands. The importance of the *coup d'état*: the object attacked is not the palace but the television building.

The power of numbers is in their superiority as a law over other laws. It is in the difficulty of overcoming an unending incomprehensible mass. A hundred perish and are replaced; a thousand fall and are already replaced; a million die and ten million are on the way.

Warsaw, 1983
Translated from the Polish by Adam Czerniawski

Readers International announces a remarkable series in contemporary world literature. Each hardcover volume, by subscription, is just £4.50 *(Retail prices average £8.50).*

MY MERRY MORNINGS
by Ivan Klíma

Your subscription begins with these witty stories of Prague today, *My Merry Mornings* by Ivan Klíma – an original and gifted new voice from inside Czechoslovakia who is well-known in Europe but virtually unknown in English. Klíma was a popular young writer during the 1968 Prague Spring. His works now circulate inside his country in hand-typed "padlock editions," the Czech form of *samizdat*. "*My Merry Mornings* is one of the lovely and significant works of fiction that fade from memory very, very slowly" – Josef Skvorecký, author of *The Engineer of Human Souls.*

It will be followed every other month by a different RI selection, six hardcover originals during the year, each priced specially at **£4.50** + 50p postage (compare retail prices in parentheses). **Chile:** *I Dreamt the Snow was Burning* by Antonio Skármeta. "One of the best pieces of committed literature to emerge from Latin America" *Le Monde* (£9.00). **South Africa:** *A Ride on the Whirlwind*, Soweto youth in revolt, by black poet Sipho Sepamla. "So powerful is the story and so strongly drawn are the urgent passions of its characters that the reader's interest is constantly held" *Worldview* (£8.00). **Nicaragua:** *To Bury Our Fathers* by Sergio Ramírez, the country's foremost prose artist and now a Sandinista political leader. "Read slowly and carefully in order to appreciate and absorb all its nuances...Mr Ramírez is as important as the substantial literary merits of his book." *New York Times Book Review* (£10.00). Also forthcoming RI selections by Palestinian, Filipino and Polish writers – each a commanding voice that demands to be heard.

Many of these works were initially banned at home or written in exile: RI is committed to publishing literature in danger. Each is from the past 10 years; each is new here. Subscribe now and give these gifted writers a voice in English – and yourself a powerfully good read at a very modest price.

READERS INTERNATIONAL
8 Strathray Gardens,
London NW3 4NY

Please begin my subscription to RI's new series, beginning with *My Merry Mornings*. Every other month I receive a new hardback, each at the £4.50 subscriber price (+ 50p postage). At any time I may cancel my subscription simply by writing to you.

Name

Address

Town   Postcode

☐ my cheque to Readers International for £5.00 enclosed.
SPECIAL SAVINGS: I want to save money, & save RI billing costs, by paying £21.00 plus postage for my first six volumes in your annual series.
☐ I enclose my cheque for £24.00, incl. postage   G 2

GERMAINE GREER
WOMEN AND POWER
IN CUBA

I came to Cuba with my heart in my mouth. Ever since my first contact with the 'Third World', in Jamaica in 1971, I had been aware how burningly important it is for the developing nations that Cuba not be a fraud or a failure. As the years passed and I wandered through slums in Bombay, past windowless huts in Morocco, Tunis and Yucatan, through the dust of Uttar Pradesh and the infested dirt of the Brazilian north-east and the menace of Bogota and the Guatemalan highlands, every step showed me that paternalist development aid is worse than useless. In the eighties, as the external debts of the developing countries mushroom over them while their people grow steadily poorer and the number of landless multiplies daily, the need of a genuine alternative is agonizing. If Cuba had shown me nothing but the institutionalized poverty and bureaucratic rhetoric and repression that Western mega-media taught me to expect, a brain-washed militarized population living by hypocrisy and fear, the dark future would show no sign of dawn. If Cuba's was really a revolution of the people, then even if a malignant power should blast Cuba out of the Caribbean, its people will be invincible.

My arrival coincided with the Fourth Congress of the Federation of Cuban Women, the FMC. Billboards and posters announced it all over Havana. *Toda la fuerza de la mujer en el servicio de la revolución* ('The entire women's force in the service of the revolution'). The logo was an art nouveau-ish montage of Kalashnikov rifles and Mariposa lilies. I was not keen on the implications of either. On the Rampa, the flood lit exhibition pavilion was turned over to the exploits of women. Banked television sets showed colour videos of the history of Cuban women, and a succession of booths displayed everything from the techniques of screening for breast cancer to scent and hair curlers. Women whose bottoms threatened to burst out of their elasticized pants tottered round the exhibits on four-inch heels, clutching their *compañeros* for support. Their nails and faces were garishly painted. Their hair had been dragged over rollers, bleached, dyed and coloured. Their clothes, including their brassières, were all two or three sizes too small and flesh bulged everywhere. Most people rushed past the educational exhibits to where a painted, conked, and corseted trio bumped and ground its way through an amorous rhumba. At the sight of an unattached woman, the loose men began a psst! psst! and beckoned to me, as if I had been a dog.

The next day, my minder from the Ministry of Exterior Relations came to take me to the Palacio de Congresos for the first session of the FMC Congress. Security was tight. I was directed to a press box in the back of the vast auditorium, with no facilities for simultaneous translation. A policeman ordered me not to put my tape-recorder up on the parapet. Later I discovered that one such instrument had been accidentally knocked off and narrowly missed braining a delegate seated thirty feet below, but then and there it seemed that Cuba was determined that I would see little and understand less. The whole day was taken up with the reading of the *informe central*, the 157-page official report to the congress. The reader was Vilma Espín, president of the FMC, alternate member of the Politburo, member of the Central Committee of the Communist Party, and wife of Raul Castro, Fidel's brother. She read correctly and quietly, a calm, matronly figure hard to associate with the slender girl who had organized the medical support system during the *lucha clandestina* and joined the guerrilla fighters in the Sierra Maestra. I complained that she was hardly a charismatic speaker. 'She doesn't have to impress us,' answered one of the delegates. 'We know her. She is our Vilma.'

Alongside her, in the front row of the serried ranks of office-bearers on the dais, sat Fidel Castro, quietly reading through the report. I expected him to make some formal rhetorical statement, as befits a totalitarian figurehead, putting in a token appearance for the Association of Townswomen's Guilds before leaving to take care of more pressing matters of state. To my surprise, he sat there quietly the whole day long, reading, caressing his beard, thinking and listening. The next day he was there again. As one of the delegates waxed eloquent on discrimination against women in the workplace, a man's voice interjected. 'This is the heart of the problem, isn't it? Women's access to work!' I looked about, wondering who owned these mild, slightly high-pitched tones. It was Castro, whom I soon learned to call what every Cuban calls him, Compañero Fidel. He was leaning forward earnestly, intent on participating in the debate, not leading but participating. If anything, the discussion became less formal and more spontaneous, as delegates held up their hands for recognition and described precise problems of access to work. The women claimed that they were considered more likely to absent themselves from work, because of their family responsibilities. Fidel pointed out that men still refuse to shoulder their part of the burden of housekeeping and child-rearing as laid down by the Cuban Family Code. The women pointed out that in fact the absenteeism of women workers was often less than that of men, and certainly no greater. Fidel pointed out that women shoulder a double duty, which is unequal, and the women argued that they were not prepared to give it up. Sometimes when the head of state wagged his hand for recognition, the chairperson ignored him. At other times, the delegates noisily disagreed with him, crying, 'No, no!,' some even booing.

I had been prepared for the chants of Fidel! Fidel! but nothing had prepared me for this. I thought ruefully of Margaret Thatcher and Indira Gandhi, each incapable of listening, especially to someone who disagreed with her. And all the time Fidel made jokes, selected funny comparisons, continually pressing the delegates to give concrete, living examples. Their carefully prepared statements went all to pieces. We discovered that women did not want men to have the same leave to absent themselves from work for family reasons, because they would abuse it and use the time to visit other women—or at least the delegates thought they might—and thus one of the most fascinating contradictions in Cuban sexual politics was drawn out in a public forum of 1,400 participants.

All afternoon the debate surged on, with Vilma at the helm steadily working through the order paper. And all the next day. When delegates complained that if the day-care centres closed down for any one of a hundred reasons—lack of water, pollution of the water supply, sickness of staff, deterioration of the building, communicable illness—women were called away from hospitals and factories, schools and voluntary work, to take care of their children. Because the day-care centres did not operate on the free Saturdays, which fall every two weeks, women were effectively prevented from undertaking the extra voluntary work that led to distinction and party membership. Fidel noticed that the Minister of Labour and Employment and the Minister of Education had not bothered to attend the Congress.

'They should be hearing this,' he said.

'Watch,' said one of the Cuban journalists.

After lunch the chairs on the dais had all been moved up, and lo! the ministers in question had appeared to answer the women's demands. When the Minister for Education complained of lack of trained infant teachers, Fidel reminded him that he was using statistics from the Second Party Congress and up-dated them for him, thus destroying the excuses. Everyone but the ministers, who could fall back only on silly compliments and party slogans, enjoyed it enormously.

When the sessions rose, the women leapt to their feet, waving the coloured nylon georgette scarves and matching plastic flowers they had all brought with them, pounding maracas, bongos, conga drums and cowbells, clapping their hands and singing fit to bust, *Para trabajar, para estudiar, para defender nuestra libertad! Firmes con Fidel! Firmes con Fidel!* Hips gyrated, scarves flashed, flowers wagged. The syncopated thunder roared round the huge building, sucking the tiredest professional congress-makers out of their offices to watch as the women put on a turn that would have shamed a Welsh football crowd into silence. They were so delighted—with the occasion, with Fidel, but above all with themselves—that I forgot how clumsy some of the women looked in their harsh-coloured and badly-made synthetic suits and the crippling high heels they thought appropriate to the situation. I abandoned my posture of superiority and let myself be impressed.

Each lunchtime, 1,400 women swarmed into the commissaries of the vast building and forty minutes later they swarmed out again into group and regional meetings in preparation for the afternoon sessions. They gave hundreds of interviews for Cuban television, to be used gradually over the ensuing months, for daily papers, for women's magazines, for regional newsletters, for books. The youngest delegate was sixteen, the oldest ninety-something. They were ready to work all day and all night if necessary. My questions to Vilma Espín had to wait ten days for answers, but late on a Saturday afternoon I was called to her office, to spend two hours discussing what the questions meant. The written answers and tape-recording of our discussion were delivered to me first thing on Monday morning.

The first evening the delegates were taken to a ballet. They arrived stomping and chanting, sat chatting eagerly about the day's doings, and when the dancing had started and silence was finally imposed, a good proportion of them went straight to sleep, waking up only to applaud wildly. While exhausted *delegadas* slumbered around me, I watched Dionea, a man-eating plant composed of Josefina Menendez and the *cuerpo de baile*, to music by Villa-Lobos, as it ate three male dancers dressed as glittering mothy creatures, with horribly erotic gestures. This was followed by the world *première* of *Palomas,* a ballet choreographed by the Chilean exile Hilda Riveros especially for the Fourth Congress of the FMC. The story ran straight down the party line; the dancers mimed birth, the mother mimed ecstatic admiration of her child. She was joined by her mate and mimed ecstatic admiration of him. They simulated spontaneous conjugal relations on the floor. She then went off for her militia training, and mimed something rather like *kung fu* in strict unison with the *cuerpo de baile.* Then she and her fellow soldiers were joined by their mates and mimed heterosexual fulfilment in unison.

The delegates snored through the whole thing but woke up with a start to watch the eighth wonder of the world, Alicia Alonso, sixty years old and virtually blind, dance a *pas de deux* with Jorge Esquivel to music by Chopin. Her line was exquisite, and if once or twice things went slightly wrong, such as when she slid out of a lift and down Jorge Esquivel's nose, so that his eyes streamed with tears, the audience had no intention of feeling, let alone showing, any dissatisfaction. Alicia Alonso came back to Cuba at a time when artists and skilled technicians were leaving in hordes. She promised her people a world-class ballet and she kept her promise. She danced in complete confidence on a stage she could no longer see, borne up less by Esquivel's strong arms than by the love and loyalty that surrounded her.

This was early days, but already I could feel something unfamiliar and very special about Cuba. The absence of theatricality that I noticed in Vilma and Fidel was part of a complex of attitudes. People did not sell themselves as they do in consumer society. Life was not soap opera, but real. There was no competition or character assassination, as people jockeyed for limelight. They spoke not to persuade or bamboozle, but to explain. They had not our prurient interest in domestic and sexual affairs. No one was quite sure how many children Fidel might have had, or, for that matter, Vilma. Public functionaires were assessed on their performance of their public duty, and did not have to drag their bed partners around with them, miming domestic bliss. Life without gossip magazines and advertising seemed wonderfully uncluttered. There was no equivalent of Princess Diana's latest outfit or Elizabeth Taylor's latest wedding or the American president's haemorrhoids. Doubtless there are some Cubans who think life would be more interesting if murder and rape were reported in the newspapers and convicted criminals were paid a working man's earnings over ten years to describe their activities in lurid detail, but most of the people I met know the other culture from glimpses of Miami television and find it crazy and perverse. The slice of American culture they get from Miami includes late-night pornographic videos, which do nothing to improve the US image. Some Cubans, the ones who steal designer jeans off foreigners' clothes-lines in Miramar and offer to change pesos for dollars, giving five times the official exchange rate so that they can buy ghetto-blasters in the dollar shops, obviously envy the hyper-stimulated life-style of capitalism, but all the Cubans I met and talked to were more interested in Ethiopia and Guatemala than in Michael Jackson.

A Chilean exile explained to me, 'I could have stayed in West Germany. They were paying me a fortune, but what could I do with it? Invest in the latest parsley cutter? Life is exciting here, even if I have very little money. There is always something to do, and it's exciting. People are creating their own future. If I got sick in Germany I could lie and rot. Here, if I don't show up at the *tienda* for my rations, people are straight round to help.' Her bath was kept permanently full of water to flush the lavatory, for Havana has a chronic and crippling water shortage, just another minor inconvenience that women have to deal with, but it made no dent in Elisabeth's fierce loyalty to Cuba. As we sat on her tiny balcony, drinking *añejo sobre las rocas*, while people flowed in and out of the tiny apartments above, beside and below us, and the old red buses, affectionately known as *guaguas,* groaned and shrieked down the hill, disgorging streams of workers, she said, 'It's a hard life, but a good life.'

The Cubans are involved after all in a much bigger adventure than sex, speed and smack could possibly supply. Their morale is towering, even if their energy should occasionally flag, as they negotiate the daily obstacle course which is life in a poor country, cursed by an irreplaceable investment in a single crop—sugar—and strangled by the American blockade which has cut off the only cheap source of supply for all the goods a single-crop economy does not produce. Every Cuban will tell you that underdevelopment is a feature of minds and hearts as well as economies. As Cubans struggle to develop logistical and communicative skills, they encounter inefficiency and confusion at all levels of social organization. The response is not irritability and hostility, but tolerance and mutual assistance.

Because of rationing, limited supplies of essential commodities and the unreliability of transport (given shortage of vehicles and spare parts), queueing is a way of life, but Cubans do not try to jump queues or stand guard to see that no one else does. Instead they have developed a characteristic solution to an intolerable situation. When you arrive at the *tienda,* to find fifty people already waiting for their ration of rice, beans, oil, crackers, fruit juice or whatever other commodity is on sale that day, you simply ask who is *el último.* When another person arrives, and you are asked the same thing, you are free to go about other business and return when the queue has moved up. People less pressed chat, criticize the authorities, flirt and clown around. When you come back the person who was behind you will call you to your place. This ad hoc system involves co-operation and a degree of awareness of other people, neither often found in rich countries. Even on my last day in Cuba, when I found a hundred people queuing at the hotel cashier's desk, I could hardly prevent myself from panicking, thinking I had no time to pack because I would be queuing for two hours or so (given the mean speed of such transactions in Cuba). However, I tried asking *el último* and went about my other chores. When I came down, the honeymooners behind me waved me to my place, by now only four from the head of the line. As I had screamed and ranted at the hotel management about their inefficiency, while they politely defended a system I condemned as hopeless, I felt truly ashamed.

It may seem that all this has little to do with women and political power in Cuba. In fact, it has everything to do with it. The people meet constant daily frustrations with calm and co-operation because they do not feel that they are the result of corruption, caprice or incompetence on the part of a separate ruling class, but aspects of problems which afflict a twenty-five-year-old nation with a heritage of ignorance, disease and poverty.

The first priority of the Cuban revolution was to combat illiteracy, disease and malnutrition, thus bringing the Cuban population to a condition in which they could exercise the duties of popular government. Despite the enormous drain of human and other resources in maintaining a convincing defence posture, they have achieved those basic aims, largely by voluntary work undertaken alongside the desperate struggle to make the sugar economy profitable despite falling world prices, and to cope with the effects of the US blockade.

My first duty in Cuba was to check the validity of Cuban claims about health and education, so I hired a car and slipped off into the countryside, driving through town after small town, checking the *policlinico* (the community hospital), the water supply, the electricity cables, the health status of the inhabitants, the intensity and productivity of the industry and agriculture. I turned up back streets, wandered into sugar mills and factory forecourts, stopped to watch militia training and the volunteer brigades grubbing up garlic and packing tomatoes in boxes. Nobody stared, nobody tried to beg, but people by the roadsides cheerfully accepted lifts. *La guagua está mal*—'The bus isn't working'—was the usual explanation. Everyone I saw was healthy, busy and quietly self-confident. Occasional unpleasantnesses helped me to realize that I was not dreaming. A boarding-school cook, coming back from collecting his daughter who spent the weekend with her psychologist mother and lived with her father during the week, told me he would not let her marry a negro.

'Oh, popi,' said the ten-year-old indulgently, shaking her head at this foolishness.

Everyone was interested in the progress that was being made. They explained to me about the difficulties of industrializing sugar production—'humanizing the work,' they called it. Questions about plant genetics and animal diseases got intelligent answers, if not from parents then from the children.

In all Cuba's struggles, women have been in the front line. During the *lucha clandestina* women organized medical supplies and treatment and taught school in the Sierra Maestra. Fidel has always acknowledged that without the help of women in building up the underground organization which victualled, supplied and protected the guerrillas in the fifties, they would never have been successful. Celia Sánchez, who was waiting with supplies, petrol and transport for the arrival of the yacht, *Granma,* which brought Fidel back to Cuba in 1956, became his aide in the closing years of the war, and took part in several battles. She chose to work as Secretary to the Council of State when the Revolutionary Government was set up. Every little girl in Cuba grows up with an impressive series of role models, going back more than a hundred years before the revolution: Rosa La Bayamesa, a captain in the war of independence; Paulina Pedrosa and Carolina Rodriguez, supporters of José Martí's revolutionary party in the 1890s; Emilia Rodriguez, leader of the *Partido Popular Obrero* (The Workers' Popular Party) in the 1920s, and dozens more. The struggle to oust Batista threw up more still, like Lydia Doce and Clodorinda Acosta Ferrais, who were only twenty years old when Batista's police threw their bullet-riddled bodies into the sea. The all-woman *Peloton Mariana Grajales,* formed in September 1958 and named after the mother of the *maceo* who led the Revolutionary War of 1868-78, held one of the most exposed positions on the highway between Havana and Santiago de Cuba and was involved in some of the bitterest fighting of the war. Women fought at the Bay of Pigs; Cira García Reyes, leader of the FMC in the region, lost her life there.

On 23 August 1960, the female network which had contributed so much to the rebel effort was officially instituted as the Federation of Cuban Women, the FMC. By spreading out over the countryside, they were to consolidate the revolution by convincing the passive and fearful that they could construct a new society. Peasant women like Nadividad Betancourt Marten led groups of women who travelled from village to village in their regions, politicizing women like themselves. The FMC organized the push for literacy in Cuba,

215

working as volunteer teachers in peasant huts up and down the island, teaching more volunteers who taught others. Women conducted the 'Battle for the Sixth Grade', and when that was won, they went on to help all kinds of people achieve the standard of ninth-grade education.

The US blockade is a disaster which popular endurance and initiative have turned into a blessing, for nothing less brutal could have protected Cuba from becoming another impoverished would-be consumer nation. The ridiculous attempt to invade, known by the Cubans as the Victoria de Girón and by the Americans as the Bay of Pigs débâcle, gave all Cubans a sense of external threat and national heroism. The strangely explosive epidemic of haemorrhagic dengue fever, involving a mutant strain similar to one that is normally found in Asia, which swept through the province of Havana in 1981, producing thousands of cases within a week, was met by mobilizing all the mass organizations to isolate cases and run improvised field hospitals in all kinds of public buildings. The hypothesis of germ warfare was obvious, but the Cubans wasted no time in investigating whether it was another gift from the CIA dirty tricks department; they were more interested in their own preparedness and efficiency in overcoming it, as they did. The disease vanished from Cuba as suddenly as it came.

It would be quite wrong to imagine, however, that there was no resistance to the full incorporation of women in the development process. For many people the only notion of the good life was derived from the bourgeois example; moreover, the legacy of the past included male unemployment, especially during the seven months of the year when the cane was not being cut, while women struggled to feed their families by domestic work, by working in the tobacco industry and by prostitution. Slave women had not been protected from brutalizing toil, therefore the right to manual labour was not one that Cuban women were on the whole particularly anxious to win. There had been opposition to the presence of women fighters in the Sierra, but for some reason, perhaps his dependence on Melba Hernández and Celia Sánchez, Fidel insisted on women's full participation in the struggle, in the victory and in the glory. In 1965 he was already defining women's liberation as 'a revolution within the revolution.' It is generally assumed that the authority for the revolutionary Cuban conception of women's role is the writings of Marx and Lenin, against 'the base, mean and infamous denial of rights to women' and inequality of sexes. To be sure, Cuba follows the Russian line on abortion, contraception, neo-Malthusianism, women in the workplace, divorce, child care, education and maternity leave. But there are aspects of sexual politics in Cuba that are distinctly Cuban, and owe nothing to the Russian paradigm.

Sexual politics in Cuba are complex. It is not enough to say that the Cuban man is macho or even extremely macho. Chances are that whatever the Cuban male is, his mother has had far more to do with the development of his personality than his father. A joke in a Cuban girls' magazine sums the conundrum up perfectly. 'Your boyfriend is terribly macho,' says one. 'Yes,' simpers the other. 'Aren't I lucky!' Cuban sociology does not express itself in detailed examinations of the psychopathology of everyday life, so it was difficult for a visitor to gain any clear idea of the reality behind the body language of male-female interaction. Officially, Cuba is a totally heterosexual country. There are no homosexual partnerships, no people living alone, no one-parent families. There are no published figures to illuminate the reality behind this impossibility, just as there are no figures on rape and crimes against women or sex-related offences generally. Certainly, when work is over, the streets of Havana fill with couples, hand in hand, kissing, giggling, wandering through Coppelia (a complex of pavilion and garden covering a whole block and totally given over to the sale and consumption of ice cream) or attending any of the dozens of free amusements that socialism supplies—museums, aquaria, literary *tertulias*, concerts....

The situation is complicated by a severe housing shortage, with a typically Cuban solution. People in need of privacy to make love can go to one of several *posadas*, where at very reasonable rates they can hire a room, a bed and clean sheets by the hour, and order food and beverages to the room. Nobody asks questions about the couples, who may be married to each other, married to others, unmarried, engaged or one-hour stands. The only inconvenience is that, as with everything in Cuba, there is a wait, sometimes a three-or four-hour wait. Couples sit in the waiting-room, smoking, necking, chatting, until the next horizontal space becomes free. Anyone who remembers Lenin's scornful dismissal as bourgeois the demand of feminists like Inessa Armand and Alexandra Kollontai for the right of free love will see that, in this matter at least, the Cubans have gone their own way.

The Cubans have accepted that adultery is their national sport. Men boast of it. A man otherwise intelligent, cultivated and reasonable will tell you that when a pretty girl works for him or near him he will do his best to get near her and 'be with her' as often as he can, but his attentions to his wife will continue at the same intensity. The implication is that he can satisfy both, and there can be no significant objection to the spreading of so much happiness by his so potent art. The men seem to be totally caught up in this fantasy, which explains why they have the temerity to call unattached women across to their sides as if they were loose puppies. A foreign woman alone in Havana might well interpret the staring and gesturing of men as signs of aggression, hostility and low esteem for women, especially if she is accustomed to the North American or north European version expressed in whistling, cat calls and sexist comments.

Cuba's boast of advances in its progress towards complete equality for women seemed to me invalidated by the overt interference by Cuban men in my freedom to sit in a darkened cinema by myself or stand waiting for the lift in a hotel lobby. However, after a few days I began to realize that male aggression in Cuba was different. If I clearly expressed my displeasure or lack of interest in the proceedings, the men appeared startled and embarrassed and tended to disappear or, indeed, flee. Men told me that Cuban women quite enjoy approaches of this kind and often flirtatiously provoke them, and I did see some evidence for the truth of this claim. Women on the other hand told me that if I had protested, when I was harassed in the cinema, the people sitting around me would have taken my part. One of the men involved might have found himself the victim of a citizens' arrest and eventually subject to up to fifteen years' detention in a work centre. This is a rather different reason for not creating a scene than what prevails in England, where the people around me would most likely dismiss the uproar as evidence of my hysteria and exonerate the man for lack of evidence other than my protest.

It stands to reason that male aggression towards women would be modified by the salutory reflection that any woman may be a salaried officer of the Fuerzas Armadas Revolucionarias. Most women are trained in the militia and actively involved in the public surveillance duties of the *Comités para la Defensa de la Revolución.* However, male-female relationships in Cuba are different from those I grew up with, principally because, like Cuba itself, they are Afro-Latin. The Africans who were shipped to Cuba left behind them intricate family structures in which the relationships of siblings and cross-cousins through the female line were at least as important as patrilineal relationships, and the mother-child relationship possibly the most intense and durable of all human bonds.

In the slave society, where men and women were bought and sold like cattle, women were used as brood animals, often fecundated by their owners rather than the men of their choice and prevented from setting up any viable, legitimate family structure. The legacy of this persists in all Afro-American societies, where first births are often very early, where the nuptial bond is fragile and mothers—and mothers' mothers—supply the only stability in the child's experience. Doubtless, feminist chauvinists will sneer at an impression based on two weeks' acquaintance; nevertheless I must say that there seems to me to be less hositility in male-female relations in Cuba than, say, in northern Europe. Cuban women would agree. They staunchly refuse to entertain a notion of sexual politics which postulates any significant degree of male-female hostility. Even when Compañero Fidel suggests that the greatest obstacle to women's complete equality is the attitude of men to the work traditionally done by women, the women prefer to stress other 'objective' factors. Cuban men, for all their flirtatiousness, seem to like and respect women. One way of interpreting the emphasis on men's strength—machismo, as Cubans are themselves ready to call it—is as an attempt to counter-balance the dominance of women in family and kin relations.

It is notable that one of the sources of friction in the day-to-day workings of the friendship between the Cuban cockerel and the Russian bear is the Russians' treatment of women. Almost more important than Marx and Lenin in the genesis of the Cuban revolution is the figure of José Martí, the national hero of Cuba, a man of high culture and clear and coherent political ideology, who adored women. He died fighting with the Mambi Army in 1895, but his personality permeates Cuba still. When accused of being a Marxist after the attack on the Moncada Barracks in 1952, Fidel claimed that the sole designer of the attack had been José Martí. Martí believed that no cause that women supported could be defeated, and no side could be victorious which did not have the support of women. Martí's feminism was based on a chivalrous ideal of the pure, cultivated, disinterested woman, an ideal drawn from bourgeois notions of women as weaker, nobler and less sexual than men, but which had a special relevance in a society in which women had never been protected from degrading physical toil. His notion of male/female complementarity relied upon an extreme polarity, but he also argued that one source of the brutality of capitalist society was that it suppressed feminine feeling in women *and* in men. He found American feminism erring in its over-emphasis on the same coarse self-seeking that characterized the perversion of the American dream of a free and egalitarian society. If they achieve their aims, he asked, *Dónde estará el aroma de las rosas?* ('Where will the roses' scent be?') Present-day Martí scholars argued with me earnestly that society needs the feminine qualities, which when pressed they defined as self-abnegation, sensitivity, enthusiasm, '*espirito*' and tenderness. *Cuál es la fuerza de la vida y su única raíz sino el amor de la mujer?*('What is the force of life and the only reason for living, if it is not the love of a woman?')

To Martí's enduring influence, then, we may attribute the emphasis that Cuban feminists lay on feminity. Women who have been trained to kill will be wearing pearlized nail polish and lipstick when they do it. The perennial shortage of acetone in Cuba probably means that the nail polish will be chipped, unless the solider has had time to got to the beauty parlour, for acetone is supplied to the nation's manicurists. Even the heroines of work, who cut cane, go down the mines and drive huge cranes, are depilated, deodorized and scented. One of the first problems tackled by the FMC was devising a way of supplying Cuban women with the resources for making pretty clothes out of the scanty fabric supplies. Seamstresses and tailors were trained and given the facilities for carrying on trade as licensed artisans in a state scheme. At the FMC Congress, some of the foreign journalists were intrigued that so many women were wearing suits of various styles in a particular shade of kingfisher blue Courtelle. Was it a uniform of some sort, they asked. In fact it was simply that the blue was one of the few vivid shades available, and literally hundreds of women had chosen it.

For a feminist like me who considers that the combination of dazzle with drudgery is one of the most insidious ways in which women in our society are subject to stress, the multiplication of contradictory demands upon the Cuban woman is a cause for concern. Women who are expected to be prepared to kill are also expected to be flower-like; the Mariposa must accompany the Kalashnikov. The brain surgeon, the politburo member and the chief of police must also be ready to sit by their children's beds in hospital, comforting and caring for them, their attention for the moment undivided. The Cuban women are proud that they can handle all this. They see theirs as the force of the flower that in growing towards the light shatters the rock. To Martí's question, *Hay hombres que se cansan, cuando las mujeres no se cansan?* ('Are there men who tire when women do not?'),they answer yes.

As I travelled around the provinces of Havana, Matanzas and Pinar del Rio, alone in a hired car, I talked to dozens of women, hitch-hiking without fear in their own country, to join their parents, their *novios*, their husbands, separated from them by the demands of the revolution. They were shy, but not frightened to talk.

Pilar was typical. She is twenty-three, and has nearly finished her studies in medicine at the University of Havana. Next will come work in a remote part of the island or *internacionalismo*. She had hitched a ride with me to visit her husband, studying a hundred kilometres away at the University of Matanzas. When I suggested that so much separation now and a prospect of indefinite separation to come was a bit hard on a marriage, she said, 'We can handle it. We were sweethearts for eight years, and it was always like this.' I pushed a little harder, saying how hard it was to give men the attention they demanded after a week's hard work. She grinned and I noticed how pale she was and how white were her gums.

'Sometimes, I've been in the operating theatre all night and I

221

have to grab my bag and get out here on the road. I haven't time to wait for the *guagua* and it's always so crowded—I just can't face the trip standing up.'

I probably should have concentrated on the pot-holes and let her go to sleep, but instead I asked if she might not have been anaemic.

She seemed slightly startled by the thought. 'Possibly. I've got an IUD.' She knitted her brows. Cuban girls can be fitted with IUDs on demand if they are sixteen or over. Pills, some made from steroids derived from locally-grown hennequin (sisal), are also available, and there is a move to switch to them. IUDs in a young population are always problematic, but absolutely no publicity is given to such matters in Cuba. Juvenile pregnancy is such a pressing problem that the emphasis is all on prevention.

We talked about housework.

'A man wants a wife, doesn't he? Not a maid,' she said stoutly. I got to know other women like Pilar, hard-working party members, serious and committed in everything, including their sexual relationships. As I watched her walking towards her husband's dormitory over the burnt grass, I hoped she would find his room clean and his clothes washed when she got there. The older women told me, 'Oh no. If she wanted to be at all comfortable, she would have had to set to and clean him up.' The young women said, 'Of course,' but it sounded more like ideology than fact. As Pilar walked away, I called out, 'Take care of yourself!' She gave me a white smile, and slightly ironic shrug.

It would be perfectly possible to argue that Fidel Castro's revolution exploits women. Socialist revolution exploits everybody. 'From each according to his capacity, to each according to his need.' Every ounce of courage, patience, energy, determination and intelligence is needed if Cuba is to realize her own aims.

The burden ought to fall on men and women impartially. In addition to their salaried and professional work, men and women both undertake voluntary work in the service of the revolution. Men and women are involved in the constant watch kept in Cuban streets by day and night, so that in the event of an attempted insurrection or invasion or an epidemic the Cuban people can be mobilized from the street up; as a by-product, crime has disappeared off their streets.

Men and women volunteer to clean the streets and plant public gardens in their free time; on a Sunday morning in every town in Cuba, you may see gangs of women, gangs of men and mixed gangs sweeping away leaves, burning waste paper, hauling trash. Such voluntary work is particularly onerous for women because in addition to their paid work, they are also working unpaid in the home. As the level of general culture and the standard of living has risen, the amount of housework to be done has increased exponentially. Cubans are fanatically clean. When it became possible to wash garments every time they were worn, because water, soap and garments were all present in sufficient supply, all Cuban garments were so washed. The traditional Cuban diet involves a good deal of preparation and long cooking, as well as the the hours of waiting at the *tienda* for the monotonous supplies. The state helps by providing meals at the place of work, and in schools and day-care centres, where pre-school children stay from seven to seven p.m. and eat two full meals and two snacks. Working women carry a card which enables them to go to the front of the food queue, not because they deserve some free time but to make it possible for them to cram all the duties expected of them into the inelastic twenty-four hour day.

There is very little time left over for even more voluntary work in the grass-roots organization of *Poder Popular,* the ultimate legislative power in Cuba, even if we do not take into account the time and money the Cuban woman must spend on her other duty of keeping pretty and attractive. It is the more remarkable then that two million members of the FMC voted to be allowed to train with the *Milicia de las Tropas Territoriales*, the volunteer home guard, who train one Sunday a month. Women's record as *cumplidoras*, with full attendance at work and invariably fulfilled production quotas, is consistently higher than men's. And yet at the first sign of *fiesta,* the Cuban woman is ready to stick a frangipani behind her ear and rhumba the night away. Even the Cuban sugar allowance, four pounds of sugar per person per month, could not generate this kind of energy in a disaffected population, although it clearly goes some way to causing a serious health problem of massive obesity, especially in women over forty.

T hose people who ask, 'But in Cuba are men relinquishing political power so that women can take it up?' are projecting a curiously corrupt notion of political power on to the post-revolutionary process in Cuba. Revolutionary socialists are involved in re-making political power in such a way that it is genuinely wielded by the masses. While enemies of the revolution may persist in believing that power is still concentrated in the hands of an oligarchy, the people themselves are working hard to create the administrative structures which will promote the expression of the collective will and translate it into state policy.

Outsiders may assume that Cuba is actually a dictatorship masquerading as a democratic republic and that real power is vested in the politburo or the Central Committee of the Communist Party; such in fact is not the case. In 1976, Cubans voted in a referendum to accept a socialist constitution which enunciated the principle by which the popular assemblies became the ultimate legislative power in the land. Those of us accustomed to seeing democratic processes subverted by lobbying, patronage and secret government would assume that the huge machinery of *Poder Popular* could do little but rubber-stamp legislation originating in the inner recesses of the Communist Party. In fact, the grass-roots-level assemblies do originate the legislative process, follow it through and participate actively in the drafting of legislation. For such a cumbersome system to work, the enthusiastic participation of large numbers of people for frequent and long sessions is indispensable, yet the system has produced the new housing law in Cuba, which has less to do with socialist ideology than the pragmatic expression of the people's will. Rather than nationalize housing, the Cubans have chosen to own their own homes, amid a multitude of special considerations regarding leasing, letting and inheritance, all designed to protect the right to own one's home and prevent speculation or profiteering.

Democratic centralism, if earnestly undertaken, is the system which produces the least return for the most massive expenditure of human resources. Frequent long meetings, with the intervening struggle to study unfamiliar matters, such as housing law, contract, equity, conveyancing and alternative adminstrative systems, as in the case of the 1985 *Ley de las Viviendas* (Housing Law), must arrive at unanimity, much as juries do, by long argument and counter-argument. The amateur legislators—for only the full-time functionaries are paid—must struggle to keep the process under control, agreeing agendas and then following them through. The process demands what Cuban women have least of—time—yet, even so, twenty-seven per cent of delegates in *Poder Popular* are women. This is more significant than the presence of women on the Central Committee of the Communist Party; nevertheless of 119 members and seventy-one alternates, twenty-seven are women, seventeen of them full members. Women formed twenty-two per cent of the delegates elected at the Second Party Congress, an increase of fifty per cent over the First Party Conference. The Third Party Congress this year will probably be attended by a high proportion of women and elect more female members of the Central Committee.

If we look at the profile of women's participation in leadership activities, contradictory trends emerge. From their first participation in the youth movement of the José Martí Young Pioneers, we will see that little girls are fifty per cent of the members and 66.3 per cent of the troupe leaders. In the *Federación de los Estudiantes de las Escuelas Medias* (The Federation of Secondary School Students), women are fifty-seven per cent of the membership and sixty-one per cent of the leadership, while at university level they are fifty-nine per cent of the student enrolment but only forty-eight per cent of the leadership. Thus, as women become numerically dominant in the rank and file, they are outnumbered in the leadership. Women are only forty-one per cent of the Young Communists, the highly selective organization and training ground for future members of the Communist Party of Cuba. The disparities can be understood in two ways: the increasing proportion of female leaders in the younger age groups may reflect a general tendency to increasing female participation in the future; the troupe leaders among the Young Pioneers may continue as leaders until they find themselves on the Central Committee of the CPC. (In December 1984 the FEEM elected a national committee composed of six women and three men with women for president and vice-president.) The negative interpretation of the same data leads to the conclusion that as little girls approach puberty their ascendancy over the boys, who develop social and communicative skills more slowly, disappears, to be replaced by passivity and participation only in an ancillary capacity, in proportion as they become aware of and involved in sexual activity.

The price Cuban women pay for teenage sexual activity is very high: analysis of statistics supplied in the *Anuario Estadístico de Cuba* (1981) shows that not only were nearly 52,000 of the nation's 187,500-odd births in 1976 to mothers aged between fifteen and nineteen, but a further 10,000 of the total were unaccounted for, probably to mothers below the age of fifteen, the only category not specifically mentioned. Abortions have settled at about 100,000 per year, and about a quarter of them are carried out on women under nineteen. More than 400,000 girls of less than nineteen years old are already married, accounting for the largest proportion of divorces, currently running at about 3.2 per thousand per year, while marriages stand at about thirteen per thousand. Of the nation's 3,371,000 women over fifteen, about 1,400,000 are legally married, while half as many are living in informal unions. Of Cuba's 575,000 or so girls under nineteen, 52,000 are already legally married, while 87,000 are living with a man, and a further 25,000 describe themselves as divorced or separated.

The data are incomplete, but they point to a situation in which young women find themselves with domestic and family responsibilities just at the time when they should be gaining professional experience and qualifications. To the problems of evolving sexuality and the contradictoriness of the female role as both active comrade and sex object are added the divided attention of the young mother and the unavoidable drain upon her time and energy. The state gives all the help that legislation can provide, with free birth control, free abortion on demand and free day-care facilities, but it cannot alter the emotional reality of juvenile marriage, parenthood and divorce and the young women's own attitudes towards them. Babies are accepted in day-care from forty-five days old, but mothers are not, and should not be constrained to give them up for twelve hours a day, an impossibility in any case if they wish to breast feed.

It must not be thought that it has taken an outsider to detect the series of interlocking factors militating against women's full incorporation in the development of the Cuban state. The FMC is a high-relief organization, with vociferous representation at all levels of local, provincial and state administration. Its members, *las federadas*, are known throughout the country, and although their demands may cause consternation, as does their present campaign to allow husbands to be granted leave from work to accompany sick children in hospital, it is understood that they will eventually have to be met. Cuba's commitment to the full social, political and economic equality of women is a fundamental aspect of Cuban socialism. Insofar as the system is not one of draconian imposition, but of pragmatic accommodation of the people's will and transformation of social realities at a pace with which the ordinary people (who are the ultimate cause and purpose of the revolutionary process) can keep up, women's full emergence into political life depends upon their own redefinition of their life aims with a consequent alteration of the psychopathology of everyday life. Put in the simplest terms, this means that women will have to demand more of men.

There are some indications that the young Communists are leading the way in this. In sex education discussion groups involving both sexes it is generally agreed that emotional relationships should be built on a more intimate and committed basis. Cuban feminists have begun to reject the idea that men should help with women's work, and have begun to demand sharing all aspects of family building, involving men much more in the activities of parenting than has traditionally been the case. It is understood that progress towards women's equality is a struggle against entrenched attitudes and obsolete but enduring concepts of appropriate sex roles. An older Cuban man may tell you that he accepts the idea of his responsibility towards his children and their mother or mothers, and yet give curiously vague answers to direct inquiries about how often he sees his children and how much time he spends with them. He may tell you that his wife accepts his absenteeism and his sporting attitude to extra-marital conquests, but it is unlikely that his wife will agree with him. The *delegadas* stoutly maintain that as women have economic independence they no longer have to tolerate humiliation and would reject any husband whose infidelity was discovered, but their anxiety about male fickleness could not be concealed. When I argued that male adultery was impossible without serious flaws in female solidarity, they refused to see the point. They would not agree either that if women were really monogamous men would be unable to find partners for adultery, or that men's promiscuity was anything but 'natural'. *Él es hombre* is the sexist explanation they give for male perfidy. They could not see that women's vulnerability to men's infidelity was an aspect of sexual colonialism. The Cuban woman has all her emotional eggs in one basket; she is psychic one-crop economy, direly threatened by male sanctions, in particular the withdrawal of affection and intimacy, but the suggestion that she protect herself by cultivating other kinds of emotional satisfaction and other sources of esteem was not taken. There was very little emphasis placed by the FMC on sisterhood. No one ever discussed the single woman, a rare creature in Cuba in any event.

There is an inherent contradiction in Cuba between the socialist ideals of the revolution and the bourgeois paradigm of the nuclear family, which is what most Cubans take as the basic unit of the modern state. In the nuclear family the child is confronted by only two adults contrasted by sex. The tendency towards polarization is unavoidable. The duplication of effort in the nuclear family is directly connected to the family's role as the principal unit of consumption in consumer society. Each household is destined to acquire a complete set of all the consumer durables considered necessary for the good life, and per capita consumption is therefore maintained at its highest level. In sex as in consumption the nuclear family emphasizes possession and exclusivity at the expense of the kinds of emotional relationships that work for co-operation and solidarity. Even the best-educated Cubans seem unaware of the arguments of Marx and Engels against monogamy. They regret the instability of marriage, and work towards enculturating young people to delay the formation of exclusive sexual partnerships until they should be mature enough to undertake long-term commitment, when perhaps they ought to be spending more time reducing the psychic damage done to young people, young women especially, by the breakdown of these early relationships, so that they are less vulnerable in future.

One of the heroines of the revolution, Haydée Santamaría, killed herself after her husband began a public affair with a younger, more glamorous woman. Although she was the founder of the Casa de las Americas, and widely respected throughout Latin America, she could not recover from this blow to her self-esteem. Yet Cuban feminism shows no signs of any attempt to reduce women's psychic dependence upon their success in heterosexual relationships by strengthening cameraderie among women or teaching them that in order to live with men they must learn to live without them. As the standard of living rises women's work increases, and their dependence upon the sexual relationship with their husbands will increase as households diminish in size.

There are difficult days ahead for the Cuban woman, but as long as the ideology of revolution is lively and sincere, ways will be devised to deal with the new stresses. In the meantime Cuba remains the only country in the world where women may take any job they wish to do at the same rate of pay as a man, earn any qualification they are prepared to study for, carry their own weapons in the army and rise to the rank of colonel, dress as they please and accept or refuse men's attentions as they please, terminate or continue a pregnancy as they think fit, knowing that they will have help to carry out whichever course they should decide to follow.

Perhaps the true extent of women's power in Cuba is best illustrated not by quoting numbers on the central committee, but in a homely example which shows how important women are to Cuba. Every sexually active woman in Cuba at risk of contracting cervical cancer is given her smear test every two years. Every year hundreds of women's lives are saved by prompt treatment, while in England, Equal Opportunities Commission or no, women are dying because they have not had their smears, because they did not have them often enough, and because they were not informed when the cells were seen to be abnormal. The British health service could not cope with the demand if all the women who should ask for smear tests did, and presented themselves for further treatment. Yet little Cuba manages it. Follow-up and recall are carried out at street level by the FMC and the Committee for the Defence of the Revolution, while the state institutions supply the technical facilities. This may not be evidence of power as it is commonly perceived by capitalist societies, but access to the technology in order to save your own life is the kind of power women want. It is real power, unlike the authoritarian fantasies that pass for power in most of the world. And the women of Cuba struggled for it, defined it and exercise it on their own behalf. It remains to be seen now whether Cuban women will raise their own standard in the world forum and show the other emergent nations how to harness the strength and tenderness of women in the remaking of our tired and guilty world. As Cuba's leaders have always realized, survival is too desperate a matter to be left to half the world's population. We need to see Federations of Women of every nationality mobilizing in the streets of every city, town and village in the world, *para trabajar, para estudiar, para construir nuestra libertad!*

GRANTA

"England's best-selling, most influential literary magazine."—TIME

AVAILABLE, AT LAST, IN AMERICA

In February 1983, Penguin Books in Britain began publishing GRANTA, the paperback magazine of new writing. The response was immediate:

> "A magazine absolutely charged with life and risk." —GEORGE STEINER
>
> "A courageous literary magazine." —GRAHAM GREENE
>
> "GRANTA has rapidly become the premier literary magazine of Britain—and mainly because it is for writers and readers—not critics and academics." —JOHN FOWLES

ISSUE AFTER ISSUE, four times a year, GRANTA has published the most engaging, talked about writing in Britain today:

AUTOBIOGRAPHY: Saul Bellow, Doris Lessing, Raymond Carver.

TRAVEL WRITING: Paul Theroux, Gabriel Garcia Marquez, Jan Morris.

FICTION: Nadine Gordimer, Italo Calvino, Anita Brookner, Jayne Anne Phillips.

POLEMIC: Milan Kundera on the failure of the West, Salman Rushdie on the revival of the Raj, Mario Vargas Llosa on cheap intellectuals.

REPORTAGE: James Fenton looting the US embassy in Saigon, Michael Herr traveling across Europe with Wim Wenders, Stanley Booth with the Rolling Stones, Redmond O'Hanlon loose in the jungles of Borneo.

IN THE LAST YEAR and a half, each issue of PENGUIN GRANTA has sold out within seven days. In the last year and a half, each issue of GRANTA has been read by more people than any other literary or political magazine published in the UK today. More than the TLS. More than the New Statesman.

AS OF JULY 1985, GRANTA IS AVAILABLE IN AMERICA

For only $12, you can get a year's subscription, 4 issues each the size of a paperback book, and, at no additional cost, the First US Edition. A single copy of GRANTA sells for $6.95 in bookstores: you save over $22, unless you subscribe for 2 or 3 years and save as much as $60. GRANTA will come to you on approval for three months; during that time you may, if dissatisfied, cancel your order and your money will be refunded in full.

Please send me GRANTA for: ☐ 1 yr. at $12 ☐ 2 yrs. at $22 ☐ 3 yrs. at $30

Name

Address

City　　　　　State　　　　　Zip

☐ Check enclosed ☐ Bill me later

GRANTA: 13 White St., New York, NY 10013

DAVID HARE
NICARAGUA:
AN APPEAL

When a certain senior Nicaraguan politician was received at the Foreign Office by Lord Carrington, who was then Foreign Secretary, he was told how worried the British government was that Nicaragua was supplying arms to the rebels in El Salvador.[1] With five hundred miles of common border, said Lord Carrington, it is inevitable that people will be crossing back and forth with guns. The senior Nicaraguan politician replied that if Lord Carrington looked at a map of Central America, he would see that Nicaragua had no common border with El Salvador. It must be Guatemala he was thinking of.

Henceforward somewhat disadvantaged at this meeting, Lord Carrington nevertheless went on to assert that with the FSLN in power he was worried about the future of democracy in Nicaragua. The Nicaraguan diplomat replied that with Mrs Thatcher in power he was worried about the future of democracy in England. Carrington is said to have had the grace to smile and reply, 'I take your point.'

To arrive in Nicaragua is at once to be disoriented, for since the earthquake in 1972, there has been, and is still no proper city of Managua. There are ruins, there are suburbs, there are scrubby bald patches of land, but there is no heart. For the announcement of the elections last February long lines of people trailed in from the countryside. They were visible for miles off in all directions even from what is meant to be the centre of the town. They arrived, listened, and dispersed, once more in lines, once more visible for hours after they had left the square. The occasion was anti-climactic. I heard no good rhetoric in Nicaragua. In private the ministers of the government are witty and humane, but in public they do not always sparkle. The purpose of rhetoric is to persuade people to an argument of which they are not sure, or to which they are not yet converted. But the Nicaraguan citizen already knows clearly the two main realities of his life: that he is poor and that he is under threat from the United States of America.

---

[1] This is the text of a speech delivered at the London concert, *A Night for Nicaragua*, on 13 January 1985, to raise money for the Nicaragua Solidarity Campaign, 20 Compton Terrace, London N1.

It is often hard to see why one of the two greatest military powers in the world should feel that its way of life is being subverted by a country in which the people so plainly wanted, and to a large extent still admire their own revolution. But it is so. The CIA's handbook on the management of local assassinations is written in a prose style which finds its respectable echoes in the report of Kissinger's joke commission. And casual instances of news distortion signify as much. There is a patisserie in a suburb of Managua where they bake fresh French bread, for which people not unnaturally are willing to stand in line. An American TV news team filmed the queue, then put out a story on the US evening news, headlined BREAD LINES IN NICARAGUA.

The images of colonialism are so simple and drastic in this part of the world that anecdotes form themselves effortlessly into parables. A Matagualpa theatre director had to go to New York to pay a royalty for the privilege of copying out one of Nicaragua's own national classic plays. A Hollywood film company decided to make a film about the Sandinista revolution called *Under Fire*. A considerable success, it was seen in many countries in the world. But the American distributors asked so much money in advance that the Nicaraguans could not themselves afford to show it.

As you see, there is no good will here. There is bitter hostility. For it is essential to the United States' present idea of itself that all revolutions are malign. It has presumably forgotten its own. It refuses to understand that in Nicaragua free enterprise is encouraged. Coffee plantations are extensively privately owned. There is official opposition. A conservative newspaper is published daily. Observers held the recent elections to be as fairly administered as was possible. Yet it is essential to the Yankees' idea of their own democracy to go on typing this regime as exclusively Soviet-inspired.

'There are', says the Nicaraguan Ambassador to the United States, 'more Marxists in the University of London than there are in the whole of Nicaragua.' I doubt this. Marx has plainly been an inspiration to the revolution. So has Sandino. So has Jesus Christ. All three men share a certain ambiguity: they are open to a bewildering variety of interpretations. There is a belief, which to

233

us may seem naive, that by taking the best from each the Nicaraguans may make a compound which is all their own. They think that by avoiding the language of ideology, they may also avoid its terrors. They will take technology from the West, scientists from the East and practical help from any part of the world which is willing to provide it. I cannot emphasize enough tonight how much that support means. A border guard, not far from Ocotal, wept when we presented him with a transistor radio, because he could not believe that anyone would think it worthwhile to come so far to give him a simple present.

It is hard at this distance to convey the feeling of a country where half the inhabitants are under twenty-one, where everyone has known war, and where there is an almost universal certainty that nothing can be as bad as the past. At the mass, people no longer kneel to pray. To kneel is to humble yourself, and throughout America the Church has so long been implicated in the order of things that worshippers feel God will understand that they can no longer make a gesture they associate with their old behaviour towards the ruling class. The Liberation Mass is a jumble of politics, rock music and personal confession which I found jarring and ugly. I asked one of the devout whether he did not feel that the church should be a place of sanctuary, of peace and quiet, where you would have time to think about the essentials of life and death. Only in the West, he replied, would you think this. For there the Church is the one place set aside for these things. But in Nicaragua, where every day our thoughts are on whether we shall live or die, the last thing we need is a place for more of the same. What we need is a place of celebration.

I found that to travel through the country was often depressing, because you are so aware that the history of revolutionary experiments in our century has not been a happy one. Yet a visit to neighbouring Honduras brought upon me a much profounder despair. There the United States has been invited in and has begun to set up military bases. War games have begun, on a borrowed football pitch which once claimed to be an independent republic. In the Cafe Chico in Tegucigalpa, I attended a reception given by the Honduran government, for two hundred men in dark suits with gold propelling pencils. The President of Honduras gave up alcohol twenty-five years ago: now he is constantly looking at his watch to see how long it is since he last had a drink. I asked one of his minor officials if the Hondurans did not fear receiving the same treatment as the Vietnamese. Surely, I said, the North Americans will inflate your economy and destroy your culture, then when their own domestic needs change, they will betray you. No, he said, for this time the difference is that we will be in control. We will let them in for a while, but they have agreed that when we ask them to go, they will. But is it not true, I said, that when President Reagan was due to arrive in Honduras, US Secret Service men were sent ahead to disarm the Honduran guards who were waiting at the airport, supposedly to protect him? What more perfect image can there be of the distrust fundamental to any relationship between a cold war superpower and its self-deceiving satellites?

The families of the disappeared, who told us how their relatives had been dragged from their homes and shot, or taken from the streets, did no more than testify to something in the air. A major US intervention in the area is ironically far more clearly foretold in Honduras than in Nicaragua. Although Nicaragua is everywhere preparing for war, it is in Honduras that people have begun lying to one another and to themselves. In the famous words of a US military man in Vietnam: 'In order to protect this village, it will first be necessary to destroy it.'

An interest in foreign affairs has for some years been out of fashion in England. The modern newspaper employs as few foreign correspondents as possible, for they are, in the best possible sense, out of control. They bring unwelcome news of a world which is difficult, and whose diversity and vitality contrast with the politics of selfishness which is now the orthodox practice of the West. Our own national life is marked with a vengeful self-righteousness. It is constantly pretended that the privileged classes of the West are under some sort of unspecified threat. That they are in some way hard done by. That they have not been allowed to express their genius to the full. That they are entitled to more than they are getting. On the back of this feeling, politicians have ridden to power. News of how little everyone else in the world is getting can only confuse and disorient the domestic electorate. The suggestion that the battle-lines may be re-drawn between the old ideologies is vigorously resented.

David Hare

Dismantling the cold war represents a real challenge to the brainpower and imagination of our rulers: worse, it represents a threat to jobs—to the only jobs which are safe in modern England: jobs for indifferent politicians. Too close an examination of the map may only reveal where Nicaragua actually is.

It is obvious to everyone that we can learn from Nicaragua. Where politics is identified with need, it becomes more than politics. But never forget, they also need us. Our help. On behalf of the organizers of this event I ask you to give as generously as you dare.

THE DAY THE UNIVERSE CHANGED

James Burke's sumptuously illustrated examination of the Western view of life. It explores the way we think, the way we feel, the way we are. It could change the way you see the world.

FROM BOOKSELLERS £14.95

James Burke

BBC PUBLICATIONS

NOTES FROM ABROAD

Christopher Hitchens
Nicaragua

T owards the close of *Memoirs of a Revolutionary,* Victor Serge—faced with a miserable Mexican exile, and oppressed by the spread of totalitarian ideas—offers a number of reflections on the fate of the betrayed Russian revolution and the 'socialist experiment':

It is often said that 'the germ of all Stalinism was in Bolshevism at its beginning.' Well, I have no objection. Only Bolshevism also contained many other germs—a mass of other germs—and those who lived through the enthusiasm of the first years of the first victorious revolution ought not to forget it. To judge the living man by the death germs which the autopsy reveals in a corpse—and which he may have carried in him since his birth—is this very sensible?

I went to Nicaragua, as I had gone to Cuba, Angola, Zimbabwe, Grenada and other such *loci*, not as a tourist of revolution but as an amateur biochemist. How were the bacilli doing? What germs were emerging as the dominant strain? In other words, would Nicaragua turn into another example of frowsty barracks socialism, replete with compulsory enthusiasm, affirming only the right to agree?

I went to Nicaragua determined not to come away saying things like, 'You have to remember the specific conditions—the blockade, the sabotage, the CIA....' The Sandinistas make large claims for a revolution in liberty—socialism with a human face—and for a new kind of American state that fuses the best of two opposing world systems. This time, they seemed to say, would be different. It didn't seem patronizing to take them up on it.

*M*anagua is a famous hell-hole that, with its sprawling *barrios* and its crass, nasty Intercontinental Hotel, combines the worst of the Third World and the tackiest of the New. In between—nothing much. Until the Sandinistas cleared the rubble from the 1972 earthquake, there were the beginnings of an urban jungle in the real sense. Lianas and creepers were everywhere, and there was the exciting prospect that snakes, parrots and pumas would move in to midtown. How like the Macondo of Márquez that would have been—what stirring copy.

But they don't tell you how beautiful the country is outside its capital. In the interior there are cool colonial verandas and courtyards, mountain resorts, lava plains, jungles and forests. Nicaragua is a caesura between the Atlantic and the Pacific, precariously built on an earthquake fault. The great volcano at Masaya, with its enormous crater full of swirling green parrots, makes such a hypnotic inhaling noise that the Spanish conquerors put up a huge cross to ward off the breath of the Evil One. This is a land of miraculous virgins and frantic rumours. Tranquility is found only on the shores of the giant inland ocean of Lake Nicaragua, where Pablo Antonio Cuadra wrote his *Songs of Cifar* and *The Sweet Sea*—the lake is the Aegean of his Odyssey—and where the fishermen do their millennial stuff. This is also where various American adventurers of the last century planned to build the first isthmian canal, and incorporate Nicaragua as a slave state into the Union. Not far from the lake and the volcano is Monimbo, an Indian town where, in legend and in fact, the insurrection against Somoza and the Americans began.

*N*icaragua has always impelled its writers into politics, or exile, or both. Ruben Dario had to leave the stifling backwardness of the country in order to conduct his experiments in modernism. The novelist Sergio Ramirez spent much of his life in Berlin. The poet Rigoberto Lopez—seeing no future at all—killed the elder Somoza in what he must have known was a suicide attack. It is perhaps no surprise that the last Somoza held the intelligentsia in such utter contempt that he succeeded in fusing its writers and intellectuals into a united front opposed to his rule. But when the Somoza dynasty collapsed, the unity it inspired disintegrated as well. It followed, I felt, that the writers in Nicaragua might turn out to be an especially sensitive register of the country's affairs, and I ended up spending most of my time there talking to two men, Sergio Ramirez and Pablo Antonio Cuadra, at one time friends and still mutual admirers, who between them exemplify the depth of the Nicaraguan revolution and the intensity with which its failings are felt. Ramirez, the nation's leading novelist and one of the few non-uniformed members of the Sandinista directorate, serves as Vice President to Daniel Ortega and was the founder of *Los Doce,* the Group of Twelve which mobilized civilian and intellectual support for the revolution. His novel *Te dio miedo la sangre? (Were You Scared of the Blood?)* is published in English as *To Bury Our Fathers.* Pablo Antonio Cuadra is a poet who also publishes the review *El Pez y La Serpiente (The Fish and the Snake)* and edits the literary supplement of the right-wing anti-Sandinista news-sheet *La Prensa.* A disillusioned ex-supporter of the Somoza family, Cuadra counts himself a supporter of the 1979 'Triumph', which he now regards as a revolution betrayed.

Sergio Ramirez was acting President on the night that I saw him, because Daniel Ortega had winged off to Moscow. Our five-hour conversation was interrupted only three times—twice by calls from Ortega and once by an earth tremor which first removed and then replaced the smiles on the faces of the guards. I, who knew no better, decided to take their relative insouciance at face value. Ramirez, on the other hand, sprang to his feet and ordered the doors thrown open. In an earthquake zone, you are ever ready for the moment when you may have to stand under the lintel. Also, a door temporarily shut can become a door permanently jammed. The two threats of an earthquake framed our discussion in other respects, if only by analogy: like every Sandinista, Ramirez expects that one day the *Yanquis* will bring the roof down; and, like most visitors, I wanted to know whether some of the 'temporary expedients'—censorship, informing and conscription—would harden into features of a permanent system.

Considering that Ramirez was, as acting President, speaking on the record in a week when the White House had announced economic sanctions against Nicaragua, he displayed considerable candour and scepticism about the course of the revolution. But so, sometimes, does Fidel Castro (who also likes late-night sessions with foreign guests). 'Before the "Triumph",' Ramirez recalled, 'there were many discussions about writing and culture. We felt that we might have the first opportunity really to test ourselves in a society where writers have always had a role. But there was a temptation to develop a "line", and I call it a temptation because of the old idea that art should "serve". We knew of the negative experiences of other socialist and Third World countries. We decided, instead, on a policy of complete creative freedom.

'At our first assembly of writers in the national palace I made, and later published, a speech. I warned that we don't need a recipe for writing. I don't mind experiments by our "workshop" poets, though there is a risk of doggerel. The result of an individual's intimate work, though, must not be despised.'

I saw what he meant about the workshop poets, when I came across a stanza by Carlos Galan Pena of the Police Complex Workshop, writing to his beloved Lily:

you and I are the Revolution
and I am filled with my work
and you spend hours and hours
...in the office of propaganda.

The most that can be said of this is that Ernesto Cardenal's Ministry of Culture is encouraging people who have never thought of themselves as writers before.

I ask Ramirez about the dismal situation of the writer in Cuba, most notably the persecution of the poet Heberto Padilla. Ramirez is rather cautious: it is 'necessary to be present'—involved—in a revolution; those who defect to the other side—as Padilla did in fleeing to the United States—have in essence surrendered. But Padilla is 'not a bad poet,' Ramirez adds, 'and there are rights to which everyone, even those who criticize the revolution, must be entitled.' Even so, it was interesting to learn that, during the first five years of the revolutionary government, he did not write at all: Ramirez—who otherwise describes his whole literary endeavor as a conscious struggle against the seductive influence of Gabriel García Márquez—was afraid during this period of producing a politicized or didactic prose.

I suggest that it is almost axiomatic that writing can only exist in a pluralist society, and mention Orwell's remark that the imagination, like certain wild animals, is unable to breed in captivity. Ramirez agrees with enthusiasm: 'We don't censor the cultural section of *La Prensa*' (revealing that they do censor the rest of it). He admires Milan Kundera, for instance, and cannot blame him for choosing exile over living under a military occupation. But Kundera is also 'simplistic—totalitarianism doesn't come only from the East.'

A totalitarianism of a different sort is evident in Ramirez's *To Bury Our Fathers,* which deals with two generations of Nicaraguan life under the *ancien régime.* Ramirez claims that every incident in the novel actually took place, at least in the sense that oral history has established certain episodes as having 'actually happened', and the humour with which he accepts a reported event as fact is typical of a country that lives on myths and rumours. The brain of Nicaragua's greatest poet, Ruben Dario, for instance—its dimensions were reputedly enormous, a 'fact' that greatly impressed the provincial minds of the time—has gone missing, and every now and then fresh gossip about its whereabouts goes humming on its rounds. And nobody knows where Sandino is buried. His body was interred hugger-mugger by the American-trained *Somocistas* who betrayed and murdered him, and ever since strenuous, fruitless efforts have been made to locate his grave (which may well be under the runway of Managua airport).

Rumour and myth are, however, also the most formidable enemies of the Sandinistas. The CIA manual written for the right-wing terrorists and discovered before the last US presidential election is obviously strong on such matters as assassination, the use of local criminal networks and the techniques of economic sabotage. But it is equally strong on spreading slander and alarm. Stories about Sandinistan orgies, or the nationalization of the family, are standard; one of the most illuminating, though, is the story of the Virgin of Cuapa. On 8 May 1981 a local sacristan in the town of Cuapa named Bernardo found himself in conversation with the Virgin Mary. In a succession of appearances, she told him about the suffering Nicaragua has had to endure since the earthquake: 'if you do not change,' she is meant to have said, 'Nicaragua will continue to suffer and you will hasten the coming of the Third World War.' Our Lady showed a shrewd grasp of contemporary politics, especially in describing the Sandinistas as 'atheists and Communists, which is why I have come to help the Nicaraguans. They have not kept their promises. If you ignore what I ask, Communism will spread throughout America.'

This is of a higher standard than the usual Christian Democratic miracle. In its pedantic toeing of the US State Department line (especially the artful bit about the Sandinistas not keeping their promises) it outdoes Fatima in 1917 or the repeated counter-revolutionary uses of the blood of San Gennaro. Despite official attempts to dismiss the episode—the liberation theology faction has also denounced it as 'bourgeois Mariolatry'—the Virgin of Cuapa, in some sense, lives. She is a decisive weapon in the campaign to get peasants to join a *vendée* run by their former masters.

Ramirez smiles and admits that 'as a writer, I of course believe in the Virgin of Cuapa.' The Sandinistas, in any case, possess what they consider to be a more potent icon: the spirit of Cesar Augusto Sandino, whom nobody in Nicaragua would dare oppose. Even his former enemies pay homage to him in their pamphlets and broadcasts, and one presumes that they would not bother to counterfeit a bankrupt currency. Disgruntled stall-holders who dislike the regime will tell you that, in spite of everything, they feel prouder to be Nicaraguan these days. One is, in vulgar terminology, either a Sandinista or—one of Sandino's favourite expletives—a *vendepatria*: a vendor of the fatherland, selling off the country.

What is his government's greatest mistake? There is a large repertoire to select from, he replies, but chooses to answer by way of an episode elaborated in his forthcoming book about Julio Cortázar. 'On the day that we took over the American-owned mines on the Atlantic coast, Julio was with us. I wanted to show him what we had found. There were files on every worker. One, for example, was the file of a man who had laboured there from 1951 until one week before "the Triumph". He was listed as having been fired. Under the heading REASON FOR DISMISSAL was the entry "Killed in an accident". I can show you this surreal file and many others like it. They would sack dead workers in order to avoid paying compensation to the family. And we also captured the records of the 'personal tax' that the owners paid to Somoza in order to get away with it. The relationship his regime enjoyed with the United States was indulgent to the point of carnality.

'The mines themselves were worthless—another piece in the Somoza museum of horrors. The machinery was useless—fit only to be worked by the cheapest labour. Nationalizing gained us nothing. But we did it to show that an era had ended. It was an act of love as much as hatred. Maybe it was a mistake.'

In Chile and Argentina, he says, the middle and upper classes are a powerful social force, organized and capable of exerting influence. In Nicaragua, they are a mere shadow thrown by foreign influence, an 'appendage of the United States'.

Vendepatrias, in fact?

'I don't like such simplistic phrases.'

'*O*h, doesn't he?' Pablo Antonio Cuadra, in his dingy office at *La Prensa Literaria,* talking about his old friend Sergio Ramirez ('*un bueno hombre de letras*'), dismisses anti-Americanism as a local contagion. Admittedly, the hemisphere is dominated by the United States, but it is too easy to blame the *Yanquis* for everything. 'In any case, Sergio should be writing, not trying to be a politician. The FSLN have thrown away the revolution—the most magnificent moment that Nicaragua ever had.' Cuadra is prepared to say that the situation is actually worse than it was ten years ago under Somoza, 'if you omit his last few weeks of terror and bombing' when he ordered his own capital to be strafed from the air.

How different would it be if the United States invaded?

This, he says, is 'a horrible question. The Americans might negate even the original revolution. But to imitate the Soviet Union is the most macabre thing of all.'

More macabre than a *Somocista* restoration?

'*Sí.* It is more difficult to remove.'

Nevertheless, Cuadra is not a particularly expert political observer. At one point, he was a nationalist, enthusiastically supporting the Somoza dynasty; towards the end of the Somoza terror, Cuadra wrote a defence of Ramirez's literary faction, *Los Doce,* which got him into hot water. And when he finally gave his support to the revolution, he was seen in the worst possible light: a late joiner. *La Prensa,* the paper Cuadra now writes for, is a vulgar, sensational, superstitous right-wing propaganda sheet, publishing lies and distortions on a scale that even Western diplomats find embarrassing; it also carries Cuadra's name on the masthead—under the sonorous title of 'Don Pablo Antonio'—as its director, together with Jaime Chamorro. The Sandinista party paper *Barricada* used to be edited by Carlos Chamorro, his brother. *Nuevo Diario,* the other leftist daily, is edited by Xavier Chamorro, another family member. Chamorro, Chamorro and Chamorro....

Is there not something inescapably political about Latin American contemporary writers—Neruda, Fuentes, Márquez, Cortázar, Vargas Llosa, even Borges? Is this automatically unhealthy?

Not at all, he replies: every one of us has been politicized, and life itself is political. But very few of these writers have mixed their literary work with their politics—except for Neruda, for whom it was his downfall as a writer. Even Márquez keeps his polemics in a separate compartment. It is, in other words, not politics that must be avoided, but politicization.

Cuadra recalls the first assembly of Nicaraguan writers where

Ramirez repudiated a 'line' or a 'recipe': 'Cortázar was there and so was I. There were great proclamations about artistic freedom from Sergio and Ernesto Cardenal. I even had Cuban friends who said that this might have a positive influence in Havana. But within a year, *Ventana* was publishing Fidel Castro's notorious speech to the intellectuals, saying that "nothing against the revolution was permitted."' *Ventana* is the Sandinistas' literary and cultural magazine—edited by Daniel Ortega's wife, and described by Ramirez as 'boring'.

*R*amirez says that Cuadra is a great poet who doesn't understand revolution. Cuadra says that Ramirez is a great novelist who has become intoxicated by politics. Ramirez and Ernesto Cardenal say that the restrictions on liberty result from the exigencies of war and blockade, and from the threat of invasion. Cuadra says that they result from a dogmatic, ideological tendency inherent in the FSLN. Ramirez says that Nicaragua will not become 'like Bulgaria'. Cuadra grants that so far there is no imposed socialist realism, but points out that many of his contributors are asking to be published anonymously: there is a general tendency towards 'the correct'.

It is possible to conclude rather glibly that both men are right, and that Nicaragua is becoming a hybrid or a compromise. Mario Vargas Llosa, for example, takes the view that the Sandinistas will become like the ruling party in Mexico, the so-called Institutional Revolutionary Party, which retains the lion's share of power and patronage without acquiring a total monopoly. This sort of diagnosis—arguably true for the moment—treats a very volatile present as somehow static. Ramirez doesn't want conformity and Cuadra doesn't want the forcible reimposition of a right-wing dictatorship. Both men may be optimists.

In spite of the brave and, I believe, genuine aspirations of Sergio Ramirez, there are symptoms of an encroaching orthodoxy in Nicaragua. During our conversations, for example, he used the terms 'one-party society' and 'closed society' as synonymous. Today's Nicaragua is, at least in the cities, a multi-party *society*. The posters and emblems of the Conservatives (who are really conservative) and the Liberals (who are not really liberal) are everywhere. Likewise those of the Communists. But it is also a one-party *state*. All the power worth having belongs to the FSLN; the broadcasting station and the armed forces are both officially called 'Sandinista'. Foreign policy, despite some anomalies, is directed pretty solidly towards the Warsaw Pact. And in cultural matters, a sort of dull utilitarianism is creeping in. Even Ramirez is not proof against it. Denying newsprint to the opposition, for example, is due to 'the rationing of scarce resources'. The unavailability of books and magazines, except from Eastern Europe, is due to 'the lack of foreign currency'. There is some truth in these claims. But they are, equally, just the sort of euphemisms that led, through many false dawns, to the Zhdanovization of culture in Cuba.

On 6 April 1984, Ernesto Cardenal wrote to his friend Lawrence Ferlinghetti from the Ministry of Culture, promising that censorship of opposition newspapers would end the following month when the elections began. It didn't. Father Cardenal is a devout Catholic and was a friend of Thomas Merton (two qualifications he shares with Pablo Antonio Cuadra), and these facts are often cited, by observers like Graham Greene, as proof of Cardenal's commitment to freedom and pluralism. Why not as proof of his readiness to believe anything—like his wide-eyed admiration of the austere absence of materialism among the Cubans?

In numerous respects, the Sandinista revolution *is* its own justification. Despite some exaggerated claims, the achievements in social welfare and education are spectacular and moving. So is the fact that, after half a century and more of tutelage, Nicaragua is no longer a mere 'ditto' to the wishes of the United States. But the only way to justify the gradual emergence of a one-party-state is by continual reference to the neighbouring fascisms and the menace of imperialist invasion. And I would rather leave that job to the cadres of sincere, credulous, self-sacrificing American youth who are everywhere to be found in Nicaragua ('Look, man, the people care more about full bellies than about freedom in the abstract'). The Americans' motive for being there is generally religious, and likewise their method of argument. I have seen this movie before, most recently in Grenada: Maurice Bishop abolished such independent media as there were, and then had no means of appealing to the people when his own turn came.

The contortions and ambiguities of the Left are familiar. What about those of the Right? Pablo Antonio Cuadra told me, almost visibly squirming, that the worst thing the CIA had ever done was to finance and train the *contras,* the *Somocista* terrorists in the north: nobody who has seen the *contras'* work can doubt that, if they came to power, they would emulate the ways of the military governments in Guatemala and El Salvador if they got the chance. And military regimes—especially in Latin America—are just as hard to remove as Stalinist ones. In addition, no regime in Latin America has shown an interest in social welfare or education or merely raising the economic 'floor'—the elementary subsistence level on which most people have to live the one life that is allowed to them.

This is why no conversation with a Sandinista lasts for more than a few minutes before coming up against the name of Salvador Allende. By allowing his murder, and thus by welcoming a dictator into Chile, Dr Kissinger and his *confrères* inadvertently educated a whole generation of Latin American radicals. Pluralism is now seen by many of them as a trap or a snare: an invitation to make yourself vulnerable, a none-too-subtle suggestion of suicide. Stand in the middle of the road, and you get run down. Did not Sandino surrender to his murderers under a guarantee of safe conduct? The fact that this argument can lead to disastrous results (as it did with Maurice Bishop, who used it all the time) does not diminish its force or its relevance.

And the Nicaraguan opposition does not believe in democracy. Its leaders will tell you so. The Cardinal dislikes the revolution because it promises free education and teaches Darwin in the schools ('atheist indoctrination'). The rightist parties, and most of the centrist ones, are mostly organized around one *caudillo,* and say openly that they would be happy to come to power by whatever means available—by force or with the aid of a foreign government. Most deplorable in many ways are the American liberals, who have now voted to aid the *contras* to avoid being accused by Reagan of 'appeasing' the Communists. These people never thought of Central America as a 'critical' problem when it was a sweltering, superficially tranquil serfdom. To deem a country worthy of your attention—and, possibly, of your military—only when it explodes from misery and neglect: this is the highest and most callous form of irresponsibility. North American *bien-pensants* have more to apologize for than they can ever realize. As Victor Serge puts it:

> A feeble logic, whose finger beckons us to the dark spectacle of the Stalinist Soviet Union, affirms the bankruptcy of Bolshevism, followed by that of Marxism, followed by that of Socialism.... Have you forgotten the other bankruptcies? What was Christianity doing in the various catastrophes of society? What became of Liberalism? What has Conservatism produced, in either its enlightened or its reactionary form? If we are indeed honestly to weigh out the bankruptcy of ideology, we shall have a long task ahead of us. And nothing is finished yet.

What, then, of the bacilli? The healthy ones are still alive, and still circulating. As Ramirez said to me: 'Without the confrontation with the United States, we could put Nicaragua under a glass bell and experiment in freedom.' Or alternatively, as Cuadra said: without some of the pressure from abroad things might be proceeding further along the Castroite path. Both men are still free to speak, and both of their futures will be significant monitors of Nicaragua's progress or its decline.

The critical, forensic finding seems to me to be this. Nicaragua has witnessed six years of revolutionary government, after half a century of the Somozas, and more than a century of humiliating colonial subordination. It has done so with hardly any acts of vengeance and without a massacre; capital punishment has been abolished, even though some Sandinistas now say they wish they *had* shot the *Somocista* old guard instead of releasing it to reincarnate in

Honduras and Miami. Nicaragua has not avoided all the mistakes and crimes of previous revolutions, but it has at least made a self-conscious effort to do so. The Stalinist bacilli are at work all right, but they do not predominate as yet and there is nothing that says they have to. Perhaps one should beware, anyway, of biological analogies. On the shirts and badges of the American 'advisers' in Honduras is a monogram which pre-dates Marx and Lenin and, probably accidentally, has an echo of the elder Simon de Montfort. Emblazoned with a skull and crossbones, it reads 'KILL 'EM ALL—LET GOD SORT 'EM OUT!'

THE EDINBURGH REVIEW

A lively magazine of international literature and ideas

No. 67/68: Tom Leonard on James (B.V.) Thomson
Janet Daley on Mark Rothko
Margaret Yourcenar on The Black Brain of Piranesi
Scottish, Irish and American fiction

No. 69: Interview with Michel Foucault
George Davie on Scottish Philosophy and Robertson Smith
Poems of Roque Dalton
New Scottish and Irish short stories

No. 70: Article on Alexander Trocchi
Story by Kathy Acker
Jenny Turner on Laurie Anderson
Reviews of British and American contemporary fiction

'Mr Kravitz has produced an exciting magazine, international in its vision . . .' _The Scotsman_
'. . . enough rough edges to strike some sparks.' _City Limits_

Subscriptions: Inland, one year, £10; Overseas, one year, £15.
Buy two gift subscriptions and get a third free.
State which issue you wish to start with.
Cheques payable to EUSPB.

Send to: EDINBURGH REVIEW, 1 BUCCLEUCH PLACE, EDINBURGH EH8 9LW.

LETTERS

Secrets

To the Editor

Clive Ponting's 'Crown Jewels' document and the analysis of it by Peter Greig ('Revelations', *Granta* 15) provide a catalogue of the deception, dubious legality and incompetence which characterize the run-up to the sinking of the Argentine cruiser *General Belgrano* during the Falklands campaign.

They make us face the distasteful truth that on 1 May 1982 British Foreign Secretary Francis Pym signed a letter questioning the legality of sinking the Argentinian aircraft carrier without warning, while on the following day in Washington he told the world's press that 'no other military action is envisaged for the moment other than making the Total Exclusion Zone secure.' We have the War Cabinet receiving advice that sinking the carrier would be beyond the legal protection offered by Article 51 of the United Nations Charter, yet proceeding with the plan only to be frustrated by military error. We have the remarkable suggestion that of two signals recalling the Argentine fleet to home waters, one was successfully interpreted and decoded, only to be misconstrued by naval intelligence, and the other was intercepted but appears to have lain on a desk at GCHQ while the most important decision of the war was taken.

None of these provide plausible explanation, however, for the British government's deceptions, which began with John Nott's first announcement on 4 May, went on through the General Election, and continued.

So why all these lies? Not to protect Francis Pym. His head has already rolled for different reasons. Probably not because of international law: a defence of retaliation to an Argentine order to sink British ships had already been prepared. Not to protect the intelligence service from charges of incompetence: the Franks Committee already largely blamed them for failing to anticipate the invasion.

This unanswered question is the motivating force behind the continuing campaign by Labour MP Tam Dalyell and others. Are we to believe that the one intercepted signal which might have altered the course of the war was not decoded until days after the *Belgrano* had been sunk? Was the War Cabinet really not told that the *Belgrano* had altered course for home eleven hours before the torpedo was eventually fired? Did the peace plan which had been keeping busy the American Secretary of State, the British Foreign Secretary and the entire Peruvian government really not reach the British Prime Minister until too late?

If answers to these questions are the reasons for the British government's reluctance to tell the whole truth, its members would do well to study Watergate. Its lesson is that it can only be a matter of time.

Stuart Prebble
Manchester

To the Editor

Peter Greig's mysterious account of
the sinking of the *Belgrano* is as
interesting for what it fails to reveal
as for the new information it
reports.

What Peter Greig obscures, in a
curious sequence of speculative
passages, is that both the
intelligence-gathering machinery at
GCHQ and the intelligence analysts
at the Northwood Naval Station
made, apparently, three mistakes.
The first mistake is well-known: on
1 May, GCHQ intercepted and
decrypted the Argentine fleet order
calling for an attack on the British
task force involving two groups of
the Argentine fleet; the intelligence
analyst at Northwood wrongly said
that the *Belgrano* was also ordered
on the attack. The second mistake
also involves the Northwood
intelligence analysts: on receiving
the intercepted and decoded
Argentine signal from GCHQ that
the attack had been called off, an
intelligence analyst said that the
signal was of uncertain meaning and
did not pass it on. The third
mistake, however, is more
spectacular. On 2 May, GCHQ
intercepted the signal—one that
could not possibly be read as being
of uncertain meaning—*confirming*
that the Argentine attack had been
called off: but this signal was never
decoded. To appreciate the
significance of this omission, one
must bear in mind that of the
hundreds of signals intercepted *and*
broken by GCHQ, this, by an
extraordinarily apparent

coincidence, is the only one that was
not decoded. The irony is apparent
in the fact that Defence Minister
Michael Heseltine later learned of
the signal only on reading about it
in Arthur Gavshon and Desmond
Rice's *The Sinking of the Belgrano*.
Heseltine immediately asked for the
signal to be found, and demanded
that Sir Brian Toby, then Director
of GCHQ, appear before him and
John Stanley with it in hand—which
Toby duly accomplished, retrieving
the blue sheet of this *still* undecoded
signal from a briefcase filled with
sheaves and sheaves of other signals,
all decrypted.

If the GCHQ version of events is
to be believed, it illuminates the
government's understanding of what
constitutes an official secret and
why it decided to prosecute Clive
Ponting for what he revealed of the
'Crown Jewels': simply that the
government had made a balls-up. A
balls-up, incidentally, that resulted
in a violation of international law
and that leaves Britain liable to
being sued by the Argentine
government for the killing of 368
young soldiers.

Name not supplied

The Front Line

To the Editor

It concerns me that the focus of the
debate over politics and literature is
almost entirely related to non-
English writers, and struggles

abroad where the front-line is overt and explicit. What is at stake—the political battle, literature's role in it and how writing is shaped by politics—is no less pressing in Britain. It's simply being fought on a different front. And I believe it's all the more urgent for being a hidden front.

Attacks upon our civilization permeate my work and others', and inform that work with a certain consciousness, whatever the subject. I do not believe that British writers are without subject, nor that that subject must always be politics. But we in Britain look abroad for struggle, ignore our own and shrink from debate.

We romanticize the front-line that lies elsewhere: Nicaragua, Chile, South Africa, Poland. *Our* front-line is tricky, and demands all our attention and commitment; there is a war on, a war on consciousness and thus on reality. Our power as people is being snatched from us—overtly, as in the loss of the right to demonstrate during the miners' strike; and covertly, insidiously, by way of cuts in (writing and publishing grants. Which words will get through?

I applaud *Granta*'s internationalism. But is there not room for debate on how writing, commitment and politics exist here? Can British writers become passionate and articulate only when they stick their necks out about India, South Africa and Chile?

'Political writing' is not only writing that has a political battle as its subject. *Our* front-line is a shifting edge which at times joins the real struggle, but often diverges from 'official' politics and tracing it would be impossible. Yet I have a sneaking suspicion that there is little sense among British writers that it exists at all.

Death, decay and poverty—material, cultural, linguistic—are everywhere and spreading. The tools we use to see and understand each other are as much under attack by the state apparatus as are our health, education and social services. We do not need a single definition of what it means to resist, to make a political gesture. But resistance and gesture are necessary responsibilities here, as they are anywhere else on our planet, if we are to understand our own cultural decay.

Nicki Jackowska
Brighton
East Sussex

Notes on Contributors

Oliver Sack's last book was *A Leg to Stand On.* 'A Matter of Identity' and 'The Possessed' will be included in his forthcoming collection of 'clinical narratives', *The Man who mistook his Wife for a Hat and other Cases,* to be published by Simon and Schuster this autumn. **Dorothea Lynch** was a freelance journalist and correspondent for the *Quincy Patriot Ledger.* **Eugene Richards** is a photo-journalist and has published three books of photography. He lives in Dorchester, New York, and is a member of Magnum. **Thomas McMahon** is Gordon McKay Professor of Applied Mechanics and Biology at Harvard University; his other fiction includes the novels *Principles of American Nuclear Chemistry* and *McKay's Bees.* 'The Loves of the Tortoises' and 'The Blackbird's Whistle' will be included in **Italo Calvino**'s forthcoming collection of fiction, *Mr. Palomar,* a Helen and Kurt Wolff book to be published by Harcourt Brace Jovanovich this autumn. **Lewis Thomas** is President Emeritus of the Sloan-Kettering Memorial Cancer Center, New York. His most recent book is *Late Night Thoughts on Listening to Mahler's Ninth Symphony.* **William Broad** is on the staff of the *New York Times,* and is co-author with Nicholas Wade of *Betrayal and Truth: Fraud and Deception in the Halls of Science.* 'The Scientists of Star Wars' will be included in *Star Warriors,* to be published by Simon and Schuster this autumn. **Primo Levi**'s books include *If Not Now, When?, If this is a Man* and *The Periodic Table.* **John Berger** is a regular contributor to *Granta.* His work includes *G* and *Pig Earth.* **Tim O'Brien** is the author of three novels and the winner of the National Book Award for *Going after Cacciato.* 'Quantum Leaps' is from his forthcoming novel *The Nuclear Age,* to be published by Knopf this autumn. **Mary Gordon**'s other novels are *Final Payments, The Company of Women* and *Men and Angels.* **David Mamet** won the Pulitzer Prize for *Glengarry Glen Ross.* His most recent works are an adaptation of Chekhov's *The Cherry Orchard* and two one-act plays, *The Shawl* and *The Spanish Prisoner,* produced at the Goodman Theatre in Chicago. **Darryl Pinckney** works for the *New York Review of Books* and has recently completed his first novel. **Ryszard Kapuściński**'s most recent book is *Shah of Shahs.* **Germaine Greer**'s last book was *Sex and Destiny.* Her account of her recent experiences in Ethiopia will be published in

Granta 17. **David Hare**'s most recent play, written with Howard Brenton, is *Pravda: A Fleet Street Comedy*. **Christopher Hitchens** is the Washington correspondent for the *Nation*.

PHOTO CREDITS: (in order) Central Press, Ardea London, Popperfoto, Ardea London, Popperfoto, Jean Mohr, Chris Steele-Perkins, Bruno Barbey (Magnum), John Hillelson Agency. Each work copyright of the author: Oliver Sacks © 1985, Eugene Richards © 1985, Thomas McMahon © 1985, Italo Calvino © 1984 and translation William Weaver copyright © 1985, Lewis Thomas © 1985, William Broad © 1985, Primo Levi © 1985, Tim O'Brien copyright © 1985, Mary Gordon copyright © 1985, David Mamet © 1985, Darryl Pinckney © 1985, Ryszard Kapuściński © 1985, Germaine Greer © 1985, David Hare © 1985, Christopher Hitchens © 1985.

'Amazon' is from *Exploding into Life*, to be published by Aperture in Spring 1986. Aperture, Inc.—a non-profit charitable, educational foundation—is seeking funds to support the publication of *Exploding into Life*. Individuals interested in contributing (all contributions are tax-deductible), or in obtaining additional information about the book, may write to Carole Kismaric, Aperture, 20 West 23rd Street, New York, New York 10010.